GLOBAL REFUGEE CRISIS

Selected Titles in ABC-CLIO's
CONTEMPORARY
WORLD ISSUES
Series

For a complete list of titles in this series, please visit
www.abc-clio.com.

Books in the Contemporary World Issues series address vital issues in today's society, such as genetic engineering, pollution, and biodiversity. Written by professional writers, scholars, and nonacademic experts, these books are authoritative, clearly written, up-to-date, and objective. They provide a good starting point for research by high school and college students, scholars, and general readers as well as by legislators, businesspeople, activists, and others.

Each book, carefully organized and easy to use, contains an overview of the subject, a detailed chronology, biographical sketches, facts and data and/or documents and other primary-source material, a directory of organizations and agencies, annotated lists of print and nonprint resources, and an index.

Readers of books in the Contemporary World Issues series will find the information they need to have a better understanding of the social, political, environmental, and economic issues facing the world today.

GLOBAL REFUGEE CRISIS

A Reference Handbook, Second Edition

Mark Gibney

CONTEMPORARY WORLD ISSUES

ABC-CLIO

Santa Barbara, California • Denver, Colorado • Oxford, England

Library of Congress Cataloging-in-Publication Data

Gibney, Mark.
  Global refugee crisis : a reference handbook / Mark Gibney. — 2nd ed.
     p. cm. — (Contemporary world issues)
  Rev. ed. of: The global refugee crisis : a reference handbook / Gil Loescher, Ann Dull Loescher. 1994.
  Includes bibliographical references and index.
  ISBN 978-1-59884-455-9 (hbk. : alk. paper) — ISBN 978-1-59884-456-6 (ebook) 1. Refugees. 2. Refugees—Services for. 3. Disaster relief. I. Loescher, Gil. Global refugee crisis. II. Title.
HV640.L625   2010
362.87—dc22   2010030686

ISBN: 978-1-59884-455-9
EISBN: 978-1-59884-456-6

14 13 12 11 10   1 2 3 4 5

This book is also available on the World Wide Web as an eBook. Visit www.abc-clio.com for details.

ABC-CLIO, LLC
130 Cremona Drive, P.O. Box 1911
Santa Barbara, California 93116-1911

This book is printed on acid-free paper ∞

Manufactured in the United States of America

Contents

List of Tables and Figures

Preface

G*lobal Refugee Crisis* provides an overview of the world's migration situation, but it also offers up a different way of conceptualizing human rights—as well as refugee protection itself. There are presently upwards of 40 million people who have been forced to flee their homes because of political violence and oppression. One segment of this population consists of refugees—individuals who have left their country of nationality because of a well-founded fear of persecution. The population of internally displaced persons (IDPs) is approximately twice as large as this. However, what distinguishes refugees from IDPs is that the former have crossed a national border and have gained some form of international assistance, while the latter have not. The focus of the present work is on refugees, and we spend a considerable amount of time analyzing the meaning of refugee under international law.

In addition to examining law and current practice, *Global Refugee Crisis* places refugee protection within a much broader human rights context. After all, refugee protection is human rights protection. Yet, what differentiates the refugee phenomenon from all other areas of human rights is that it is based on protecting the human rights of others, rather than nationals of that state. In that way, refugee protection offers a more expansive understanding of the human rights responsibilities of states.

Yet, at the same time, refugee phenomenon serves as a strong reaffirmation of the principle of state sovereignty. For one thing, no state is obligated to admit any refugees. In addition, international law seemingly allows receiving states to pursue measures that will work to prevent refugees from arriving at their national borders. Beyond this, what also has to be recognized is that there is seemingly no obligation under international law to prevent refugee flows in the first place. Thus, refugee protection remains reactive. States respond—if they respond at all—only after a human catastrophe has taken place.

Global Refugee Crisis challenges several key assumptions that human rights and refugee protection have been premised on. One is the notion that Western democratic states have had to bear the brunt of the world's refugee protection needs. Another is that common, but untested, charge that there is widespread asylum abuse. And for a country like the United States that loudly proclaims itself the haven for the "the tired, the poor, the huddled masses yearning to breathe free," what is also challenged is a policy that admits vastly more immigrants than refugees.

Yet, perhaps the single strongest challenge is to the dominant approach to human rights—and along with that, to our conceptualization of refugee protection. Notwithstanding near universal declarations concerning the universality of human rights, the system that has emerged is one that has limited a state's human rights obligations to its own domestic sphere—but no further than this. This approach can most clearly be seen in the U.S. Supreme Court's opinion in *Sale v. Haitians Centers Council* where the court held that the prohibition against returning an individual back to a country where that person's life or well-being might be threatened (nonrefoulement) only applied after a person had arrived at American shores, but not before this. What is also noteworthy is that a number of other Western states have adopted similar measures that have had the effect of extending immigration control—but not refugee protection—further and further away from a state's national borders.

This territorial approach to human rights has recently been subject to serious challenge. We examine two challenges: the Responsibility to Protect (R2P) initiative and the work of the Extraterritorial Obligations (ETO) Human Rights Consortium. Both posit a proactive approach to human rights, and both are based on the principle that a state's human rights obligations do not suddenly and rather arbitrarily end at its own national border. This new approach to human rights—new only in the sense that the original intent behind much of international human rights law is finally being recognized—will have enormous implications in terms of our conceptualization of refugee protection. Most notably, this posits that all states would have an obligation to prevent refugee flows from arising in the first place.

Let me close by acknowledging the excellent and painstaking work of Rachel Elrod, without whom this work would never have been carried out.

Mark Gibney
Asheville, NC
February 24, 2010

1

Background and History

Introduction

A refugee is a person who is outside of his or her country of origin and fearful of returning home because of a well-founded fear of persecution based on race, religion, nationality, membership of a particular social group, or political opinion. The basic international instrument concerning refugee protection is the 1951 Convention Relating to the Status of Refugees (Refugee Convention). As the reader will see when we analyze the Refugee Convention, the term refugee has a well defined meaning under international law. However, what also has to be recognized is that the term is oftentimes used to describe individuals who are in a bad way and in need of assistance more generally. For example, there were repeated references to the victims Hurricane Katrina in New Orleans as refugees.

According to the latest data from the United Nations, at the end of 2008 there were 16 million refugees in the world, although only a small percentage of these would be formally recognized as such. The reason for this is that status precedes recognition. Table 1.1 presents data on the countries that presently produce the largest number of refugees. Perhaps it is no great surprise that Iraq and Afghanistan—two countries that have experienced longstanding wars—are at the top of this list.

Of course, refugees need some place else to go. In most instances, this will be in a neighboring country. Some very small number of these refugees will eventually be resettled in an industrialized Western state, but the overwhelming majority will not be, and substantial numbers will be warehoused in refugee camps

TABLE 1.1
Top Ten Refugee Producing States, 2008

Country	Number
Afghanistan	2,833,128
Iraq	1,903,519
Somalia	561,154
Sudan	419,248
Colombia	373,532
Democratic Republic Congo	367,995
Occupied Palestinian Authority	340,016
Vietnam	328,183
Burundi	281,592
Turkey	214,378

Source: UNHCR, "2008 Global Trends."

in Third World states for many years. Thus, one of the great fictions is that the bulk of refugees are housed in the industrialized countries of the West, which in turn has elicited repeated complaints of compassion fatigue. In fact, the exact opposite of this is true. Figure 1.1 presents data on those states that housed the largest number of refugees at the end of 2007.

Altogether, less than 10% of present-day refugees are in countries where the per capita income is more than $10,000, while fully half are in countries with a per capita income of $2,000 or less. The larger and more obvious point is that countries that are the most poorly equipped to handle refugee flows due to their own economic insecurity are the same states that have been forced to provide the lion's share of refugee protection.

A separate but related category consists of Internally Displaced Persons (IDPs). Much like refugees, IDPs have been forced to flee their homes and their livelihoods and move some place else in order to secure safety. However, what differentiates IDPs from refugees is that the latter have crossed their own national borders, while the former have not. Figure 1.2 presents an overview of the world's refugee and IDP population over the course of the past two decades.

The IDP phenomenon has truly been remarkable. Roberta Cohen, one of the leading experts on this subject, has pointed out that when first counted in 1982, there were 1.2 million IDPs in only 11 countries. However, in just four years, this total had increased to 14 million, and by 1997 there were more than 20 million IDPs in 35 to 40 countries (Cohen 2007). Cohen attributes this startling increase in IDPs to the internal conflicts that began after the end of the Cold

FIGURE 1.1
Major Refugee Hosting Countries, End 2007

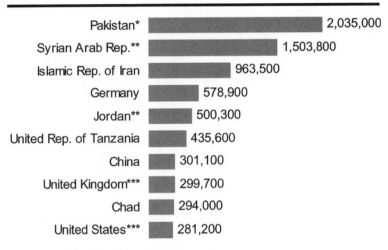

Pakistan*	2,035,000
Syrian Arab Rep.**	1,503,800
Islamic Rep. of Iran	963,500
Germany	578,900
Jordan**	500,300
United Rep. of Tanzania	435,600
China	301,100
United Kingdom***	299,700
Chad	294,000
United States***	281,200

* *Includes Afghans in a refugee-like situation.*
** *Government estimate.*
*** *UNHCR estimate based on 10 years of individual recognition of asylum-seekers. Figure excludes resettled refugees.*

Source: UNHCR Statistical Yearbook 2007.

War, growing from less than 10 in 1960 to almost 50 internal conflicts in 1992. At the end of 2008 it is estimated that there were 26 million IDPs, or approximately twice the number of refugees in the world. Table 1.2 presents a breakdown of IDP populations by continent and it includes in parentheses the number of countries in that region that are being monitored for IDP populations. To put some specificity to this, the countries with the largest number of IDPs in 2008 included: Sudan 4,900,000; Colombia 2,650,000–4,360,000; Iraq 2,840,000; Democratic Republic of Congo 1,400,000; and Somalia 1,300,000. Note that some countries, such as Iraq and Sudan, have large number of both refugees and IDPs.

To be clear, in some instances the decision not to cross a national border and assume the mantle of refugee is one that the fleeing individual makes on his or her own accord. However, in many other instances this decision is not made by the individual himself or herself, but by larger political (and military) forces.

FIGURE 1.2
Worldwide Refugee and IDP Population, 1989–2007

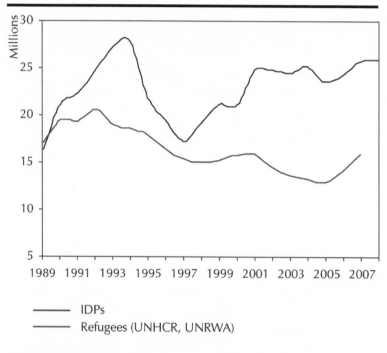

——— IDPs
——— Refugees (UNHCR, UNRWA)

Source: IDMC, Global Overview of Trends and Developments in 2008.

TABLE 1.2
Breakdown of IDP Population by Continent

Country	Number
Africa (19)	11.6 million
Americas (4)	4.5 million
Middle East (6)	3.9 million
South and South-East Asia (10)	3.5 million
Europe and Central Asia (13)	2.5 million
Total: (52)	26.0 million

Source: IDMC, Global Overview of Trends and Developments in 2008.

Certainly one of the most visible manifestations of this took place in the aftermath of the first Persian Gulf War where massive numbers of Kurds in the northern part of Iraq were desperately trying to flee from the advancing Iraqi army, only to be turned away by force at the Turkish border. If these individuals had crossed over into Turkey, they would have been considered as refugees. However, because of their failure to leave their country—a failure that was certainly not of their own choosing—they remained IDPs. However, because of the great deal of worldwide attention that was given to this particular situation (because of the Persian Gulf War itself), this group of IDPs received vastly more attention and resources than would otherwise be the norm.

However, what this also suggests is that, for the most part, IDPs are virtually invisible to the international community. One longstanding rationale for this inattention is that internal displacement is invariably a short-term event. Cohen provides a strong argument against this position:

> Civil wars can go on for decades, disrupting not only the lives of the individuals concerned but whole communities and societies. In such cases, both the areas left behind and the areas to which the displaced flee suffer extensive damage. In the areas that have been vacated, property and land are neglected, and community structures collapse as the population thins (Cohen 2007, 19).

Cohen continues:

> In the areas to which people flee, the displaced quickly strip forests and grasslands for housing and fuel, with long-term economic and ecological effects ... When flight is to urban areas, social services, water supplies, and sanitation facilities become overburdened, especially when the population doubles or triples in size. Since most conflicts and displacement occur in the world's poorest countries, the already weak infrastructure rapidly deteriorates sometimes to the point of collapse (Cohen 2007, 19).

Although our focus is on refugees, it is important to note that the only thing that differentiates this population from IDPs is the simple (or not so simple) act of crossing a national border. What

TABLE 1.3
Countries with Most IDPs as a Percentage of Their Population

Country	Percentage
Cyprus	Up to 23%
Somalia	13%
Sudan	12.4%
Iraq	9.6%
Colombia	5.7–9.3%
Zimbabwe	4.2–7.4%
Azerbaijan	6.7–7.1%
Georgia	5.7–6.3%
Lebanon	2–9%

Source: IDMC, Global Overview of Trends and Developments in 2008.

also has to be considered is that the decrease in the number of refugees (as has happened in the last few years) is not necessarily a positive thing, particularly if this only means that the number of IDPs continues to increase. Table 1.3 presents data on IDPs as a percentage of various countries' population.

The last term we will introduce is asylum (or refugee) seeker. The term asylum is typically understood in the sense of a right of a refugee to enter a country and to remain there on a permanent basis. As is oftentimes repeated, while all refugees have a right to seek asylum, no country has a legal obligation under international law to grant refugee status (Goodwin-Gill 1996, 289). However, all states are under an obligation not to send a person back to a country where his well-being or life would be in serious risk (refoulement). For our purposes, we will refer to an asylum seeker as one who claims to be entitled to the protection against refoulement. This, of course, is the legal definition, but it also needs to be pointed out that in receiving societies the term asylum seeker has a decidedly negative connotation with an overtly racist meaning.

The History of Protecting Refugees

By way of brief history, the notion of refugee protection not only has ancient roots but the principle of protecting the necessitous stranger is something that can be found in virtually all religions. However, international refugee protection only arose with the rise of nationalism (but also statelessness) in the late nineteenth and early twentieth century and then in the aftermath of World War I.

The international community's first effort to formally address this issue was the High Commissioner for Russian Refugees, created by the League of Nations in 1921 to deal with the massive social dislocations brought about the Bolshevik Revolution and the collapse of the Ottoman Empire. The Norwegian explorer and humanitarian, Fridtjof Nansen, was elected to the position of High Commissioner and he is renowned for the Nansen passports that he was able to procure for refugees. Notwithstanding these and other efforts, the refugee crisis persisted, and over the course of the next three decades, there were no less than nine international bodies that were created to deal with refugee issues.

World War II and its aftermath created even greater numbers of refugees and even greater political problems for dealing with these. In 1950, the Office of the United Nations High Commissioner for Refugees (UNHCR) was created. UNHCR has functional responsibility for administering international refugee assistance, although for both political and historical reasons the decades-long Palestinian refugee situation has been dealt with by another UN agency, the United Nations Relief and Works Agency for Palestine Refugees in the Near East (UNRWA). The statute of the UNHCR assigns responsibility to the agency of providing international protection for refugees and seeking permanent solutions for the problems of refugees. In pursuing this work, the UNHCR monitors and reports on states' refugee status determination processes as well as the overall treatment of asylum seekers, and the agency makes representations to governments on protection concerns either on behalf of individual asylum seekers or larger groups. In seeking durable solutions to refugees' problems, the UNHCR attempts to help those who wish to return home (voluntary repatriation) and to assist reintegration into their home communities. However, if this is not feasible or if voluntary repatriation is not likely to take place in the foreseeable future, the UNHCR works to settle refugees within the region (local settlement). However, for refugees who can neither return to their country of origin nor safely remain in their country of refuge, the third and last option is third country resettlement. To be clear, there are great difficulties with each of these options, particularly as states have become increasingly more resistant to housing refugees.

Unlike some of the other international human rights treaties, the Refugee Convention does not provide individuals with the possibility of challenging their own treatment, nor has the UNHCR been given the authority to adjudicate individual claims in the same manner as the Human Rights Committee and some of the other UN treaty bodies. On the other hand, it is well accepted that the contracting states give great deference to the UNHCR's interpretation of the Convention, and in this regard the *UNHCR Handbook* is widely considered to have substantial authority even if it is not legally binding.

The Post-War Human Rights Revolution

Although there have been visions of human rights in all societies and throughout history (Lauren 2003), what brought about the present-day human rights revolution was the devastation of World War II, and the horrors of the Holocaust in particular (Morsink 1999). Certainly, the most noteworthy achievement was the creation of the United Nations, dedicated to preserving international peace and security as well as the protection of human rights. In addition, many of the most important international human rights instruments were drafted during this period of time, including the so-called "International Bill of Rights" consisting of the Universal Declaration of Human Rights (UDHR), the International Covenant on Economic, Social and Cultural Rights (ICESCR), and the International Covenant on Civil and Political Rights (ICCPR)—along with the 1951 Refugee Convention.

What are human rights? Although there are varying ideas on this, one of the most elegant has been provided by the legal philosopher Michael Perry (1998) who has described human rights as based on the principle that there are certain things that you do not do to people (i.e., torture and kill) and certain other things that you do to and for them (i.e., feed, clothe, house, and educate). Before the advent of the human rights revolution, the manner in which a government treated its own people was in large part viewed as being a purely domestic matter that was considered outside the purview of the rest of the international community. In that way, the only rights that individuals possessed were those that their own government was willing to give to them. But what if that government granted few political rights—or worse, if it carried out all manner of atrocities against its own people? For the most part, the international community simply looked the other way.

In that way, the fundamental change that arose in the post-war period was the understanding that all human beings have human rights. What simply does not matter is where a person lives, the kind of government this person lives under, whether that particular state has signed and ratified none or all of the major international human rights treaties, and so on. But what was equally important was the understanding that the international community could no longer turn a blind eye and ignore human rights violations based on the idea that this was in the domestic sphere of a state.

It is within this broader context that the 1951 Refugee Convention needs to be viewed. Yet, in a number of ways, refugee protection served as a precursor to what we now know as human rights. For one thing, while the International Bill of Rights and most of the other international human rights instruments were novel undertakings, as mentioned earlier, the 1951 Refugee Convention had been preceded by a number of attempts by the international community to deal with what appeared to be a never-ending refugee crisis. The Refugee Convention precedes the human rights revolution in another way as well. In its essence, refugee protection is human rights protection—only this protection now has to be provided by a state other than one's own. The larger point is that this concern with others, which goes to the very essence of human rights, has long been manifested in the form of refugee protection. One might even go so far as to say that it took centuries for the notion of human rights to catch up with principle and practice of refugee protection.

Yet, it would be a mistake to equate refugee protection generally, and the 1951 Refugee Convention in particular, only with humanitarian concerns. For one thing, the treaty itself is a political document in the sense that it was originally limited to one place (Europe) and one time (events occurring before 1951). There is another political element to the Convention and it relates to the heavy emphasis it places on the protection of civil and political rights (CPR), but to the near exclusion of economic, social, and cultural rights (ESCR). This demarcation was not the result of any accident, but reflected political considerations, particularly in the context of the Cold War (Hathaway 1991, 7).

Finally and more broadly, refugees and refugee protection are very much hostage to larger political phenomena. Bill Frelick (2007) has suggested that there have been three distinct refugee paradigms. The first is the exilic period from 1948 to the 1990s. During this period of time, Western states actively encouraged refugee flows, especially from communist states. Frelick uses the Vietnamese exodus from the mid-1970s onward as the model for this period. With at least some cooperation by the communist government in that country, large numbers of Vietnamese were able to gain access to first asylum countries as Thailand and Malaysia. However, these camps only remained open and receptive to these refugee flows because of the promise that a large percentage would be resettled in Western states, which is exactly what took place.

However, following the end of the Cold War, Western states began to take a decidedly more jaundiced view of refugee populations. Or to state this more bluntly, refugees no longer served the foreign policy interests of Western states. As a result, there were several different ways that this situation was approached including: temporary protection (as opposed to permanent asylum arising out of refugee status determinations); cross border humanitarian assistance, often in the form of creating humanitarian corridors in various conflict zones as well as the establishment of safe areas in refugee-producing countries; and finally, humanitarian intervention in such countries as Iraq (1991), Haiti (1994), Bosnia (1995), Serbia (1999), and (belatedly) in Rwanda (1994).

As Frelick points out, in most of the humanitarian emergencies of the 1990s the international community pursued policies that were designed to prevent refugee flows.

> While the rhetoric—and undoubtedly the motivation—of many actors in the international community was humanitarian and predicated on the idea of attenuating the causes of refugee flows, in reality it was often powerful governments, the protagonists with a vested interest in avoiding refugee flows, who became the major sponsors of "protection" or "prevention" schemes inside countries that generated refugee flows or potential refugee flows. The UN agencies involved in peacekeeping and humanitarian response, and their NGO partners often found themselves trying not only to protect internally displaced persons (IDPs) within their country of origin, but also working to prevent their escape (Frelick 2007, 37).

The third and final paradigm began on September 11, 2001, and it continues to the present time and what marks this stage is the deep suspicion, and even fear, of refugees. Frelick suggests that the most obvious sign of this new paradigm shift is the decrease in asylum applications, noting that in one year alone, from 2003 to 2004, worldwide asylum applications decreased 22 percent, from 508,100 in 2003 to 396,400 in 2004, and overall, there has been a 40 percent drop since 1991. In terms of specific countries, it is noteworthy that the United States and Canada received 48 percent fewer asylum requests in 2004 than in 2001. Frelick explains what is behind this phenomenon:

> Under the security paradigm, refugees are devalued to the point where providing asylum or intervening to provide source-country solutions are trumped by the desire to keep terrorists out. As with the previous paradigms, these are not formalized international-community positions, but rather represent general trends, for which there will certainly be exceptions (Frelick 2007, 47).

In sum, the human rights revolution following the massive horrors of World War II attempted to make a new world order. What was recognized for the first time in history was that all individuals had human rights by the mere fact of their humanity. However, what the international community has continued to struggle with has been assigning responsibility for the protection of those rights. In some strange and even perverse way, the protection of human rights has in large part been left with the state that has committed the human rights violation in the first place. To point out what should be obvious: this system of human rights protection has not worked—and in all likelihood, it will never work.

Refugee protection provides a different approach to human rights protection. For one thing, the Refugee Convention was a product of this same time period and this same kind of thinking about creating a world that was vastly different from the Holocaust and the other horrors of World War II. But more importantly, refugee protection represents one of the few instances where one state takes responsibility for protecting the human rights of others. When it works well, it displays humanity at its very best. However, what must also be said is that there have been far too many instances when it has not worked well.

The 1951 Refugee Convention

Because of the central role that it plays in this realm, we will spend some time analyzing the 1951 Refugee Convention. On one level, the Convention (reprinted in Chapter 6) is a rather simple and straightforward international treaty. The treaty begins by defining the term refugee (Article 1) and then sets forth a catalogue of rights for refugees and obligations for receiving states in Articles 3–34. We will take these issues up in this order but we begin our analysis of the Convention by pointing out two things.

The first is that like virtually all other international law instruments, many of the terms (i.e., "well-founded fear" and "persecution") are vague and uncertain and the effort here will be to bring more definite meaning to them. The second point is that one of the unique features of the Refugee Convention is that although some of the rights set forth in the treaty are absolute—most notably, the right of a refugee not to be penalized for unauthorized entry (Article 31) and the right not to be subjected to refoulement (Article 33)—other rights are not absolute, but rather, are dependent on other factors. For example, the Convention distinguishes between refugees who are lawfully present, lawfully residing, and finally, those who are habitually residing in the receiving state—and it provides additional rights for refugees as one goes up this scale. Furthermore, certain other refugee rights are relative in the sense that they depend on how other non-nationals are treated by the host state. For example, the right to public housing (Article 21) and the right to freedom of movement (Article 26) are both dependent upon the extent to which other non-citizens are afforded these same rights. Finally, there are certain things that exclude a person from refugee protection altogether, but also an additional set of actions through which refugees will come to forfeit their refugee status, along with all the rights that go with being a refugee.

According to Article 1 of the Refugee Convention (as supplemented by the 1967 Protocol, reprinted in Chapter 6, which removed the temporal and geographical restrictions in the 1951 treaty), the term refugee applies to any person who

> owing to a well-founded fear of being persecuted for reasons of race, religion, nationality, membership of a particular social group or political opinion, is outside the country of his nationality and is unable, or, owing to such fear, is unwilling to avail himself of the protection of that country; or who, not having such nationality and being outside the country of his former habitual residence as a result of such events, is unable or, owing to such fear, is unwilling to return to it.

It is perhaps noteworthy that the Convention does not make any specific reference to political violence, although two later regional refugee instruments do. The refugee definition adopted in 1969 by the Organization of African Unity (reprinted in Chapter 6) also includes people fleeing "external aggression, internal civil strife, or events seriously disturbing public order." Similarly, the Cartagena Declaration of Refugees in 1984 (reprinted in Chapter 6) covering Central American refugees extends the 1951 Refugee Convention by including "persons who have fled their country because their lives, safety or freedom have been threatened by generalized violence, foreign aggression, internal conflicts, massive violations of human rights or other circumstances which have seriously disturbed public order."

There remains disagreement with regard to whether the Refugee Convention itself provides protection to those merely fleeing civil war and political violence (Zolberg et al. 1989). However, note that many countries that will not grant refugee status under the Convention on this basis have been willing to provide what has come to be called complementary protection, which is based broadly on humanitarian grounds, including political violence back in the country of origin (McAdam 2007). There are a few things to note about such practices. One is that in some countries the numbers receiving complementary protection will be much larger than those recognized as Convention refugees. A second point is that the protections and benefits for these individuals will invariably be far fewer than they are for Convention refugees. A third point relates to the political confusion engendered by such practices in the sense that the general populations in these countries are being given two diametrically opposed messages. The first is that these individuals are not refugees. But this message is then seemingly negated by allowing large numbers of these non-refugees to remain in this country. Perhaps it is no wonder that refugee and asylum practice has been such a political powder keg in those states.

Alienage

We begin with the requirement under the Convention definition that a refugee is someone who is outside his or her country of nationality, or origin. Note that the definition does not require that an individual had to flee his or her country because of a well-founded fear of persecution, although in many instances this is exactly what has taken place. Rather, the Convention also gives leeway for a person to develop the well-founded fear while this individual is already outside his or her country of nationality. One situation might involve a military coup that occurred while an individual was outside his or her country of nationality, and this person is now fearful of returning home. This category of refugees is commonly referred to as *refugees sur place*. Another situation is where a person, while in another country, expresses or adopts certain views or engages in certain activities that would now place him or her in danger if he or she is returned to his or her country of nationality. However, what would certainly raise questions is whether this individual was politically active before, the idea being that someone who otherwise appeared apolitical before departing but who then turns into a sharp critic of the ruling regime after leaving that state might simply be manufacturing these views for purposes of gaining refugee status. On the other hand, refugee law also recognizes that individuals should not be put to the test of having to prove that they are bona fide refugees by having to engage in behavior that could get them harmed or killed. Thus, both law and state practice try to calibrate whether seemingly newfound expressions of political dissent are real or not.

"Well-Founded Fear"

The second requirement of the refugee definition is that the claimant must have a well-founded fear. Most of the debate in this realm has centered around whether this term is referring to a subjective fear, an objective fear—or both. According to the dominant view, the term fear is referring to the claimant's actual state of mind, although what must also be proved is that this particular state of mind was in fact well-founded, which is to say that there was some objective criteria upon which this (subjective) fear could be based. One of the most important considerations, then, is the credibility of the claimant. Essentially, is the asylum seeker believable?

The other view is that this standard denotes a purely objective criterion. The proponents of this view argue that relying on subjective factors might result in similarly situated individuals being treated differently on the basis of their degree of fearlessness. They also argue that such an interpretation would result in the denial of protection to many applicants who are unable to express their own experiences and fears effectively. This would be particularly apt in the case of children who are refugee claimants or those who, perhaps because of their own previous treatment by national authorities, have great difficulty articulating in front of immigration officials in another country.

A separate, but related, issue is the threshold of risk. In the vast majority of cases the central issue is what will happen to a person if he or she is returned to his or her country of nationality. More particularly, will this individual be persecuted on the basis of one of the five Convention grounds—or is there a strong likelihood that this person will be free of such treatment? How much risk is too much risk?

Although there is no set answer to this issue, there are several parameters that have generally been agreed upon. For one thing, the mere chance or the remote possibility of being persecuted is insufficient to establish a well-founded fear. On the other hand, an applicant need not show that there is a clear probability that he or she will be persecuted. Rather the governing standard that seems to be emerging is that the person seeking recognition as a refugee must show a real chance or reasonable possibility of being persecuted. The UNHCR has provided this analysis:

> A substantial body of jurisprudence has developed in common law countries on what standard of proof is to be applied in asylum claims to establish well-foundedness. This jurisprudence largely supports the view that there is no requirement to prove well-foundedness conclusively beyond doubt, or even that persecution is more probable than not. As a general rule, however, to establish "well-foundedness," persecution must be proved to be reasonably possible (UNHCR: 1998, par. 17).

In its decision in *INS v. Cardoza-Fonseca*, the U.S. Supreme Court provided this analysis to the meaning of well-founded fear.

> That the fear must be "well-founded" does not alter the obvious focus on the individual's subjective beliefs, nor does it transform the standard into a "more likely than not" one. One can certainly have a well-founded fear of an event happening when there is less than a 50 percent chance of the occurrence taking place.

The Court then proceeded to use this example from the writings of refugee scholar Atle Grahl-Madsen:

> Let us ... presume that it is known that in the applicant's country of origin every tenth adult male person is either

put to death or sent to some remote labor camp. . . . In such a case it would be only too apparent that anyone who has managed to escape from the country in question will have a "well-founded fear of being persecuted" upon his eventual return.

Although mathematical probabilities provide some useful concreteness to this issue, it is important to underscore that refugee protection is anything but taking chances with the lives and well-being of others.

In establishing a well-founded fear, another issue relates to whether the individual who is facing the prospect of being persecuted could simply move to another part of his or her country and enjoy relative safely there. This is termed the internal flight alternative (IFA) and it is based on the idea that there is no need to seek refugee protection in another country when there are other areas of the claimant's home state where these same ends could be achieved. One of the problems with establishing whether there is an IFA or not is that it is not known whether those parts of a country that were safe will remain as such, or whether violence will follow a person (or a larger group of people). The UNHCR has settled on something resembling a middle ground:

> The fear of being persecuted need not always extend to the whole territory of the refugee's country of nationality. Thus in ethnic clashes or in cases of grave disturbances involving civil war conditions, persecution of a specific ethnic group may occur in only one part of the country. In such situations, a person will not be excluded from refugee status merely because he could have sought refuge in another part of the same country, if under all the circumstances it would not have been reasonable to expect him to do so (*UNHCR Handbook* 1979, par. 91).

In situations not involving civil conflict, it is expected that the requirement of seeking an IFA will generally be pushed harder.

Persecution

Oddly enough given its use in the Refugee Convention, there is no universally accepted definition of what constitutes persecution.

What is clear is that there is a direct connection between the notion of persecution and international human rights standards and there seems to be common agreement that the prospect of the denial of certain rights such as freedom from torture, the right to life, and liberty of the person, would constitute persecution. However, after this there is much less agreement.

One of the continual challenges in determining the meaning of persecution is to distinguish instances of persecution from legitimate prosecution by government officials. For instance, say that a small group of dissidents attempts to assassinate their country's leaders and are not successful. Assuming they are able to flee the country, should these would-be assassins be recognized as refugees? Their obvious fear is that if they were returned to their home country they would be brought to trial (assuming that governmental authorities would provide even this much due process of law) and subjected to severe criminal penalties, and perhaps even death. Undoubtedly, many would think that this would be a perfectly proper disposition of such a matter and that this scenario would be a proper form of prosecution—and thus would not constitute persecution. On the other hand, what if this group sought to remove a brutal dictator—the likes of Adolf Hitler or Pol Pot—and what if there was no other way of changing the ruling government? Would this still constitute lawful prosecution, or has this now moved into the realm of persecution?

Beyond this situation, it is not unknown for states to apply criminal penalties for purposes that would be considered illegitimate in most other countries. For example, a state's criminal law might outlaw certain forms of political or religious expression, or else treat certain ethic groups in a discriminatory fashion as was the case of the white apartheid regime in South Africa. There might also be instances where a state pursues legitimate governmental ends, but the effect of its policies falls more heavily on certain religious or ethnic groups. One common example is where a state has a policy of universal military service, but such practices are contrary to the beliefs of certain religions such as Jehovah's Witnesses. If those who refuse to serve are imprisoned, is this prosecution or persecution? Finally, there might be instances where a country applies a law of general applicability and it does so in a nondiscriminatory manner. However, what if it is difficult for a criminal defendant to get a fair trial? Or if the penalties are excessive by international standards? As a general rule, in determining whether a national criminal law constitutes prosecution or persecution will depend quite heavily on the conformity of this law with international human rights standards.

One final issue relates to the degree of government involvement in persecution. Note that the Convention does not specify or demand any connection between government authorities and the sources of persecution. Still, the clearest cases of persecution occur when state agents are actively involved. The other extreme is where there is a private dispute between two individuals. There is general agreement that refugee status is not warranted in these cases. However, the more difficult situations are those that fall between these two extremes: (1) where there is state sponsorship of the harm, (2) where the state tolerates the harm, and (3) where the state is simply not able to offer protection, either because it is overwhelmed with other matters or is otherwise a failed state. There are two schools of thought on this. The accountability model holds that the prospective treatment that would be afforded to a refugee claimant would only constitute persecution if the state could be held accountable under international human rights law. This would generally cover the first two categories. The protection approach, as its name suggests, focuses more on the protection needs of the individual and less on attributions of state responsibility and would in most cases cover the third situation as well.

The Nexus Requirement

The last element of the refugee definition we will look at is the so-called nexus requirement, namely, that the persecution the refugee would face would be based on one of five enumerated grounds: (1) race, (2) political opinion, (3) nationality, (4) religion, or (5) membership of a particular social group. What this means, quite simply, is that if the refugee claimant can prove persecution, but cannot tie this in with one of these five factors, he or she will be denied refugee status. The significance of this limitation depends on how broadly or narrowly the different grounds for persecution are interpreted.

Race

The first nexus ground is race. The Refugee Convention never defines this term, although the *UNHCR Handbook* provides that: "the term race ... has to be understood in its widest sense to include all kinds of ethnic groups that are referred to as 'races' in the common usage." This definition is consonant with the definition set forth by the International Covenant on the Elimination of all Forms of Racial Discrimination (ICERD), which defines racial discrimination as:

> any distinction, exclusion or preference based on race, colour, descent, or national or ethnic origin which has the purpose or effect of nullifying or impairing the recognition, enjoyment, or exercise on an equal footing of human rights and fundamental freedoms in the political, economic, social, cultural or any other field of public life.

Despite this common agreement on the meaning of race, the term will oftentimes not immediately translate into the granting of refugee status. Thus, although there is little question that South African blacks suffered severe persecution based on their race at the hands of the white apartheid government, the dominant thinking would question the appropriateness of proving refugee status on this basis alone. Yet, given the enormous disparities between South African blacks and whites in terms of such things as infant mortality, tuberculosis, per capita educational expenditures, household incomes, and so on, this might simply reflect the Refugee Convention's disfavor for protecting economic, social, and cultural rights.

Political Opinion

A second nexus ground is political opinion. The clearest case is the political dissident who expresses views in opposition to the ruling government. However, political opinion should generally be interpreted much broader than this to include opinions on any matter in which state policy is involved. Note that a person is not required to express a political opinion outright, either through speeches or in writing. Rather, persecution on the basis of political opinion not only encompasses individuals who openly express strong opinions on matters that are clearly political, but it includes political behavior as well.

Some of the most troubling cases concerning this nexus arise in the context of civil wars, especially those citizens who have a strong desire to be left alone. The question addressed by the U.S. Supreme Court in *INS v. Elias-Zacarias* was whether a refugee claimant from Guatemala who did not want to fight for either the government or for opposition forces—and who was fearful of reprisal by both sides—was expressing a political opinion by and through his neutrality. The Court held that neutrality, by itself, did not constitute a political opinion. Furthermore, it ruled that even if it could be assumed that neutrality did rise to the level of a political opinion, the refugee claimant would have to offer some kind of proof that his feared persecution was based on this, rather than on some other basis.

Nationality

The term nationality is not to be understood as citizenship, but refers primarily to an ethnic or linguistic group within that society. According to the UNHCR,

> Persecution for reasons of nationality may consist of adverse attitudes and measures directed against a national (ethnic, linguistic) minority and in certain circumstances the fact of belonging to such a minority may in itself give rise to a well-founded fear of persecution (*UNHCR Handbook* 1979, par. 74).

Religion

The Convention ground of persecution on account of religion covers believers and nonbelievers alike. While states are prohibited from interfering with religious beliefs, or forcing religious beliefs on those who are without, it can place limitations on religiously motivated conduct when such limitations are necessary to protect public safety and order. Earlier we made note of the common governmental practice of imprisoning those who refuse military service based on their religious beliefs. Is this persecution on account of religion, or are individuals free to believe whatever they wish—but only so long as their actions do not interfere with general governmental policy?

Membership of a Particular Social Group

The drafting of the Refugee Convention provides little insight on what the intent or aim of this last nexus happens to be. Some scholars and commentators take the position that social group is intended as a catch-all phrase that would include any and all other forms of persecution that are not covered by the other categories. At the other extreme are those who take the position that this ground serves mainly to clarify certain elements in the other nexus grounds. This, however, makes the term in large part superfluous. The more common approach is to take a position in between where social group does not encompass every definable group in a population no matter how loose or seemingly non-existent the connection, but limit this to certain kinds of characteristics.

According to the dominant view, the characteristic that defines a social group must be one that the members of the group either cannot change (because it is an innate attribute or because the attribute that defines the group refers to some past actions or experiences shared by the members) or else should not be required to change because it is so fundamental to their identity. As described by Guy Goodwin-Gill:

> In determining whether a particular group of people constitutes a "social group" within the meaning of the Convention, attention should ... be given to the presence of linking and uniting factors such as ethnic, cultural, and linguistic origin; education; family background; economic activity; shared values, outlook and aspirations. Also highly relevant are the attitudes to the putative social group of other groups in the same society and, in particular, the treatment accorded to it by State authorities. The importance, and therefore the identity, of a social group may well be in direct proportion to the notice taken of it by others—the view which others have of us—particularly at the official level. The notion of social group thus possesses an element of open-endedness potentially capable of expansion in favour of a variety of different classes susceptible to persecution (Goodwin-Gill 1996, 47–48).

Thus far, we have treated the nexus grounds in isolation from one another, but in many instances a refugee applicant can validly make a claim on more than one ground. For example, the individual who refuses to fight might be expressing a religious belief as well as a political opinion. Likewise, a woman who refuses to wear certain kinds of dress (such as the full burka), could be expressing a political opinion as well as a religious belief—and at the same time be considered to be a member of a social group that consists of women who oppose having their means of dress dictated to them by the government.

We close by mentioning two other matters. The first is that there will be instances when a person is attributed certain political or religious views by governing authorities that, in fact, this person does not have. It would make a mockery to deny refugee status to an individual on the grounds that the government's persecution is based on mistaken beliefs. Rather, what is essential is not whether the refugee has the attributes the government thinks he or she has, but whether the persecutor perceives that this person has these attributes—and it likely to persecute this individual on the basis of these (mistaken) attributes.

A second issue relates to whether the claimant's fear or risk of harm is shared by large numbers of other citizens. It is often said that the size of the group does not matter. However, in terms of actual state practice there frequently has been the demand that an individual prove that he or she has somehow been singled out for persecution beyond what a host of other people in that society suffer from.

Exclusions

Article 1(F) of the Refugee Convention identifies three categories of individuals who because of their past actions are considered to be undeserving of refugee protection, although in many instances these individuals will face prosecution if and when they are returned to their country of nationality. An individual falling into any one of these categories is not a refugee, and thus, not entitled to any of the rights enshrined in the Convention, including the prohibition against refoulement.

The first category applies to those who have "committed a crime against peace, a war crime, or a crime against humanity." Crimes of peace include planning, preparing, initiating, or participating in an unlawful war. Crimes against humanity are generally associated with war, but these may arise outside this context and include such international crimes as murder, rape, the forcible transfer of a population, and other inhumane acts that are committed as part of a widespread or systematic attack directed against any civilian population.

The second category applies to any person of whom there are serious reasons to consider that he or she has committed a serious non-political offense. What constitutes a serious non-political offense is not defined, but this exclusion should be read in the context of extradition law upon which it is based. In determining whether a crime is political or non-political, what needs to be determined is the nature of the crime, its alleged purpose, and the causal connection between the crime and the alleged political purpose. Thus, a crime will not be considered as a political crime if the act in question is grossly disproportionate to its alleged political objective.

The third and last category of excludable persons consists of those who have been considered guilty of acts contrary to the principles and purposes of the United Nations. It is not clear what this exclusion adds that is not covered by the first one in the sense that those who carry out war crimes and crimes against humanity would be doing so contrary to the principles and purposes of the United Nations. In all, the three exclusions demand serious reasons for denying refugee protection.

Exceptions to Nonrefoulement

Article 33(2) of the Convention provides two exceptions to the duty of nonrefoulement (analyzed below in more detail), both of which seek to protect the safety and security interests of the receiving state:

> The benefit of the present provision may not, however, be claimed by a refugee whom there are reasonable grounds for regarding as a danger to the security of the country in which he is, or who, having been convicted by a final judgment of a particularly serious crime, constitutes a danger to the community of that country.

The first exception authorizes a country to return a refugee— even one who would then face the prospects of persecution—if there are reasonable grounds for believing that this person would pose a security risk to the receiving state and its inhabitants. Given the stakes involved, such a determination should be undertaken with utmost care. For one thing, it should not be assumed that a particular individual would be a security threat simply on the basis of group membership or affiliation alone. In addition, such determinations should be made with regard to a particular person and not on the basis that a mass influx of refugee claimants who are seen as posing a grave threat to the national security of that state.

The second exception authorizes a state to return a refugee who having been convicted by a final judgment of a particularly serious crime constitutes a danger to the community of the receiving state. Note that this exception only applies to crimes of a particularly serious nature. In addition, the state must show that this individual constitutes a present danger. Thus, while a prior conviction is a necessary condition, it is not a sufficient condition in order to return an individual back home.

Cessations

A basic premise of the Refugee Convention is that international protection is a surrogate for national protection and is only warranted if and when national protection is not available. Thus, the cessation clause is premised on the idea that refugee protection should be removed when this protection is no longer warranted. Article 1(c) addresses five different scenarios when international protection is no longer considered necessary or justified because of the proof of adequate national protection.

The first is re-availment of national protection, most notably, the renewal of a passport from the refugee's state of nationality. According to the *UNHCR Handbook*, in the absence of proof to the contrary, a refugee who has obtained or renewed a passport will be presumed to avail himself or herself of the protection of his or her former country, although the Handbook also notes three factors that need to be considered: voluntariness, intent, and actual re-availment.

The second basis for cessation is the re-acquisition of nationality. The third is acquisition of a new nationality other than the refugee's (new) country of nationality. In this instance, protection will be provided by a state other than the country of nationality or the state that has granted refugee status. The fourth cessation ground is re-establishment in the country of origin and the focus here is on whether the refugee has maintained sufficient connections with his or her former home, oftentimes in the form of repeated visits, which would indicate the re-establishment, once again, of a citizen-government relationship. All four of these grounds for cessation are based on the idea that the refugee's conduct is proof positive of the removal of persecution.

The final ground for cessation is the only one out of the hands of the refugee and it relates to a fundamental change in the country of origin. The usual manifestation of this change is a substantial improvement in human rights conditions at home, although this cessation should not automatically and readily be applied at the slightest change in the political winds. Rather, there must be strong evidence that the changes are deep seated and not ephemeral and there should also be substantial reason to believe that the refugee who would be returned would not face the prospect of persecution once again.

Refugee Rights

Nonrefoulement

As noted earlier, the Refugee Convention sets forth a number of rights that refugees are to enjoy, although many of these rights are dependent on the particular status of the refugee. However, we begin with what is certainly the most important of all refugee rights and this is protection against refoulement, which is set forth in Article 33(1):

> No Contracting State shall expel or return ("refouler") a refugee in any manner whatsoever to the frontiers of territories where his life or freedom would be threatened on account of his race, religion, nationality, membership of a particular social group or political opinion.

A state's duty against nonrefoulement extends to all refugees who are within its jurisdiction who meet the criteria for being a refugee. One of the problems is that it is impossible for government authorities to know whether a particular refugee applicant is in fact a bona fide refugee without examining the facts and basis of that individual's claim. Therefore, to effectively implement the duty against nonrefoulement, states must provisionally extend this right until such time that a final determination of refugee status has been made. As this has been explained by the UNHCR:

> Every refugee is, initially, also an asylum seeker; therefore, to protect refugees, asylum seekers must be treated on the assumption that they may be refugees until their status has been determined. Otherwise, the principle of non-refoulement would not provide effective protection for refugees, because applicants might be rejected at borders or otherwise returned to persecution on the grounds that their claim had not been established (UNHCR, Note on International Protection, UN Doc. A/AC.96/815 (1993), par. 11).

Rights Owed to Refugees Physically Present in the Receiving State

As noted earlier, many of the rights provided to refugees by the Convention are dependent on the status of that particular refugee. We begin with the right set forth in Article 31 that provides that all refugees who are physically present in the receiving state are to be free from punishment because of unlawful entry. This provision is based on the realization that bona fide refugees are rarely able to comply with immigration requirements, although actual state practice seems to show that this provision is oftentimes ignored. The effective implementation of Article 31 requires that it be applied to asylum seekers as well, until and unless it is determined through a fair process that an individual does not meet the criteria of a refugee. However, this does not mean that a state cannot impose certain restrictions on the movement of asylum seekers during the time in which the refugee determination process is taking place, although such restrictions must relate to a recognized and legitimate state objective. In addition to this, detention of refugees and asylum seekers is permissible for the purpose of provisional investigation of identity and circumstances of entry. However, it does not authorize detention throughout the asylum procedure and alternative measures should always be considered first. As the UNHCR has advocated, the detention of refugees and asylum seekers is an exceptional measure that should only be used in extraordinary circumstances and applied against particular individuals when this is found to be necessary to achieve an important governmental objective. Thus, mass and indiscriminate detentions are invariably not justifiable or warranted.

Rights Owed to Refugees Lawfully in the Contracting State

A number of rights, including Article 18 (self-employment), Article 26 (freedom from movement), and Article 32 (expulsion), are provided to refugees lawfully in the host country. While national laws concerning the requirements for entry and stay should be taken into account, the decisive issue is the actual relationship between the receiving state and the refugee. Although disputed by some governments, it is quite clear that an asylum seeker who has submitted to all necessary investigations and submitted documentation or statements in support of his or her claim must be deemed lawfully present in the receiving state. The asylum seeker's presence would cease to be lawful upon a final decision to deny refugee status. However, until such time, the state must treat the asylum seeker as a lawfully present refugee and provide those rights set forth in the Convention.

Rights Owed to Refugees Lawfully Staying in the Contracting State

Those refugees who are not only lawfully in a country's territory but who are lawfully staying are entitled to additional rights including freedom of association (Article 15), the right to engage in wage-earning employment and to practice a profession (Article 17), and the right to access to housing (Article 21). The term lawfully staying denotes legal residency of some continuity and length. However, it is not synonymous with permanent resident status. Refugees who have been admitted and treated as refugees for some period of time and whom no other state will assume responsibility over are to be considered as lawfully staying in a receiving state and to be afforded rights commensurate with that status.

Rights Owed to Refugees Residing in the Contracting State

Finally, a few rights are reserved for refugees who reside in the receiving state. Habitual resident refugees have a right to legal aid and to receive national treatment in regard to the posting of security for costs in a court proceeding (Article 16[2]). And after a period of three years residence, such refugees are also exempted from both requirements of legislative reciprocity (Article 7[2]) and any restrictive measures imposed on the employment of aliens (Article 17[2]).

Interface with International and Regional Human Rights Instruments

The Refugee Convention serves as the primary means of ensuring human rights protection for refugees. However, this does not mean that refugees—but also refugee claimants and even those denied refugee status—thereby forfeit all other forms of human rights protection. What we look to in this section is the manner in which the Refugee Convention interfaces with other international and regional human rights instruments.

Nonrefoulement

As we have noted before, nonrefoulement is the linchpin of the 1951 Convention and this same principle is embodied in other human rights instruments as well. Most notably, Article 3(1) of the Convention Against Torture and Other Cruel, Inhuman or Degrading Treatment (CAT, reprinted in Chapter 6) provides: "No State Party shall expel, return ('refouler') or extradite a person to another State where there are substantial grounds for believing that he would be in danger of being subjected to torture." Although the language is quite similar to that in Article 33 of the Refugee Convention, there are also some notable differences. The most obvious is that the CAT does not have a nexus requirement in the same manner as the Refugee Convention. Thus, those making a claim under CAT are not required to prove that the harm they face if returned to their country of nationality (or any other country) is based on race, religion, and so on.

Another major difference between the two instruments is that there are no exceptions to CAT as there are in the Refugee Convention. Recall that under Article 1(F) of the Convention, a person could be excluded from refugee status altogether for having previously committed certain international crimes; while under Article 33(2) a refugee could be returned because he or she posed a security threat to the receiving state notwithstanding the persecution that he or she might endure. In contrast to this, the CAT does not have any exceptions to the prohibition against returning a person to a country where there are substantial grounds for believing that a person might be tortured. What this means, then, is that even individuals who themselves have directed and/or carried out gross and systematic human rights abuses would be protected from being sent back home if it appeared that this individual might be subjected to torture.

Note, however, that there has been some recent challenge to this principle. For example, in *Suresh v. Canada*, the Canadian Supreme Court ruled that "We do not exclude the possibility that in exceptional circumstances, deportation to face torture might be justified" (par. 78). Within the United Nations, both the Human

Rights Committee (HRC) and the Committee Against Torture have sharply criticized the Canadian government for this position, with the former making these pointed remarks in its Concluding Observations to Canada's state report:

> The Committee is concerned by the State party's policy that, in exceptional circumstances, persons can be deported to a country where they would face the risk of torture or cruel, inhuman or degrading treatment ... The State party should recognize the absolute nature of the prohibition of torture, cruel, inhuman or degrading treatment, which in no circumstances can be derogated from. Such treatments can never be justified on the basis of a balance to be found between society's interest and the individual's rights ... No person, without any exception, even those suspected of presenting a danger to national security or the safety of any person, and even during a state of emergency, may be deported to a country where he/she runs the risk of being subjected to torture or cruel, inhuman or degrading treatment. The State party should clearly enact this principle into its law (HRC 2006, par. 15).

Beyond *Suresh*, the practice of extraordinary rendition has severely tested the meaning of Article 3, as several Western states, and the United States in particular, have engaged in far-ranging and geographically far-flung programs that have resulted in those suspected of supporting international terrorism being sent to countries that have a long and ugly history of carrying out torture.

Although the CAT's nonrefoulement provision is in many ways considerably broader than the Refugee Convention's provision, what must also be said is that, in a technical sense, the prohibition against return only applies to torture as such, while the Convention applies to persecution much more broadly. What this means is that persons who might be subject to severe pain or even death that would be carried out by private actors might not qualify for protection under CAT, unless it could be shown that such ill-treatment was to be carried out at the instigation of or with the consent or acquiescence of a public official.

The International Covenant on Civil and Political Rights (ICCPR) does not have a specific provision against nonrefoulement. However, the Human Rights Committee, the treaty body in the United Nations that monitors enforcement of this international treaty, has interpreted such an obligation, placing special emphasis on Article 7, which provides: "No one shall be subjected to torture or to cruel, inhuman or degrading treatment or punishment." As mentioned earlier, the HRC criticized the Canadian Supreme Court's ruling in *Suresh*, which held that the prohibition against nonrefoulement might not be absolute.

Finally, although there is no specific nonrefoulement provision in the European Convention, the European Court of Human Rights (ECHR) has reached the same conclusion as the HRC. In its landmark decision in *Soering v. United Kingdom*, the ECHR ruled that states were prohibited from sending a person to a country where there are substantial grounds for believing that the person faces a real risk of being subjected to torture or to inhuman or degrading treatment or punishment. Furthermore, the Court has also held that no derogation can be made against this prohibition, even in times of public emergency threatening the life of the country. Thus, in *Chahal v. United Kingdom*, the Court ruled against the deportation of a Sikh separatist who was viewed by British authorities as a security threat, holding that "the activities of the individual in question, however undesirable or dangerous, cannot be a material consideration."

Racism

As noted at the outset, the term asylum seekers has become a pejorative term in Western states and it is reflective of the kinds of racism that many of those seeking refugee status have had to face. All of these countries are a state party to the Convention on the Elimination of Racial Discrimination (CERD), which provides under Article 2(1): "States Parties condemn racial discrimination and undertake to pursue by all appropriate means and without delay a policy of eliminating racial discrimination in all its forms, and promoting understanding among all races." Governments that continue to ignore the racial animus so often directed against asylum seekers and refugees are simply not living up to their obligations under CERD.

Detention

The Refugee Convention imposes certain restrictions on the detention of asylum seekers and refugees and these are buttressed by other human rights treaties that prohibit the arbitrary deprivation of liberty, most notably, Article 9 of the ICCPR. The key here is that the deprivation of liberty must be carried out to achieve a legitimate government interest. Using detention as a means of dissuading refugee flows does not meet that standard. This is not to suggest that there are no other policy grounds that a receiving state could invoke. For example, it might be valid for a state to use detention in order to verify the identity of asylum seekers, to determine the basic elements of their claim for protection, and to make sure they do not pose a risk to the society. In addition, there might be instances in the removal process where a rejected asylum seeker could be detained in order to ensure that this person does not abscond into the general population.

However, what is not acceptable under the law is the massive and indiscriminate detention of all asylum seekers based on some vague national security grounds. Likewise, the indefinite detention of those who are denied refugee status but who cannot be returned to their country of nationality is likewise not warranted.

Economic, Social, and Cultural Rights

As noted earlier, the Refugee Convention provides certain rights depending on a refugee's particular status. Yet, as part of a general restrictive trend towards asylum seekers, a number of countries (Western states in particular) have taken to restricting access to economic and social benefits. While states enjoy a certain degree of latitude in such matters, they must not adopt policies that effectively amount to a violation of the prohibition against nonrefoulement.

To reiterate, refugees, asylum seekers, and even those whose claims for refugee status have been rejected do not leave their human rights at the borders of the receiving state (or would-be receiving state). In that way, since nearly all recipient countries are a state party to the International Covenant on Economic, Social and Cultural Rights, any denial of these rights to these individuals will constitute a violation of international human rights law.

Rights of the Child

A substantial portion of the world's refugee population is comprised of children, and these children benefit from the provisions of the Convention on the Rights of the Child (CRC). One of the key provisions of the CRC is Article 3, which stipulates that the child's best interest must be the primary consideration in all actions that affect them. Beyond that, Article 22(1) provides that a child seeking refugee protection must be given appropriate humanitarian assistance, while Article 22(2) imposes an obligation on state parties to cooperate with the competent authorities in finding parents of unaccompanied refugee children. Finally, Article 37 sets forth particularly stringent conditions dealing with the detention of children.

Domestic Procedures

The 1951 Refugee Convention does not specify how a state is to implement the provisions of the treaty, although under general international law, each state party has an obligation to carry out its treaty obligations in good faith. In an effort to assist states on these matters, the UNHCR has recommended that states should: adopt formal and uniform procedures for making refugee determinations; seek to ensure that decision makers are well versed in the relevant international instruments; assist applicants in pursuing their claim; and finally, give rejected applicants the opportunity to appeal and to remain in the country while the appeal is pending.

Establishing Eligibility

For a whole host of reasons, including sudden flight, refugee claimants are oftentimes not able to provide substantial documentation in support of their claim. For this reason, one of the keys to the refugee determination process is careful consideration of the claimant's own testimony. As a general rule, the applicant bears the responsibility for proving he or she is a bona fide refugee. However, it is generally accepted that a fairer approach is one in which this burden is shared with competent authorities in the receiving state. In addition, as the *UNHCR Handbook* points out, because of the inherent difficulties facing the claimant as well as the consequences of a wrongful determination, it is generally agreed that the applicant should be given the benefit of any doubt.

Decision-making in this realm is fraught with difficulties. Not only must the adjudicator be generally knowledgeable with conditions in the claimant's country of origin, but he must also be sensitive to the unique situation faced by the applicant himself or herself. There are at least two major problems that complicate this process even further. The first has already been alluded to before and it relates to a deep-seated fear that many refugee applicants have of government officials quite generally, in nearly all cases due to their previous treatment in their former country, which is then carried over to immigration officials in the receiving state.

The second issue is how authorities should deal with refugee claimants who are thought to be lying and/or who have used false documents in order to gain entry into the recipient state. In many instances, state authorities will summarily deny the application. However, this ignores several factors. One is that an applicant might exaggerate his or her story because the enormous (and justified) fear of being sent back home. All of us tell lies—and we do so even when our life and well-being are not in the balance. Beyond this, what adjudicators need to be reminded of is the fact that without false travel documents, a good number of asylum seekers would not even have the ability of being able to gain access to most states in order to be able to present their claim in the first place. Because of this, there has grown to be a heavy reliance on professional smugglers who provide the refugee seeker with the necessary documents and along with that the story that is to be conveyed to immigration officials in the receiving state. The larger point is that inconsistencies and even proven lies (including false travel documents) should not automatically lead to the rejection of an asylum claim. The adjudicator needs to find out whether there are reasonable explanations for inconsistencies, misrepresentations and even falsehoods. In particular, immigration officials need to discern how central these things are to the refugee seeker's claim.

Denial of Asylum Hearings and Accelerated Procedures

A growing number of states have adopted measures that either deny asylum hearings altogether or else provide for accelerated proceedings. The ostensible aim of these measures is for receiving states to have to spend little or no time and resources on claims that are thought to be manifestly unfounded.

Most Western states have denied access to asylum procedures altogether in situations where responsibility for assessing an application for asylum could have been assumed by another state. This is generally referred to as the principle of "first country of asylum" or "safe third country," and the idea at work here is that the refugee claimant should now be denied the opportunity to present a claim because this could have been (and should have been) done in the safe country this individual previously had passed through. Thus, if an asylum seeker from Iraq had a brief layover at Heathrow Airport in the United Kingdom, and then proceeded to fly to Oslo, Norway, the Norwegian government would deny the ability to file an asylum claim on the basis that this individual had passed through a safe country.

It should be pointed out that there is no obligation under international law for a state to re-admit non-nationals and many safe countries have done exactly that. The term refugees in orbit has been coined to describe refugee claimants who are repeatedly bounced around from recipient country back to safe country back to recipient country, and so on. To help address this problem, states have adopted various bilateral and multilateral re-admission agreements that determine which state among the contracting parties shall be responsible for assessing certain refugee claims.

In addition to the safety of countries that asylum seekers have passed through, many Western states have developed the notion of safe countries of origin, which has meant that asylum seekers from these countries will either be barred from making a claim altogether or else will be subjected to accelerated procedures or different evidentiary standards. Although the notion of safe countries of origin has a certain intuitive feel, in practice these policies have been questionable at best and unlawful at worst. One problem is the lack of transparency that invariably has marked this process, but an even more serious problem is that a number of the countries that have been placed on various countries' lists of safe countries—Algeria in the 1990s represents one of the most egregious examples—are certainly anything but this.

Finally, receiving states have adopted a number of measures that are aimed at, or which effectively prevent, would-be refugees from reaching their borders altogether, manifesting what Matthew Gibney describes as a form of schizophrenia about refugee protection:

> A kind of schizophrenia seems to pervade Western responses to asylum seekers and refugees; great importance is attached to the principle of asylum but enormous efforts are made to ensure that refugees (and others with less pressing claims) never reach the territory of the state where they could receive its protection (Gibney 2004, 2).

The two most important means of instituting this non-entrée policy (Hathaway 2005, 291) are the application of visa requirements and the institution of carrier sanctions. A visa requirement is essentially permission to travel to a receiving state and it allows a country to decide whether to allow individuals (or certain individuals) from a particular country to travel there. Typically, states institute visa requirements against countries that produce refugees—invariably countries experiencing gross and systematic human rights violations—but what is important to note is that there are no exceptions for those in need of refugee protection. Of course, what this means is that many refugees (or would-be refugees) are effectively prevented from leaving their country of origin altogether. Moreover, in order to make these visa requirements an effective bar against entry, states have imposed sanctions on carriers (airlines, boats, etc.) that have brought aliens to their borders without visas or with improper travel documents. In addition, states have also started to send their own agents into foreign waters and even on to foreign land in an effort to enforce these restrictions. We will discuss this in much greater detail in Chapter 2.

All of these measures have gone far in significantly reducing the ability of individuals to flee their country of origin—at least legally. As a result, a growing problem has been asylum seekers who arrive at a country's borders with either no documents or forged documents. Some governments have responded to this by assigning persons who lack valid travel documents to accelerated asylum procedures and/or by subjecting these individuals to mandatory detention. However, what these governments have failed to acknowledge is that those in need of refugee protection will oftentimes need to resort to such measures in order to gain entry into another country. Thus, what should be reiterated are the provisions in Article 31(1) of the Refugee Convention, which provides that the lack of appropriate documentation or the use of fraudulent documents does not, by itself, render a claim abusive or fraudulent and should not be relied on to deny access to refugee proceedings.

Returned Refugees

Obviously, not all those who apply for refugee status will be successful. States have no obligation under international law to allow rejected applicants to remain, nor do they have a responsibility to provide a home for those whose status as a refugee has ceased. The UNHCR has adopted the view that the preferred option for dealing with these situations is voluntary repatriation that is carried out in safety and dignity. However, one of the continuing concerns is that repatriation that has been labeled (by the government itself) as voluntary has been anything but—and, thus, constitutes refoulement. Returned refugees do not forfeit their human rights. Thus, any such measures must be consonant with human rights standards and under the guidance of international and regional human rights treaties.

Conclusion

This chapter was designed to do two things. The first was to provide a snapshot of the current situation. It should be no surprise that countries experiencing massive levels of political violence, including civil conflict, would produce the largest number of refugees and IDPs. However, what will be surprising to many is that most refugees are not located in the Western industrialized states. In fact, only about 10 percent are—which means that the overwhelming majority of the world's refugees are being housed in poor, developing countries.

The second thing this chapter sought to achieve was to provide the reader with an overview and analysis of the 1951 Refugee Convention. Although the Convention has been supplemented by two of the regional refugee instruments and its work complemented by other human rights treaties, it remains the central element of refugee protection.

References

Books, Articles, and Chapters

Cohen, Roberta. 2007. "The Global Crisis of Internal Displacement," in James D. White, and Anthony Marsella, eds. *Fear of Persecution; Global Human Rights, International Law, and Human Well-Being*. Lanham, MD: Lexington Books.

Frelick, Bill. 2007. "Paradigm Shifts in the International Responses to Refugees," in James D. White, and Anthony Marsella, eds. *Fear of*

Persecution; Global Human Rights, International Law, and Human Well-Being. Lanham, MD: Lexington Books.

Gibney, Matthew. 2004. *The Politics and Ethics of Asylum: Liberal Democracy and the Response to Refugees.* Cambridge: Cambridge University Press.

Goodwin-Gill, Guy. 1996. *The Refugee in International Law,* 2d ed. Oxford, UK: Clarendon Press.

Hathaway, James. 1991. *The Law of Refugee Status.* Toronto: Butterworths.

Hathaway, James. 2005. *The Rights of Refugees Under International Law.* Cambridge: Cambridge University Press.

Lauren, Paul Gordon. 2003. *The Evolution of Human Rights: Visions Seen.* Philadelphia: University of Pennsylvania Press.

McAdam, Jane. 2007. *Complementary Protection in International Refugee Law.* Oxford, UK: Oxford University Press.

Morsink, Johannes. 1999. *The Universal Declaration of Human Rights: Origins, Drafting and Intent.* Philadelphia: University of Pennsylvania Press.

Perry, Michael. 1998. *The Idea of Human Rights.* New York: Oxford University Press.

UNHCR. January 1992. Handbook on Procedures and Criteria for Determining Refugee Status under the 1951 Convention and the 1667 Protocol Relating to the Status of Refugees (*UNHCR Handbook*). HCR/IP/4/Eng/REV.1. UNHCR: Geneva.

UNHCR. December 16, 1998. "Note on Burden and Standard of Proof in Refugee Claims."

UNHCR. 1993. Note on International Protection, UN Doc. A/AC.96/815.

Zolberg, Aristide, Astri Suhrke, and Sergio Aguayo. 1989. *Escape from Violence; Conflict and the Refugee Crisis in the Developing World.* New York: Oxford University Press.

Cases and Administrative Decisions

Chahal v. United Kingdom. 2007. 108 ILR 385. [p. 33]

Human Rights Committee. April 20, 2006. *Concluding observations of the Human Rights Committee: Canada.* CCPR/C/CAN/CO/5.

INS v. Cardoza-Fonseca. 1987. 480 U.S. 421.

INS v. Elias-Zacarias. 1992. 502 U.S. 478.

Soering v. United Kingdom. 1989. App. No. 4038/88, ECHR 14 (July 7, 1989).

Suresh v. Canada (Minister of Citizenship and Immigration). 2002. 1 S.C.R. 3, 2002 SCC 1.

2

Problems, Controversies, and Solutions

In this chapter we provide an in-depth analysis of three major issues, two of which relate directly to the issue of refugee protection while the other involves a much different conceptualization of human rights that could have enormous implications in terms of refugee protection itself. We begin by addressing the issue of asylum abuse, a charge that frequently has been made in all Western states, and which has served as a basis for many of the non-entrée policies in those countries. The question we take up is whether there is any empirical proof of this claim, or whether asylum seekers come from exactly the kinds of states that one might expect: countries experiencing gross and systematic human rights violations.

The second issue involves the scope of the prohibition against refoulement. We return to a question that has been touched upon previously, namely, how far (literally) does a state's obligation to protect extend? In this section we spend a fair amount of time analyzing the U.S. Supreme Court's opinion in *Sale v. Haitian Centers Council*.

The third and final issue involves the broader issue of human rights. Although human rights are (universally) declared to be universal, the enforcement and protection of human rights has been confined by territorial considerations. Thus, the dominant thinking has been that while states have human rights obligations within their own domestic realm, they do not have the same (or perhaps any) such obligations outside their own territorial borders. Refugee protection presents a slight variant on this in the

39

sense that it is based on one state providing human rights protection to citizens of a foreign land. Still, refugee protection is itself territorially based, as evidenced by the oft-repeated principle that no state has an obligation to admit any refugees. However, within the past decade there have been some strong challenges to the territorial conceptualization of human rights, and we will explore what this has been based on, but also what the implications of this might be in terms of refugee protection more generally.

Asylum Abuse?

One of the overarching themes in this work is there is a very strong relationship between human rights violations and refugee protection and perhaps the most essential way to think about refugees is that they are a manifestation of such violations in the sense that people do not otherwise find it necessary to suddenly flee their homes in order to seek protection in some other land. More than that, because refugees are people whose human rights have not, or will not, be protected by their home state, this responsibility is then taken over by some other country.

If refugees are people fleeing from political violence, what we would expect is that those countries experiencing the worst levels of human rights violations would produce the largest number of refugees. Conversely, one would expect to see very few refugees from countries where political violence is either low or virtually non-existence. Beyond this, one of the things that could also be tested is whether there is any kind of systematic abuse of the asylum system in various states.

To test these propositions we will undertake what we will term a human rights analysis. What this analysis is intended to do is to capture two different, but related, phenomena. The first is the probability of persecution, while the second relates to the severity of persecution. Under the refugee standard an individual must prove that he or she has a well-founded fear of persecution. The problem, of course, is that it is oftentimes difficult, if not impossible, to determine exactly when a particular individual has the requisite fear. However, what we can establish through a macro-level analysis is a rough approximation of the probability of persecution based on the level of human rights violations in that country. Thus, all else being equal, individuals who live in a state that has a very high level of political violence will have a greater probability of facing persecution, while individuals who live in states where there are very low levels of human rights violations will face a much lower probability of persecution. This is not to say that there is a one-to-one correlation or that individual determinations can be based on macro-level data. On the other hand, there should be a strong correlation between levels of political violence and refugee flows. Certainly no one would be surprised that the political violence in Iraq has resulted in massive refugee flows and an enormous Internally Displaced Persons (IDP) population. In the same way, one would be greatly surprised if a peaceful country like Costa Rica suddenly produced large numbers of refugees.

The second thing that a human rights analysis provides is some insight in terms of the severity of persecution. As we discussed earlier in Chapter 1, the 1951 Refugee Convention does not define persecution, nor does it make any attempt to differentiate between different kinds of persecution. Guy Goodwin-Gill has defined persecution this way:

> Persecution within the Convention thus comprehends measures taken on the basis of one of more of the stated grounds, which threaten: deprivation of life or liberty; torture or cruel, inhuman, or degrading treatment; subjection to slavery or servitude; non-recognition as a person (particularly where the consequences of such non-recognition impinge directly on an individual's life, liberty, livelihood, security, or integrity); and oppression, discrimination, or harassment of a person in his or her private, home or family life (Goodwin-Gill 1983, 40).

Under this view, individuals who face job discrimination based on their religious beliefs would face persecution and would be considered as refugees, as would those fleeing from death and torture. What is being suggested here is that while it might not be necessary to distinguish between levels of persecution in order to make the refugee determination itself, receiving states ought to prioritize among those who are most in need of assistance. Under that approach, those facing the prospect of torture or death should receive priority over those whose claim for refugee status is based on harassment.

To test some of these propositions we will make use of one of the most widely used human rights datasets: the Political Terror

Scale (PTS) (Gibney, Cornett and Wood, 2008). The PTS ranks countries on a scale of 1–5, with the data coming from two different annual sources: the U.S. Department of State's *Country Reports on Human Rights Practices* and the Amnesty International's *Annual Report*. Countries are coded on the following scale (Wood and Gibney, 2010):

> Level 1: Countries . . . under a secure rule of law, people are not imprisoned for their views, and torture is rare or exceptional. . . . Political murders are extremely rare. . . .
>
> Level 2: There is a limited amount of imprisonment for nonviolent political activity. However, a few persons are affected; torture and beating are exceptional. . . . Political murder is rare. . . .
>
> Level 3: There is extensive political imprisonment. . . . Execution or other political murders and brutality may be common. Unlimited detention, with or without trial, for political views is accepted. . . .
>
> Level 4: The practices of Level 3 are expanded to larger numbers. Murders, disappearances, and torture are part of life. . . . In spite of its generality, on this level terror affects primarily those who interest themselves in politics or ideas.
>
> Level 5: The terrors of Level 4 have been extended to the whole population. . . . The leaders of these societies place no limits on the means or thoroughness with which they pursue personal or ideological goals.

There are a few things to note about the PTS. The first is that it only measures actual violence. In that way, it is not a measure of overall state repression. In fact, there will be some cases (the Soviet Union in the 1980s is an excellent example) where a government's repressive measures are so efficient and effective that there will be relatively few incidents of torture, political imprisonment, summary executions, and disappearances. Another point is that the PTS only measures human rights violations carried out by the state, although it also measures political violence that is carried out by those known to be associated with the state. An example of this is Colombia where the government has strong ties to various paramilitary forces. In that way, the government's PTS score will reflect these acts of violence as well. Finally, the PTS only reflects what is in these two annual human rights reports. Thus, in the construction of the index for each year, countries are scored as if the reports are accurate and complete and any biases should be evident in the indices. In addition, those who serve as coders to this project are instructed not to consider their own knowledge of a particular country. Instead, each country receives two scores—one based on the Amnesty International Report and the other on the U.S. State Department Report—and that score should only reflect what is actually in those respective reports.

We begin with the question of the relationship between levels of human rights violations and refugee flows. The following Table 2.1 has taken the data from Table 1.1 in Chapter 1 that lists the top 10 refugee producing countries for the year 2008, but adds the U.S. State Department PTS score for that year.

As you can see, four of the top five refugee producing countries were coded at a level 5—states experiencing the very highest levels of political violence. What also should be considered is that the PTS only coded ten countries that year at level 5: Afghanistan, Chad, Democratic Republic of Congo, Iraq, Israel and the Occupied Territories, North Korea, Somalia, Sri Lanka, and Zimbabwe. Thus, Table 2.1 provides affirmation that there is a strong relationship between levels of human rights abuse and the creation of refugee flows.

Although the results here are by no means surprising, they are an important means of testing whether people leave their home country because of political violence—or whether, instead, they do so for economic betterment. What this data shows is that what

TABLE 2.1
Top Ten Refugee Producing States, 2008 and PTS Scores

Country	Number
Afghanistan	2,833,128 (5)
Iraq	1,903,519 (5)
Somalia	561,154 (5)
Sudan	419,248 (5)
Colombia	373,532 (4)
Democratic Republic Congo	367,995 (5)
Occupied Palestinian Authority	340,016 (5)
Vietnam	328,183 (3)
Burundi	281,592 (4)
Turkey	214,378 (3)

drives people out of their homelands is not poverty so much—unfortunately, there are a lot of poor countries in the world—but political violence, particularly very high levels of political violence. As noted earlier, macro-level data such as this cannot be used to determine whether a particular individual has the requisite well-founded fear of persecution. On the other hand, however, one would think that states could easily establish asylum procedures whereby individuals fleeing from a level 4 or level 5 country would enjoy a rebuttable presumption that they are bona fide refugees, while they could work under the same (rebuttable) presumption that individuals fleeing from a level 1 or level 2 country are simply not refugees.

What about at the receiving end? The reason why Western states have undertaken such measures as visa restrictions, carrier sanctions, interdiction, and so on is the belief that there has been a great deal of asylum abuse. However, very little empirical analysis has been carried out on this issue. Instead, most of the proof of this charge is to be found in the denials for refugee protection made by receiving countries themselves. However, there is another way that this proposition can be tested and it is to examine where asylum seekers are coming from. If most applicants are arriving from states experiencing relatively low levels of political violence, it would be fair to say that the charge of asylum abuse does have a strong basis in fact. On the other hand, if the opposite of this is true—that is, if the overwhelming majority of those seeking refugee protection are from countries experiencing the very highest levels of political violence—then a very strong case can be made for the opposite proposition.

The empirical evidence shows that in one Western country after another, and over an extended period of time, substantial majorities of asylum seekers have come from countries experiencing gross and systematic human rights violations. In Chapter 6, there is a complete set of data presented on asylum claims for ten Western countries (United States, United Kingdom, Sweden, Netherlands, Italy, Germany, France, Denmark, Canada, and Australia) for three different time periods: 2008, 1998, and 1988. For each country, the top ten countries of origin are listed along with the number of asylum seekers from that country as well as that country's PTS score for that year. Note that this data only lists non-European asylum seekers and there are several reasons for doing this. The first is that the number of asylum seekers from other European countries is relatively small to begin with, so this is a way

of taking out some of the noise. A second reason is that, almost without exception, the European countries are reasonably safe countries, something that is reflected in the PTS scores of these states.
Finally, when the term asylum seeker is hurled at people the way
that it so often is, it is not other Europeans who are the target.
Instead, it is invariably used against non-Europeans, particularly
those who do not look European. For these reasons, we limit our
analysis to non-Europeans—for truly it is against this population
that the charge of asylum abuse has so frequently been made.

United Kingdom

What we will do here is to try to summarize some of the findings from the data in Chapter 6. We will begin with the United
Kingdom and Table 2.2 presents data on asylum applications for
2008. What is listed is the total number of asylum seekers that
year (30,065) along with the ten top states and their PTS score
for that year. Finally, and most importantly for the present

TABLE 2.2
Asylum Claims Filed in the United Kingdom, 2008

United Kingdom

Top Ten Countries of Origin	Population	State PTS Score
Zimbabwe	4,330	5
Afghanistan	3,730	5
Iran	2,585	4
Eritrea	2,345	4
Iraq	2,030	5
Pakistan	2,010	4
Sri Lanka	1,840	5
Somalia	1,575	5
China	1,490	4
Nigeria	970	4
Total Number of Asylum Applications	30,065	
% from PTS 5	48.2	
% from PTS 4	40.8	
% from PTS 3	7.5	
% from PTS 2	2.2	
% from PTS 1	0	
% from other/unscored	1.3	

analysis, what is also included is a breakdown of what percentage of asylum seekers to the United Kingdom that year were from level 5 countries, level 4 countries, and so on.

As the reader can see, the greatest number of claims were made from these three countries: Zimbabwe, Afghanistan, and Iran. Furthermore, breaking this down by PTS level, fully 89 percent of the asylum claims that year were from individuals from countries experiencing the highest levels of political violence— with 48.2 percent being from a level 5 state and 40.8 percent coming from a level 4 country. The converse of this is also true; that is, almost none of the asylum claims filed in 2008 were from individuals from relatively safe countries. In fact, asylum claims from level 1 and level 2 countries totaled only 2.2 percent of the total claims filed that year.

What also needs to be pointed out is that 2008 is by no means an aberration. In order to test this, we also computed data from 1998 and 1988 (see Chapter 6), and the results are quite similar to what they are in 2008. In 1998, there were a similar number of total asylum claims (35,180) as there were in 2008. In 1998, 65.2 percent of the asylum applicants to the United Kingdom were from level 4 and level 5 countries, while only 0.1 percent were filed by asylum seekers from level 1 and level 2 countries. In 1988, the biggest difference is that the UK only received a small fraction (3,980) of the asylum claims that it would later receive in 1998 and 2008. Still, more than half (57.8 percent) of the claims filed in 1988 were from asylum seekers from level 4 and level 5 countries, while there was not a single asylum application from a person from a level 1 country and only 4.6 percent of the total asylum applications were from people coming from a level 2 country.

The Netherlands

The Netherlands (see Table 2.3) provides the same kind of results. In 2008, individuals from two countries—Iraq (5,027) and Somalia (3,842)—produced the highest number of asylum claims. Both of these countries received a score of 5 on the PTS that year. Reflective of this, what is most stunning about the Dutch data is that nearly three quarters of the asylum claims filed in Holland in 2008 were from individuals coming from a level 5 country. Recall that only ten countries in the entire world were designated as such. At the opposite end, only 1.5 percent of the asylum claims were filed by individuals arriving from a level 1 or level 2 country.

TABLE 2.3
Asylum Claims Filed in The Netherlands, 2008

The Netherlands			
	Top Ten Countries of Origin	Population	State PTS Score
	Iraq	5,027	5
	Somalia	3,842	5
	China	563	4
	Afghanistan	395	5
	Iran	322	4
	Eritrea	236	4
	Sri Lanka	216	5
	Guinea	154	3
	Sierra Leone	129	2
	Mongolia	103	3
	Total Number of Asylum Applications	13,092	
	% from PTS 5	73.3	
	% from PTS 4	16.3	
	% from PTS 3	6	
	% from PTS 2	1.5	
	% from PTS 1	0	
	% from other/unscored	2.9	

Sweden

The third example we will use is Sweden (see Table 2.4). In 2008 there were 21,146 asylum claims filed. Like the Netherlands, Iraq (6,083) and Somalia (3,361) asylum seekers constituted the two largest groups, and as mentioned above, both were coded as level 5 countries that year. In total, 71.8 percent of the (non-European) asylum claims filed in Sweden in 2008 were from individuals fleeing from either a level 4 or level 5 country, while only 2.8 percent were from a level 1 or level 2 countries. Was 1998 an aberration? The data in Chapter 6 show that it was not. Although Sweden received far fewer asylum claims from non-Europeans in 1998 (7,545), nearly 65 percent of these claims were from level 5 countries. If we move back in time another decade to 1988, that year Sweden received 16,453 (non-European) asylum claims, the bulk of which were from Iran (5), Chile (4), Iraq (5), and Ethiopia (5). That year, nearly 45 percent of the asylum claims in Sweden were from a level 5 country (and note that

TABLE 2.4
Asylum Claims Filed in Sweden, 2008

Sweden			
	Top Ten Countries of Origin	Population	State PTS Score
	Iraq	6,083	5
	Somalia	3,361	5
	Russia	933	4
	Eritrea	857	4
	Iran	799	4
	Mongolia	791	3
	Afghanistan	784	5
	Uzbekistan	741	3
	Libya	646	3
	Syria	551	4
	Total Number of Asylum Applications	21,146	
	% from PTS 5	49.3	
	% from PTS 4	22.5	
	% from PTS 3	18.1	
	% from PTS 2	2.8	
	% from PTS 1	0	
	% from other/unscored	7.2	

there were nine level 5 countries in 1988): Afghanistan, Ethiopia, Iran, Iraq, Myanmar (Burma), Peru, South Africa, Sri Lanka, and Sudan.

Interested readers can peruse Chapter 6 for more data on some of the other Western democracies but for the most part the results are the same. In terms of the most recent data (2008), these were the percentage of asylum seekers from level 4 and level 5 countries: Italy (78 percent), Germany (77 percent), France (60 percent), Denmark (90 percent) and Australia (76 percent). The only exceptions to this trend were Canada and the United States. In terms of the former, there were 32,310 claims filed in 2008 with Mexico (8,070), Haiti (4935) and Colombia (3,130) constituting the three largest groups. Mexico and Haiti were coded at level 3 by the PTS, while Colombia was coded as a level 4 country. Reflecting this, nearly half (49.3) of the asylum applications were filed by individuals from a level 3 country.

United States

The final country we will examine is the United States, where 37,597 asylum claims were filed in 2008 (see Table 2.5).

As you can see, although a majority (56.3 percent) of the asylum claims filed in 2008 were from individuals from countries that were coded at either level 4 (50.4 percent) or level 5 (5.9 percent), this number is not as high as it is for the other Western democracies that year (excluding Canada). However, like these other countries (including Canada), there were extraordinarily few claims filed by individuals from level 1 and level 2 counties (4.1 percent total).

An earlier analysis of U.S. practice (Gibney et al. 1992) based on data from the 1980s showed that there were substantial differences between U.S. asylum practices and the country's Overseas Refugee Program (ORP) (described in much more detail in Chapter 3), with the latter being dominated by states with only low to moderate

TABLE 2.5
Asylum Claims Filed in the United States, 2008

United States			
	Top Ten Countries of Origin	**Population**	**State PTS Score**
	China	9,831	4
	El Salvador	2,789	3
	Mexico	2,713	3
	Haiti	2,078	3
	Guatemala	1,853	3
	Ethiopia	1,168	4
	Colombia	910	4
	Indonesia	894	3
	Honduras	893	3
	Iraq	809	5
	Total Number of Asylum Applications	37,597	
	% from PTS 5	5.9	
	% from PTS 4	50.4	
	% from PTS 3	38.4	
	% from PTS 2	4	
	% from PTS 1	0.1	
	% from other/unscored	1.1	

levels of political violence, whereas nearly three quarters of asylum applicants were from a level 4 or level 5 country. The assertion made then was that there was no indication of any form of asylum abuse in the United States, but if there were abuse it was practiced by the government itself. The reason for saying this is that the asylum applications were almost exactly what one might both expect in the sense that the countries most represented were individuals from some of the most violent countries in the world. In strong contrast to this, the ORP, where U.S. government officials literally go out into the world and pick and choose which refugees to admit to the United States, was seemingly driven by foreign policy considerations, as evidenced by the continued admission of tens of thousands of refugees from the (former) Soviet Union, but also in terms of continued large-scale flows from Vietnam.

Since that time, U.S. practices have become somewhat more mixed. Thus, while in 1988 an astounding 92.4 percent of the asylum applicants were from either a level 4 or a level 5 country (see Chapter 6), a decade later this number had fallen substantially to 35.7 percent (see Chapter 6), which truly does suggest that there was substantial abuse in the asylum system at that time. However, the 2008 data (see Table 2.5) represents something much closer to what one might expect.

A much greater change has recently appeared in the ORP (see Table 2.6). Applying the same kind of human rights analysis to the 2008 ORP that we did to asylum practices, what we see is that fully 71 percent of the refugees admitted to the United States through ORP were from either a level 4 or level 5 country.

The biggest reason for this is that until 2008 refugee admissions from Iraq were virtually non-existent (see Table 3.2 in the following chapter). However, after a great deal of negative publicity regarding the manner in which Iraqi refugees had been systematically ignored by the U.S. government—notwithstanding the fact that it was the U.S. invasion that certainly helped create these refugee and IDP flows in the first place—in 2008 the United States admitted 13,823 Iraqi refugees. The same is true of Burma/Myanmar, which previously had barely been represented in the ORP (see Table 3.2). However, what remains uncertain is the extent to which U.S. refugee policy will remain a (true) refugee policy, or whether other interests, particularly foreign policy interests, come to dominate once again.

TABLE 2.6
Refugee Resettlement in the United States, 2008

Country of Origin	Population	State PTS Score
Burma	18,139	4
Iraq	13,823	5
Bhutan	5,320	2
Iran	5,270	4
Cuba	4,177	3
Burundi	2,889	4
Somalia	2,523	5
Vietnam	1,112	3
Ukraine	1,022	3
Liberia	992	3
Other	4,841	n/a
Total	60,108	n/a
% from PTS 5	27.2	
% from PTS 4	43.8	
% from PTS 3	12.1	
% from PTS 2	8.9	
% from PTS 1	0	
% from other/unscored	8	

Summary

Western states are no longer desirous of receiving large numbers of refugees. On the other hand, it would be impossible for these states to renounce the principle of refugee protection. Thus, what these states have done instead is to observe the principle of refugee protection, while at the same time they have taken a number of measures to severely reduce refugee flows arriving at their borders. In order to achieve this, what these states have done is to claim that there is widespread abuse of the asylum system. However, the empirical evidence points in quite the opposite direction. As we have seen here, in every country (except Canada in 2008), the overwhelming majority of those filing asylum claims in Western countries have been from states experiencing massive levels of political violence. Of course, what is not being said is that all (or any one) of these individuals is a bona fide refugee. However, what the data do show is that there is a strong relationship between levels of political violence and the creation and maintenance of refugee flows, but also, that nearly all of those seeking refugee protection in the West are from countries experiencing gross and systematic human rights violations.

Nonrefoulement: When (and Where) Does the Prohibition Apply?

As we have noted before, although no state has an obligation to admit a refugee to its territory, under a number of international and regional human rights treaties—i.e., the 1951 Refugee Convention, but also the International Covenant on Civil and Political Rights, the European Convention, and arguably under customary international law as well—all states are under an obligation not to send an individual to a country where this person's life or freedom might be threatened. This is the prohibition against refoulement, and as we have said earlier, this is the single most important right under the 1951 Convention.

However, one of the questions that has been raised recently is how far—literally—a country's nonrefoulement obligations extend. The way this issue has arisen is that several Western states have undertaken to enforce their immigration laws outside their own territorial borders. Although many of these efforts have taken place on the high seas, other states have patrolled the territorial waters of sending states as well (Gammeltoft-Hansen 2009). Beyond this, destination states have taken a number of other measures in an attempt to regulate, and arguably even eliminate, refugee flows in the first place. One means is through visa restrictions that are backed up by carrier sanctions, while other states have taken to placing their own immigration officials in other countries. Thus, the question is whether the prohibition against refoulement applies whenever and wherever a state acts.

Sale v. Haitian Centers Council, 509 U.S. 155 (1993)

This issue was confronted directly by the U.S. Supreme Court in *Sale v. Haitians Center Council*. The case centered around the U.S. Coast Guard's Haitian interdiction program, which stopped and then returned ships from Haiti, returning all those on board.

The argument of the U.S. government was that the prohibition against refoulement only applied to aliens who had reached American shores. What the U.S. government was espousing was a territorial reading of the 1980 Refugee Act, a statute that sought to make U.S. law consonant with international law. In contrast to this, the plaintiffs claimed that the prohibition against refoulement operated no matter where a state's immigration enforcement practices were carried out, in this case, that the prohibition applied to these interdictions on the high seas. In their view, any other reading would be inconsistent with the object and purpose of both domestic and international law.

Background

Although there has been a long history of Haitians attempting to come to the United States seeking refugee protection, these numbers increased significantly in the late 1970s and early 1980s. There seem to have been at least two reasons for this. The first was the ever-increasing levels of political violence in a country that has had more than its fair share of brutality, either at the hands of the Haitian military or its long-time associates the Tonton Macoutes. A second explanation is that during this same period of time, the United States was taking in massive numbers of Cubans as refugees, and this fact was not lost on Haitians who sought to escape their own dictatorship. However, as we will explain in more detail in the next chapter, while Cubans were overwhelmingly welcomed (although in 1980 U.S. President Jimmy Carter eventually had to renege on his promise to take in all Cubans who wanted to come to the United States with open arms), Haitians were not welcomed at all, as evidenced not only by very low asylum acceptance rates but also by the policy of policing the Atlantic Ocean.

In order to attempt to regularize migratory flows from Haiti, on September 23, 1981, the United States and the Republic of Haiti entered into an agreement authorizing the U.S. Coast Guard to intercept vessels engaged in the illegal transportation of undocumented aliens to our shores. While the parties agreed to prosecute illegal traffickers, the Haitian Government also guaranteed that its repatriated citizens would not be punished for their illegal departure. The agreement also established that the U.S. Government would not return any passengers whom the U.S. authorities determined to qualify for refugee status.

On September 29, 1981, U.S. President Ronald Reagan issued a proclamation describing the continued migration to the United

States as a "serious national problem detrimental to the interests of the United States," and he suspended the entry of undocumented aliens from the high seas and ordered the Coast Guard to intercept vessels carrying such aliens and to return them to their point of origin. However, the Executive Order expressly provided that "no person who is a refugee will be returned without his consent."

In the ensuing decade, the Coast Guard conducted 22,176 interviews on board ships in the Atlantic, but of these only 28 Haitians were screened in and transported to the United States in order to file a formal application for asylum. All of the others were summarily returned to Haiti.

On September 30, 1991, a group of military leaders displaced the government of Jean-Bertrand Aristide, the first democratically elected president in Haitian history. As a result, hundreds of Haitians were killed, tortured, detained without a warrant, or subjected to violence and the destruction of their property because of their political beliefs, while thousands of others were forced into hiding. This, in turn, prompted even larger numbers of Haitians to flee. In the six months after October, 1991, the Coast Guard interdicted over 34,000 Haitians and because of the logistical problems of holding asylum hearings on board Coast Guard cutters, a temporary facility was created at the U.S. Naval Base in Guantanamo, Cuba. However, these facilities subsequently proved to be inadequate and at this juncture the Bush administration decided to forgo asylum proceedings altogether and to simply return all those it encountered on the high seas of the Atlantic. It was this policy and practice that was being challenged in *Sale v. Haitian Centers Council*.

The Majority Opinion

In Chapter 3 we spend some time explaining that under U.S. law, there are two statutes that govern refugee protection. One of these is the definition of refugee that we examined in Chapter 1, while the second provision is the withholding of deportation statute, which had been Sec. 243(h) (1) of the Immigration and Nationality Act (INA) at the time of the *Sale* litigation, but which has since been renumbered as Sec. 241(b) (3):

> The Attorney General shall not deport or return any alien . . . to a country if the Attorney General determines that such alien's life or freedom would be threatened in

such country on account of race, religion, nationality, membership in a particular social group, or political opinion.

The original 1952 version of this statute included the phase any alien "within the United States." However, during the passage of the 1980 Refugee Act, this language was removed, but also the phrase "or return" was added. What is also noteworthy is that prior to 1980, relief under Sec. 243 was discretionary. This prohibition was made mandatory by the inclusion "shall" in the phrase "shall not deport or return."

Notwithstanding these amendments, the Court held that Section 243 remained territorial:

> The addition of the phrase "or return" and the deletion of the phrase "within the United States" are the only relevant changes made by the 1980 amendment to 243 (h) (1), and they are fully explained by the intent to apply 243 (h) to exclusion as well as to deportation proceedings. That intent is plainly identified in the legislative history of the amendment. There is no change in the 1980 amendment, however, that could only be explained by an assumption that Congress also intended to provide for the statute's extraterritorial application. It would have been extraordinary for Congress to make such an important change in the law without any mention of that possible effect. Not a scintilla of evidence of such an intent can be found in the legislative history (509 U.S. at 176).

The majority supported its conclusion by examining Article 33 of the Refugee Convention, which U.S. law is based on. First, it looked to the structure and language of Article 33 and it then examined some of the drafting history of this provision.

Article 33 reads in its entirety:

Article 33.—Prohibition of expulsion or return ("refoulement")

1. No Contracting State shall expel or return ("refouler") a refugee in any manner whatsoever to the frontiers of territories where his life or freedom would be threatened on account of his race, religion, nationality, membership of a particular social group or political opinion.

2. The benefit of the present provision may not, however, be claimed by a refugee whom there are reasonable grounds for regarding as a danger to the security of the country in which he is, or who, having been convicted by a final judgment of a particularly serious crime, constitutes a danger to the community of that country.

According to the majority opinion, under the second paragraph of Article 33 an alien may not claim the benefit of the first paragraph if he or she poses a danger to the country in which he or she is located. The majority then went on to say that if the first paragraph did apply on the high seas, then no state could invoke the second paragraph's exception with respect to an alien there on the basis that an alien intercepted on the high seas is in no country at all. Thus, the Court held that if Article 33 (1) did apply extraterritorially, Article 33 (2) would create what it termed an absurd anomaly, namely, that dangerous aliens on the high seas would be entitled to the benefits of the first paragraph, while those residing in the country that sought to expel them would not. The Court then went on to say that it was more reasonable to assume that the coverage of the second paragraph was limited to those already in the country, because it was understood that Article 33 (1) obligated the signatory state only with respect to aliens within its territory.

In addition to the internal structure of Article 33, the Court also examined the language in Article 33 itself. It began by saying that the word expel has the same meaning as deport, and that deportation or expulsion can only be effectuated against those who are already within a state's territory. It then went on to say that the term return has a legal meaning that is narrower than its common meaning, and that this conclusion is reinforced by the parenthetical reference to *refouler*, a French word that is not an exact synonym for the English word return. In the words of the Court:

[N]either of two respected English-French dictionaries mentions "refouler" as one of many possible French translations of "return." Conversely, the English translations of "refouler" do not include the word "return." They do, however, include words like "repulse," "repel," "drive back," and even "expel." To the extent that they are relevant, these translations imply that "return" means a defensive act of resistance or exclusion at a border, rather than an act of transporting someone to a particular destination. In the context of the Convention, to "return" means to "repulse," rather than to "reinstate" (509 U.S. at 180–182).

Finally, the Court then turned to the drafting history of Article 33 (which in its original version was Article 28), paying particular attention to the negotiating conference of plenipotentiaries held in Geneva, Switzerland on July 11, 1951, where the Swiss delegate (Philippe Zutter) explained his understanding that the words expel and return covered only refugees who had actually entered the host country.

> Mr. ZUTTER (Switzerland) said that the Swiss Federal Government saw no reason why article 28 should not be adopted as it stood; for the article was a necessary one. He thought, however, that its wording left room for various interpretations, particularly as to the meaning to be attached to the words "expel" and "return." In the Swiss Government's view, the term "expulsion" applied to a refugee who had already been admitted to the territory of a country. The term "refoulement," on the other hand, had a vaguer meaning; it could not, however, be applied to a refugee who had not yet entered the territory of a country. The word "return," used in the English text, gave that idea exactly. Yet article 28 implied the existence of two categories of refugee: refugees who were liable to be expelled, and those who were liable to be returned. In any case, the States represented at the Conference should take a definite position with regard to the meaning to be attached to the word "return." The Swiss Government considered that in the present instance, the word applied solely to refugees who had already entered a country, but were not yet resident there. According to that interpretation, States were not compelled to allow large groups of persons claiming refugee status to cross its frontiers. He would be glad to know whether the States represented at the Conference accepted his interpretations of the two terms in question. If they did, Switzerland would be willing to accept article 28, which was one of the articles in respect of

which States could not, under article 36 of the draft Convention, enter a reservation (509 U.S. at 184–185).

As the Court pointed out, no other delegate expressed any disagreement with the position of the Swiss delegate on that day or at the session two weeks later when Article 28 was again discussed. At that session, the delegate of the Netherlands (Baron van Boetzelaer) recalled the Swiss delegate's earlier position:

Baron van BOETZELAER (Netherlands) recalled that, at the first reading, the Swiss representative had expressed the opinion that the word "expulsion" related to a refugee already admitted into a country, whereas the word "return" ("refoulement") related to a refugee already within the territory but not yet resident there. According to that interpretation, article 28 would not have involved any obligations in the possible case of mass migrations across frontiers or of attempted mass migrations.

He wished to revert to that point, because the Netherlands Government attached very great importance to the scope of the provision now contained in article 33. The Netherlands could not accept any legal obligations in respect of large groups of refugees seeking access to its territory.

At the first reading, the representatives of Belgium, the Federal Republic of Germany, Italy, the Netherlands and Sweden had supported the Swiss interpretation. From conversations he had since had with other representatives, he had gathered that the general consensus of opinion was in favour of the Swiss interpretation.

In order to dispel any possible ambiguity and to reassure his Government, he wished to have it placed on record that the Conference was in agreement with the interpretation that the possibility of mass migrations across frontiers or of attempted mass migrations was not covered by article 33.

There being no objection, the PRESIDENT ruled that the interpretation given by the Netherlands representative should be placed on record.

Mr. HOARE (United Kingdom) remarked that the Style Committee had considered that the word "return" was the nearest equivalent in English to the French term "refoulement." He assumed that the word "return" as used in the English text had no wider meaning.

The PRESIDENT suggested that, in accordance with the practice followed in previous Conventions, the French word "refoulement" ("refouler" in verbal uses) should be included in brackets and between inverted commas after the English word "return" wherever the latter occurred in the text (509 U.S. at 185–186).

According to the *Sale* majority, what the drafting history shows is that was a general consensus, and in July of 1951, several delegates understood the right of nonrefoulement to apply only to aliens physically present in the host country. In addition, the Court pointed out that there is no record of any later disagreement with that position. And finally, the Court believed that the use of the term refouler was purposeful and was intended to avoid an inappropriately broad reading of the English term return.

In sum, the Court ruled that an extraterritorial reading of Article 33 of the Refugee Convention was not warranted, either by the language in the treaty itself or by the drafting history. In its view, notwithstanding the harsh or even immoral results that might ensue from this reading, the prohibition against refoulement only applied after a refugee had arrived at a state's territorial boundaries. In that way, then, the Court upheld the government's view that the prohibition against nonrefoulement did not apply to the actions of the U.S. government while operating on the high seas.

Justice Blackmun's Dissent

The *Sale* case was an 8–1 decision, with only Justice Harry Blackmun in dissent. Blackmun began his dissent by stating that when the United States acceded to the UN Protocol Relating to the Status of Refugees (see Chapter 6), it pledged not to "return (refouler) a refugee in any manner whatsoever" to a place where he would face political persecution, and that in 1980 Congress amended U.S. immigration law to reflect the Protocol's directives. However, according to Justice Blackmun, the majority decision reached its decision by concluding that return does not mean return, and by adopting the position that the opposite of "within the United States" is not outside the United States.

Blackmun writes:

> I believe that the duty of nonreturn expressed in both the Protocol and the statute is clear. The majority finds it "extraordinary," that Congress would have intended the ban on returning "any alien" to apply to aliens at sea. That Congress would have meant what it said is not remarkable. What is extraordinary in this case is that the Executive, in disregard of the law, would take to the seas to intercept fleeing refugees and force them back to their persecutors—and that the Court would strain to sanction that conduct (509 U.S. at 189).

A Return Is a Return Is a Return

Like the majority, Blackmun begins with the language of Article 33. In his view, the terms are unambiguous. He writes: "Vulnerable refugees shall not be returned. The language is clear, and the command is straightforward; that should be the end of the inquiry" (509 U.S. 190). Furthermore, he pointed out that until the litigation in this case, the U.S. government had consistently acknowledged that the Convention applied on the high seas.

For Blackmun, the problem is that the majority insists on giving the term return a special meaning. He writes:

> It is well settled that a treaty must first be construed according to its "ordinary meaning" ... The ordinary meaning of "return" is "to bring, send, or put (a person or thing) back to or in a former position" *Webster's Third New International Dictionary* 1941 (1986). That describes precisely what petitioners are doing to the Haitians. By dispensing with ordinary meaning at the outset, and by taking instead as its starting point the assumption that "return," as used in the treaty, "has a legal meaning narrower than its common meaning," the majority leads itself astray (509 U.S. at 191).

Blackmun argues that the straightforward interpretation of the duty of nonreturn is strongly reinforced by the Convention's use of the French term refouler, which means to repulse, to drive back, or to repel. In his view, this is exactly what the government is doing in this case, and he describes the majority as reaching its conclusion in a peculiar fashion:

After acknowledging that the ordinary meaning of "refouler" is "repulse," "repel," and "drive back," the majority, without elaboration, declares: "To the extent that they are relevant, these translations imply that " 'return' means a defensive act of resistance or exclusion at a border. . . . " I am at a loss to find the narrow notion of "exclusion at a border" in broad terms like "repulse," "repel," and "drive back." Gage was repulsed (initially) at Bunker Hill. Lee was repelled at Gettysburg. Rommel was driven back across North Africa. The majority's puzzling progression ("refouler" means repel or drive back; therefore "return" means only exclude at a border; therefore the treaty does not apply) hardly justifies a departure from the path of ordinary meaning. The text of Article 33.1 is clear, and whether the operative term is "return" or "refouler," it prohibits the Government's actions (509 U.S. at 192–193).

In further support of his position, Blackmun pointed out that while Article 33 does have a geographical limitation—it only speaks in terms of where a refugee could not be sent to, but not where a refugee is coming from.

Blackmun then turned to the majority's reliance on the juxtaposition of the two paragraphs of Article 33, especially the majority's position that an extraterritorial reading of Article 33 would create an absurd anomaly. Blackmun responds:

Far from constituting "an absurd anomaly," the fact that a state is permitted to "expel or return" a small class of refugees found within its territory, but may not seize and return refugees who remain outside its frontiers, expresses precisely the objectives and concerns of the Convention. Nonreturn is the rule; the sole exception (neither applicable nor invoked here) is that a nation endangered by a refugee's very presence may "expel or return" him to an unsafe country if it chooses. The tautological observation that only a refugee already in a country can pose a danger to the country "in which he is" proves nothing (509 U.S. at 194).

The Drafting History of Article 33

Blackmun took sharp issue with the majority's reliance on the drafting history of Article 33. He began his analysis by pointing out that under widely established rules governing statutory and treaty interpretation, the plain language of the treaty is controlling, while reliance on the *travaux préparatoires* (the drafting history) is only appropriate where the terms of the document are obscure or lead to manifestly absurd or unreasonable results. Moreover, even the general rule of treaty construction allowing limited resort to *travaux préparatoires* has no application to oral statements made by those engaged in negotiating the treaty that were not embodied in any writing and were not communicated to the government of the negotiator or to its ratifying body. In terms of the accession of the United States to the Refugee Convention in particular, Blackmun noted that there is no evidence that the comments made by the Swiss and Dutch representatives were ever communicated to the United States Government or to the Senate in connection with the ratification of the Protocol.

Yet, even assuming that these statements had been known, Blackmun argues that one must place these comments within a broader context, something that he alleges the majority failed to do:

> The pitfalls of relying on the negotiating record are underscored by the fact that Baron van Boetzelaer's remarks almost certainly represent, in the words of the United Nations High Commissioner for Refugees, a mere "parliamentary gesture by a delegate whose views did not prevail upon the negotiating conference as a whole ... " The Baron, like the Swiss delegate whose sentiments he restated, expressed a desire to reserve the right to close borders to large groups of refugees. ... " Yet no one seriously contends that the treaty's protections depend on the number of refugees who are fleeing persecution. Allowing a state to disavow "any obligations" in the case of mass migrations or attempted mass migrations would eviscerate Article 33, leaving it applicable only to "small" migrations and "small" attempted migrations.
>
> There is strong evidence as well that the Conference rejected the right to close land borders where to do so would trap refugees in the persecutors' territory. Indeed, the majority agrees that the Convention does apply to refugees who have reached the border. The majority thus cannot maintain that Van Boetzelaer's interpretation prevailed (509 U.S. at 195–196).

Blackmun also makes note of the fact that van Boetzelaer's interpretation of Article 33 was merely placed on record, in contrast to formal amendments to the Convention, which were agreed to or adopted. Given this, in his view the silence of the other states should not be interpreted as indicating any kind of consent. Instead, Blackmun argued that the majority's statement that "this much cannot be denied: At one time, there was a 'general consensus,' is simply wrong. All that can be said is that, at one time, van Boetzelaer remarked that 'he had gathered' that there was a general consensus, and that his interpretation was placed on record" (509 U.S. at 197).

Yet, even if van Boetzelaer's statement had in fact been agreed to and reflected the dominant thinking, Blackmun argues that the present situation is not a case about the right of a nation to close its borders, but rather, one in which a country "has gone forth to seize aliens who are not at its borders and return them to persecution. Nothing in the comments relied on by the majority even hints at an intention on the part of the drafters to countenance a course of conduct so at odds with the Convention's basic purpose" (509 U.S. at 197) (emphasis in original). He then concludes: "In sum, the fragments of negotiating history upon which the majority relies are not entitled to deference, were never voted on or adopted, probably represent a minority view, and in any event do not address the issue in this case" (509 U.S. at 198).

The 1980 Amendments to U.S. Law

Blackmun also questioned the majority's view that the 1980 Refugee Act did not effectuate any change to U.S. law. As he points out, before 1980, 243 (h) simply provided that:

> The Attorney General is authorized to withhold deportation of any alien ... within the United States to any country in which in his opinion the alien would be subject to persecution on account of race, religion, or political opinion and for such period of time as he deems to be necessary for such reason.

In his view, the 1980 Refugee Act explicitly amended this provision in three critical respects. First, Congress deleted the words "within the United States." Second, the statute barred the Government from returning as well as deporting alien refugees. And third, the statutory changes made the prohibition against return mandatory, thereby eliminating the discretion of the Attorney General over such decisions. He writes:

> The import of these changes is clear. Whether "within the United States" or not, a refugee may not be returned to his persecutors. To read into 243 (h)'s mandate a territorial restriction is to restore the very language that Congress removed (509 U.S. at 202).

Blackmun surmises that notwithstanding the clarity of the text and the object and purpose behind Article 33 of the Refugee Convention and Sec. 243 of the Immigration and Nationality Act, the majority is driven to its conclusion because of a heavy reliance on the presumption against extraterritoriality. In response, he first notes that this reliance is misplaced because Congressional intent in favor of an extraterritorial reading of the withholding statute has been expressed—by removing the geographical scope of Section 243 by means of the 1980 Refugee Act. Beyond this, the subject matter itself is extraterritorial in nature. Blackmun writes:

> In this case, we deal with a statute that regulates a distinctively international subject matter: immigration, nationalities, and refugees. Whatever force the presumption may have with regard to a primarily domestic statute evaporates in this context. There is no danger that the Congress that enacted the Refugee Act was blind to the fact that the laws it was crafting had implications beyond this Nation's borders (509 U.S. at 206).

Furthermore:

> If any canon of construction should be applied in this case, it is the well-settled rule that "an act of congress ought never to be construed to violate the law of nations if any other possible construction remains." *Murray v. Schooner Charming Betsy,* 2 Cranch 64, 117–118 (1804). The majority's improbable construction of 243 (h), which flies in the face of the international obligations imposed by Article 33 of the Convention, violates that established principle (509 U.S. at 207).

The Purpose and Meaning of the 1951 Convention

Finally, Blackmun suggests that the majority has simply ignored the overall purpose of the Refugee Convention itself—which is to protect desperate people—and he ends his dissent on this stirring note:

> The Convention that the Refugee Act embodies was enacted largely in response to the experience of Jewish refugees in Europe during the period of World War II. The tragic consequences of the world's indifference at that time are well known. The resulting ban on refoulement, as broad as the humanitarian purpose that inspired it, is easily applicable here, the Court's protestations of impotence and regret notwithstanding (509 U.S. at 207–208).

And finally:

> The refugees attempting to escape from Haiti do not claim a right of admission to this country. They do not even argue that the Government has no right to intercept their boats. They demand only that the United States, land of refugees and guardian of freedom, cease forcibly driving them back to detention, abuse, and death. That is a modest plea, vindicated by the treaty and the statute. We should not close our ears to it (509 U.S. at 208).

Summary

When confronted with the question of the scope of nonrefoulement in a challenge to lawfulness of the Haitian interdiction program, the U.S. Supreme Court ruled that the withholding of deportation statute was territorial in nature. Thus, for individuals physically located within the United States as well as those at American borders (although this latter part remains unclear), the U.S. government does have a legal obligation not to return/send these refugees to a country where their life or freedom might be threatened. However, the Court ruled that this same obligation does not exist for refugees on the high seas. Rather, these individuals could be returned to Haiti—presumably even in the face of certain persecution and even death.

The lone dissent in this case was filed by Justice Blackmun, who argued that taking a territorial approach to this extraterritorial phenomenon was inconsistent with the object and purpose of the Refugee Convention itself. In his view, while the United States was under no obligation to admit Haitian refugees, it most certainly had an obligation not to return these individuals back home where there was a good likelihood of facing persecution. In his view, any other reading would defeat the very purpose of the law itself.

The Practices of Other States

The *Sale* decision remains the leading judicial authority on the matter of the scope of nonrefoulement. However, what is also noteworthy is that a number of other countries have undertaken practices that are similar to the Haitian interdiction program that was at issue in that case. For example, Spain has an agreement with Senegal and Mauritania to intercept and directly return irregular migrants within the territorial waters of those states, while Italy has signed a similar treaty with Libya that allows for joint patrolling in Libyan waters (Gammeltoft-Hansen 2009, 65). Beyond this, in February 2003, a British proposal for a new vision for refugee protection was unveiled that envisaged the establishment of "transit processing centres" in third countries on the major transit routes of the European Union (EU). Under this proposal, asylum seekers arriving spontaneously in the EU would be sent back for status determinations.

Certainly, Australia's Pacific Solution has garnered the most worldwide attention. The plan was developed followed the incident involving the Norwegian ship MV *Tampa*, which in August 2001 responded to a distress issued by the Australian government involving an Indonesian ship that was carrying 433 asylum seekers, most of whom were from Afghanistan. However, the Australian government refused to allow the *Tampa* to enter Australian waters, although due to the humanitarian crisis on board this directive was ignored. Subsequent to this, an agreement was reached with Papua New-Guinea and Nauru, where the asylum seekers were taken for processing. The *Tampa* incident led to three changes in Australian law. The first was the passage of the 2001 Border Protection Act, which established general interdiction powers. The second was that two amendments were passed to the Migration Act, one excising certain northern islands from its migration zone, and thus part of Australian territory where asylum claims could be filed. The second enabled Australian authorities to send interdicted asylum seekers or persons who arrived in the (now) excised areas to other countries for refugee processing (Gammeltoft-Hansen 2009, 108–109).

Notwithstanding these attempts to off-shore refugee protection, the actions of these countries should not necessarily be interpreted as a rejection of the nonrefoulement principle. Most notably, these states have sought to make assurances that international refugee protection standards are being followed. Whether this is true or not remains to be seen. However, what does seem certain is that Western states are continuing to make strong efforts to remove themselves from participating more fully in a system of worldwide refugee protection and one of the ways that they have done this is by designating certain areas—either the high seas or even parts of their own national territory—and claiming that their own obligations under international law do not apply within this geographic space.

Re-Conceptualizing Human Rights— and Refugee Protection

As we have noted throughout this work, there is a very strong connection between refugee admissions and human rights protection. A refugee flees from his/her home state due to a well-founded fear that he or she will be subjected to certain human rights violations. And because the refugee's home state does not, or will not, protect that person's human rights—and in most instances will actually be the source of these violations—it is thereby necessary for some other country to provide this protection by granting refugee status. It is this transnational dimension that differentiates refugee protection from other areas of human rights.

Yet, what is also important to note is that refugee protection and international human rights law are both based on traditional notions of state sovereignty. In terms of the latter, under the dominant approach, each state has sole responsibility for protecting human rights within its own territorial borders. The flip side to this is the notion that states do not have any human rights obligations outside those borders.

Notwithstanding its transnational nature, refugee protection is also based on a traditional conception of state sovereignty. For one thing, as we have already seen, although individuals are given the right to seek asylum, no state is obligated to admit a single refugee. Rather, states are only obligated not to send a person to a country where his or her life or freedom might be threatened—and apparently this obligation only arises if and when a refugee is either at the borders of that state or else has somehow gained entry. Beyond this, if a state does decide to admit refugees, it is that state, and that state alone, which determines how many refugees, what countries they will come from, and so on. Moreover, as we have seen in Chapter 1, although the 1951 Refugee Convention provides a series of ascending rights to refugees and asylum seekers depending on their particular legal status in the receiving country, what is important to note is that not one of the these rights will arise unless and until the refugee has gained access to the territory of this other country. Furthermore, the exercise of state sovereignty now even seems to include the ability of countries to take whatever measures they can in order to prevent refugees from ever arriving at their borders in the first place.

But the protection of state sovereignty apparently goes much further than this. Thus, there is no readily identifiable principle under international law that a state should not contribute to the creation of refugee flows in some other country, and if the policies of one state do bring massive human displacement in some other land—for example, the U.S. invasion of Iraq that has resulted in approximately two million refugees from that country and an additional two million Internally Displaced Persons—the acting state is seemingly under no obligation to help provide any kind of protection, by means of refugee admissions or otherwise.

In sum, international human rights law (and this includes international refugee law) has been based on territorial considerations. Thus, according to the dominant approach, while international human rights law restricts the domestic behavior of states, it is not clear what effect (if any) such law has on the behavior of states when they are operating outside their own borders. However, this conceptualization of human rights has recently been challenged and we will discuss two such initiatives in a moment. To be clear, what is not being challenged is the principle that each state has the primary responsibility for protecting human rights within its own territorial borders. Rather, the issue that has been raised is whether these territorial obligations comprise the entirety of a state's human rights obligations—or whether a state might also have a secondary obligation to protect the human rights of individuals in other states.

Oddly enough, perhaps, one of the things that helped raise this issue has been the U.S. conduct in the "war on terror." As the reader must know, the Bush administration has used the U.S. military base at Guantanamo Bay, Cuba, as a detention facility for hundreds of so-called enemy combatants. The primary reason for choosing this offshore site is the idea that U.S. human rights obligations will be different (and perhaps even nonexistent) in this locale than they would be if the detainees were held in some facility within the territorial boundaries of the United States.

In taking this approach, the U.S. government has espoused a territorial reading of international human rights law. Certainly, the United States cannot deny that it is a state party to the Convention against Torture and the International Covenant on Civil and Political Rights. On the other hand, the position that the U.S. government has taken is that the obligations that arise from these and other human rights treaties will only be applicable to actions that are taken within the territorial borders of the United States, but no further.

This position may (or may not) seem tenable to you, but note that this is the same position the U.S. government maintained with respect to the scope of the prohibition against refoulement in the 1951 Refugee Convention. As we discussed in the previous section, in its *Sale* decision the U.S. Supreme Court ruled that the withholding of deportation statute under U.S. immigration law had no extraterritorial effect. What this means is that while the U.S. is under an obligation not to send an individual who has arrived on U.S. soil back to a country where this person's life or freedom might be threatened, it has no obligation to offer the same kind of protection (and, arguably, no protection at all) to refugees who, for whatever reason, are not within the territorial boundaries of the United States.

Although the *Sale* decision has been sharply criticized, what also needs to be pointed out is that all states—or, more accurately, all Western states—apparently operate under the same belief that human rights are territorially based (Gibney and Skogly 2010). We have already seen some indications of this previously in terms of the number of states that are now engaged in interdiction practices outside their own border, but it is important to point out that the implications of this approach to human rights are much more far-ranging than this.

Thus, one of the most important cases in this realm is *Bankovic et al. v. Belgium et al.* (2001), an admissibility decision of the European Court of Human Rights (ECHR). The background for this case involved a 1999 NATO bombing mission over Belgrade, Serbia in which 16 civilians were killed and another 16 wounded. Although Serbia is not a state party to the European Convention, those who were injured and/or killed during the attack brought a claim against the NATO countries before the ECHR, alleging that they were victims of various human rights violations that were prohibited by the Convention.

Article 1 of the European Convention provides: "The High Contracting Parties shall secure to everyone within their jurisdiction the rights and freedoms defined in ... this Convention." According to the ECHR, at the time these injuries and/or deaths occurred, the affected individuals were not within the jurisdiction of the Contracting States, and on this basis the case was dismissed. According to the Court, the original draft of Article 1 included the term territory, and although this wording was eventually dropped, the European Convention remained territorial in scope—or to use the Court's terminology, essentially or primarily territorial. One reason for these qualifiers was that in previous decisions involving Turkey's occupation of part of Cyprus, the Court (as well as its former counterpart the European Commission on Human Rights) had given the Convention an extraterritorial reading, ruling that the Convention applied to Turkey's actions in this part of Cyprus.

The *Bankovic* court did not disavow these prior rulings, but rather, it held that in order for the Convention to apply to actions undertaken outside the territorial boundaries of the European states there would have to be some "exceptional circumstances." Although the Court never fully explained what constituted "exceptional circumstances" (never mind where this standard came from and why), what we do know from the ruling in the case itself is that dropping bombs and killing people on the ground does not rise to this level (Roxstrom et al. 2005).

Like the U.S. Supreme Court decision in *Sale* before it, the *Bankovic* decision was based on a territorial reading of human rights standards, only in this instance the territory was the entirety of Europe. And also like *Sale*, the *Bankovic* ruling caused quite a stir. The reason for this is that the case could be read to mean that when European states are acting outside of Europe, they are not bound by the provisions of the European Convention. More than that, the *Bankovic* court went so far as to say that all other international human rights treaties were territorial in scope as well. Of course, if this were true this would mean is that when a state operates outside its own borders it is exempt from any and all international human rights law.

Bankovic remains good law. However, what should also be noted is that at around the time of this ruling there began a movement away from reading international human rights treaties in a strictly territorial fashion. In terms of the ECHR itself, in *Ocalan v. Turkey*, the Court ruled that Turkish officials making an arrest of a terrorist suspect in Nairobi, Kenya, were subject to the provisions of the European Convention. According to the Court, what made this case different from *Bankovic* was that the defendant was in the actual physical custody of Turkish security forces. Beyond this, in *Issa v. Turkey*, the Court held that the Convention would apply to a situation where Turkish troops had entered on to Iraqi territory and had tortured and killed a group of Iraqi civilians. However, immediately after enunciating this principle, the Court then went on to rule that there was no conclusive proof that Turkish soldiers had in fact gone onto Iraqi territory as alleged, and it dismissed the complaint. Still, the seeds of change should be apparent.

There are other manifestations of a different interpretation of international human rights law that go beyond this. Two phenomena seem to be at work here. One simply relates to state practice. It is one thing to think about a state's human rights obligations as being restricted to its own territorial borders when states limit their operations to the domestic setting. However, it is something else altogether different when many states engage in practices outside their borders almost as a matter of course—refugee interdiction, drug enforcement, arms sales, pollution, and so on—particularly in recognition of the fact that the actions of one state can have a decided effect on the human rights protection of individuals living in other countries. Economists refer to the process of globalization, and in a way what we are speaking about here is the law's response to some of the negative consequences of globalization.

The second reason relates to the work of human rights scholars and practitioners (Coomans and Kamminga 2004; Gondek 2009; Salomon 2007; Salomon et al. 2007; Gibney 2008). In that way, there has been a growing recognition and understanding that a strictly territorial reading of international human rights treaties will oftentimes go far in defeating the object and purpose of international human rights law itself. Thus, if it is unlawful for a state to carry out torture within its territorial borders, but not unlawful to do so in some other land, then there is a very strong incentive for a state simply to move its basis of operations to some other place—as we have seen all too clearly with the practice of "extraordinary rendition" (Mayer 2008).

One of the most notable examples of this new scholarship has been Sigrun Skogly's work on the drafting of the International Covenant on Economic, Social and Cultural Rights (ICESCR). Like other international human rights treaties, the natural (but unquestioned) interpretation was that the ICESCR was territorial in scope, notwithstanding the fact that there is no mention in the treaty of either territory or jurisdiction. Furthermore, there is also language in the treaty that is certainly extraterritorial in nature, most notably Article 2:

> Each state party . . . undertakes to take steps, individu-
> ally and through *international assistance and cooperation*,
> especially economic and technical, to the maximum of
> its available resources, with a view to achieving progres-
> sively the full realization of the rights recognized in the
> present Covenant by all appropriate means. . . . (empha-
> sis supplied).

After undertaking an extensive study of the drafting process of the ICESCR, Skogly concluded that there was a general consensus among the drafters of the Covenant that the economic, social, and cultural rights set forth in the treaty could only be protected through international means. Skogly writes:

> [T]he drafting history of Article 2 (1) shows that there are
> some inconsistencies in the approaches held as to the
> concrete meaning of *through international co-operation*
> *and assistance*. However, it seems that the delegations
> were quite agreed that international co-operation and as-
> sistance is needed for the full implementation of the
> rights, and that the resources available based upon this
> co-operation and assistance should be part of the re-
> sources used for the full realization of these rights
> (emphasis in original) (Skogly 2006, 86).

We will take up this issue of reconceptualizing human rights by focusing on two recent initiatives. The first is the Responsibility to Protect (R2P) proposal that was undertaken under the lead of the Canadian government. R2P is ostensibly concerned with the issue of humanitarian intervention, but as you will see immediately, the issue of the responsibility to protect goes much further than this, and what it is based on is the idea that all states have obligations to prevent humanitarian disasters—at home, for sure, but in other lands as well. The second initiative is even more recent than this and it involves the work of the Extraterritorial Obligations (ETO) Consortium (http://www.lancs.ac.uk/fass/projects/humanrights/).

The final issue is how all this relates to refugee protection more specifically. With only rare exception (Gammeltoft-Hansen 2009), there has not been a great deal of scholarly attention given to the possible extraterritorial effect of the Refugee Convention aside from the nonrefoulement issue that has been analyzed previously. On the other hand, we will suggest that a reconceptualization of international human rights law will have enormous implications for refugee protection quite generally. Among other things, this would suggest that states have certain legal obligations to work towards the prevention and elimination of all refugee flows.

The Responsibility to Protect (R2P)

Much like refugee protection, humanitarian intervention has been a longstanding principle under international law. In addition, and again like refugee protection itself, humanitarian intervention is based on the notion of one state engaging in certain practices to protect the human rights of other people. The major distinction, of course, is that while one is based on giving physical protection by admitting refugees, humanitarian intervention is based on taking military measures in another country in an attempt to remove the causes of these violations.

Notwithstanding its long pedigree, there have been a number of problems associated with humanitarian intervention in practice. One is the continuing conflict concerning whether a particular intervention is in fact humanitarian—or whether such measures were undertaken as a means of promoting the geo-political interests of the intervening state. For example, there were three major interventions in the 1970s: Vietnam's intervention in Cambodia, Tanzania's intervention in Uganda, and India's intervention in what was then East Pakistan (now Bangladesh). Notwithstanding the gross and systematic human rights violations (and genocide in the case of Cambodia) in each of these countries, because of the previous enmity between the states involved, many scholars and policymakers refused to recognize these interventions as being humanitarian in nature.

A much different kind of problem relates to the failure to intervene. Consider, then, some of the interventions (but also the non-interventions) from the 1990s. The first involved an American-led humanitarian intervention in Somalia in 1992 as a response to massive starvation in that country. By most accounts, Operation Restore Hope represented a humanitarian intervention in its purest form in the sense that there was no geo-political end sought by the United States, and it is also estimated that the intervention saved the lives of upwards of a million. However, when the mission became more military in nature, but also when Western soldiers began to get killed as a result of this changed mission, the intervention came to be viewed as a failure and the United States and the United Nations both began to remove themselves from Somalia. What should also be pointed out is that Somalia has remained the world's basket case ever since. What is equally important is that this failure in Somalia played a central role in explaining the non-intervention in Rwanda in 1994 as well as the decidedly belated response to the ethnic cleansing in Bosnia from 1992 to 1995.

Although there were some successful humanitarian interventions in the late 1990s, including East Timor and Kosovo, there was growing dissatisfaction with the principle of humanitarian intervention itself. For one thing, although the UN Charter places responsibility for military intervention squarely on the Security Council, this body was repeatedly seen as failing in this role. Typical of the growing frustration with the whole notion of humanitarian intervention were these remarks by UN Secretary General Kofi Annan at the 2000 Millennium Summit Meeting:

> If humanitarian intervention is, indeed, an unacceptable assault on sovereignty, how should we respond to a Rwanda, to a Srebrenica—to gross and systematic violations of human rights that offend every precept of our common humanity?

Responding to the Secretary-General's challenge, in 2000 the Canadian government, along with several international foundations, created an International Commission on Intervention and

State Sovereignty that was made up of a body of distinguished academics and international policymakers who subjected the issue of military intervention to intense scrutiny. In December 2001 they published a report *The Responsibility to Protect*. At the 2005 UN World Summit, world leaders unanimously declared that all states have a responsibility to protect their citizens from genocide, war crimes, crimes against humanity, and ethnic cleansing and that as members of the international community they stand "prepared to take collective action" in cases where national authorities "are manifestly failing to protect their populations" from these four ills. In April 2006, the UN Security Council reaffirmed R2P and indicated its readiness to adopt appropriate measures where necessary.

The driving force behind the Commission's work was its deep commitment to spare the world of any more Rwandas. In order to achieve this, the Commission set forth the following four objectives:

> To establish clearer rules, procedures and criteria for determining whether, when and how to intervene;

> To establish the legitimacy of military intervention when necessary and after all other approaches have failed;

> To ensure that military intervention, when it occurs, is carried out only for the purposes proposed, is effective, and is undertaken with proper concern to minimize the human costs and institutional damage that will result; and

> To help eliminate, where possible, the causes of conflict while enhancing the prospects for durable and sustainable peace (R2P 2001, par. 2.3).

The first thing to note about R2P is that it is based on a much different notion of state sovereignty. Under the traditional approach, countries automatically enjoy the privileges of state sovereignty, no matter how gruesome or brutal state practices happen to be, and no matter what level of refugee flows these policies and practices produce. However, under R2P, sovereignty is something that states have to earn and the way to achieve this is by protecting human rights. The Report explains the nature of this change:

> First, it implies that the state authorities are responsible for the functions of protecting the safety and lives of citizens

and promotion of their welfare. Secondly, it suggests that the national political authorities are responsible to the citizens internally and to the international community through the UN. And thirdly, it means that the agents of state are responsible for their actions; that is to say, they are accountable for their acts of commission and omission (par. 2.15).

Where does the responsibility to protect lie? In the first instance, of course, it is the territorial state. As the report explains:

The Commission believes that responsibility to protect resides first and foremost with the states whose people are directly affected. This fact reflects not only international law and the modern state system, but also the practical realities of who is best placed to make a positive difference. The domestic authority is best placed to take action to prevent problems from turning into potential conflicts (par. 2.30).

However, if domestic authorities fail to meet this responsibility, that is, if this state essentially forfeits its own sovereignty, then this task is placed in the hands of the international community.

While the state whose people are directly affected has the default responsibility to protect, a residual responsibility also lies with the broader community of states. This fallback responsibility is activated when a particular state is clearly either unwilling or unable to fulfil its responsibility to protect or is itself the actual perpetrator of crimes or atrocities; or where people living outside a particular state are directly threatened by actions taking place there. This responsibility also requires that in some circumstances action must be taken by the broader community of states to support populations that are in jeopardy or under serious threat (par. 2.31).

However, perhaps what distinguishes R2P the most from present practice is that rather than being reactive, the proposal is based on a decidedly proactive approach to human rights. The Responsibility to Protect proposal posits that there are three separate, but related, obligations: the responsibility to prevent, the responsibility to react, and the responsibility to rebuild.

The first duty of states is the responsibility to prevent humanitarian disasters from arising in the first place. The report sums this up nicely: "Intervention should only be considered when prevention fails—and the best way of avoiding intervention is to ensure that it doesn't fail" (par. 3.34). How is this to be done? To begin, it is important to establish again that the primary responsibility for prevention rests with the territorial state. If states succeed in preventing humanitarian disaster within their borders, then there is no need to look any further to ensure prevention, and certainly not intervention. However, if the territorial state fails to meet its responsibility, then the states of the international community share an obligation to take whatever measures are necessary—"more resources, more energy, more competence, more commitment" (par 3.40)—to prevent humanitarian disaster.

As noted before, what R2P is seeking to avoid is the reactive nature of present practice. Currently, the international community only responds (if it responds at all) after the fact. That is, after widespread human rights violations occur and only after large-scale refugee flows and IDP populations arise. The problem, of course, is that these efforts are invariably much too late and far too little. What R2P calls for is a complete change in mindset, from what it refers to as a "culture of reaction" to a "culture of prevention," which can only be accomplished by holding states accountable for their actions and by attending to preventive measures at the local, national, regional, and global levels. As the report warns:

> Without a genuine commitment to conflict prevention at all levels—without new energy and momentum being devoted to the task—the world will continue to witness the needless slaughter of our fellow human beings, and the reckless waste of precious resources on conflict rather than social and economic development. The time has come for all of us to take practical responsibility to prevent the needless loss of human life, and to be ready to act in the cause of prevention and not just in the aftermath of disaster (par. 3.43).

The second obligation is the responsibility to react if, for whatever reasons, preventive measures have not worked, and this is where R2P comes closest to looking like traditional humanitarian intervention. Yet, as the Report makes clear, one of the great problems with those interventions that have taken place is that they are not based on any discernible standards. To fill this vacuum, the R2P initiative sets forth these six standards, based in large part on just war theory, that should be followed in all interventions: 1) just cause, 2) right intention, 3) last resort, 4) proportionate means, 5) reasonable prospect of success, and 6) legitimate authority—preferably the UN Security Council.

The third and final duty is the obligation to rebuild after an intervention takes place. As the Report points out, because this principle has long been ignored in practice, what this oftentimes has led to is a situation where an intervention might halt fighting for some period of time, but begin once again simply because conditions on the ground have not fundamentally changed. In certain ways, the responsibility to rebuild can be interpreted literally in the sense of engaging in public works projects to rebuild houses, roads, buildings, and bridges that were destroyed during the course of the fighting. Beyond this, the responsibility to rebuild also dedicates to establishing both security and the rule of law.

In short, the R2P initiative is offering up a much different vision of the world. Each state has the primary responsibility for protecting human rights within its own territorial boundaries, but if a state fails to do this—if it essentially forfeits its own sovereignty—then this task has to be undertaken by the international community. As we have seen, the goal here is to create an international system that avoids humanitarian disasters in the first place. Thus, rather than reacting to disasters after the fact, by means of refugee protection or humanitarian intervention, R2P is premised on the international community taking the necessary steps to avoid humanitarian disasters in the first place.

Extraterritorial Obligations (ETO) Consortium

The second initiative we will look at is the groundbreaking work of the Extraterritorial Obligations (ETO) Consortium, which was founded in 2007, bringing together a rare blend of scholars, nongovernmental organizations, and representatives of certain international institutions and organizations. The ETO Consortium bases its work on a set of tripartite duties, namely, that all states have an obligation to respect, protect, and fulfil human rights. Under the obligation to respect, states have an obligation not to violate human rights themselves. In terms of the responsibility to protect, states have an obligation to ensure that other actors do not violate human rights. And finally, under the obligation to fulfil, states have an obligation to provide human rights protection when this is needed.

Yet, where the ETO Consortium challenges existing orthodoxy is in positing that these obligations apply both inside and outside a state's territorial borders. Consider the prohibition against torture. Under international law it is unlawful for a state to torture an individual within its own domestic realm, but according to the approach of the ETO Consortium, this obligation would also extend to areas outside that state's territorial borders. In terms of the obligation to protect, states have an obligation to ensure that private entities under its control or jurisdiction do not torture, and once again, territorial considerations would simply not matter. To choose a real-world example, that would mean that the U.S. government has an obligation to see to it that private security firms operating in countries such as Iraq and Afghanistan do not carry out torture.

The third and final obligation is the duty to protect, which means that a state has a positive obligation to prevent human rights violations when it is within its powers to do so. Although most of the work of the ETO Consortium has been based on economic, social and cultural rights, the responsibility to protect applies in other areas of human rights as well. To stay with the example of the prohibition against torture, this would mean that states have an obligation to help prevent torture in other lands. We have already spent a considerable period of time on the prohibition against refoulement, and this provides a perfect example as an extraterritorial application of the obligation to protect.

But the Torture Convention provides other means of achieving this as well (Nowak 2010). One is that under the "prosecute or extradite" provision of Article 7, all state parties have a legal obligation to either prosecute an alleged torturer themselves or else extradite that person to a country that will do so. Note that what simply does not matter is if the torture did not occur in that country, or that neither the torturer nor the victim is a national of that state. Rather, all states have agreed to form a kind of international constabulary force to help ensure that all torturers are held accountable for their actions. Finally, the Torture Convention also has an inter-state complaint system under which one state party can file a complaint against another state party on the grounds that the latter is not fulfilling its obligations under the treaty (Article 21).

Implications for Refugee Protection

What these two initiatives—R2P and ETO—represent is a much different way of conceptualizing human rights. Under the dominant approach, human rights obligations are limited by territorial considerations. In certain ways, both refugee protection and the principle of humanitarian intervention have served as counter-examples to this approach in the sense that human rights protection came from some other state. Still, the responsibilities (assuming they are legal responsibilities) of these outside states remain quite limited. Thus, if a state decided not to admit any refugees it was under no obligation to do so. In addition, state sovereignty has been interpreted in such as way so as to allow states to engage in practices that would be detrimental to the human rights protection of individuals in other states—whether it is selling arms to repressive governments, applying visa restrictions that would prevent would-be refugees from being able to flee, or returning individuals back to a country where there is a strong likelihood of persecution, so long as this was done outside that state's territorial boundaries.

The same has been true of humanitarian intervention as well. Like refugee protection, humanitarian intervention challenges state sovereignty in the sense that one state (or a group of states) is intervening militarily in another country in order to protect the human rights of foreign nationals. Yet, humanitarian intervention poses only a mild challenge to the principle of state sovereignty most notably in that there is no obligation to intervene. And as we have seen over the course of the past few decades alone, there are a number of instances where countries have experienced massive levels of human rights violations—Sudan, Democratic Republic of Congo, Rwanda, and Bosnia, to mention some of the most egregious examples—but where there has either been no intervention, or intervention occurred well after the slaughter had already taken place.

In a seminal article more than two decades ago, Andrew Shacknove (1985) posited that there is only a small overlap between those who are victims of human rights violations and those who receive refugee protection. And as he points out, of all the human rights victims in the world, refugees enjoy a form of preferred position in the sense that they have at least some recourse to the international community in ways that other victims do not. Unfortunately, Shacknove's work has not prompted very much attention and thinking as to why so many victims are ignored, if not abandoned, by the international community. Human rights are (universally) described as being universal. Why, then, do we allow territorial considerations to override all other considerations in terms of the protection of those rights?

In certain ways, refugee protection has served as a challenge to state sovereignty, but in many other ways it has protected and fortified this principle. Refugee protection serves as a kind of safety valve for some of those denied human rights protection in their home state. However, the international community has established a system where this safety valve is not opened too much, and where the international community seemingly has no obligations or responsibilities to close the valve in the first place. In that way, refugee protection is decidedly reactive and as long as it is reactive there will always be refugees—and there will always be human rights violation. The key, then, is to eliminate human rights violations in the first place—but isn't this what international human rights law is supposed to accomplish?—and what this will do is to help eliminate the world's global refugee crisis.

References

Books, Articles, and Chapters

Coomans, Fons, and Menno Kamminga, eds. 2004. *Extraterritorial Application of Human Rights Treaties*. Antwerp: Intersentia.

Gammeltoft-Hansen, Thomas. 2009. *Access to Asylum: International Refugee Law and the Offshoring and Outsourcing of Migration Control*, Ph.D. Thesis. Aarhus University.

Gibney, Mark. 2008. *International Human Rights Law: Returning to Universal Principles*. Lanham, MD: Rowman & Littlefield.

Gibney, Mark, Vanessa Dalton, and Marc Vockell. 1992. "USA Refugee Policy: A Human Rights Analysis Update." *Journal of Refugee Studies* 5: 33–46.

Gibney, Mark, and Sigrun Skogly, eds. 2010. *University Human Rights and Extraterritorial Obligations*. Philadelphia: University of Pennsylvania Press.

Gibney, Mark, Linda Cornett, and Reed Wood. *The Political Terror Scale 1976–2008. Last accessed on January 28, 2010*, http://www.politicalterrorscale.org.

Gondek, Michael. 2009. *The Reach of Human Rights in a Globalising World: Extraterritorial Application of Human Rights Treaties*. Antwerp: Intersentia.

Goodwin-Gill, Guy. 1983. *The Refugee in International Law.* Oxford, UK: Clarendon Press.

Mayer, Jane. 2008. *The Dark Side: The Inside Story of How the War on Terror Turned Into a War On American Ideals.* New York: Doubleday.

Nowak, Manfred. 2010. "Obligations of States to Prevent and Prohibit Torture in an Extraterritorial Perspective," in Mark Gibney, and Sigrun Skogly, eds. *University Human Rights and Extraterritorial Obligations.* Philadelphia: University of Pennsylvania Press.

Roxstrom, Erik, Mark Gibney, and Terje Einarsen. "The NATO Bombing Case and the Limits of Western Human Rights Protection." *Boston University International Law Journal* 23: 55–136.

Salomon, Margot. 2007. *Global Responsibility for Human Rights: World Poverty and the Development of International Law.* Oxford University Press.

Salomon, Margot E., Arne Tostensen, and Wouter Vandenhole, eds. 2007. *Casting the Net Wider: Human Rights, Development and New Duty-Bearers.* Antwerp: Intersentia.

Shacknove, Andrew. 1985. "Who Is a Refugee?" *Ethics* 95: 274–284.

Skogly, Sigrun. 2006. *Beyond National Borders: States' Human Rights Obligations in International Cooperation.* Antwerp: Intersentia.

The Responsibility to Protect: Report of the International Commission on Intervention and State Sovereignty. 2001. Ottawa, Canada: International Development Research Centre.

Wood, Reed, and Mark Gibney. (2010). "The Political Terror Scale: A Re-Introduction and a Comparison With CIRI." *Human Rights Quarterly* 367–400.

Cases and Administrative Decisions

Bankovic et al. v. Belgium et al., App. No. 52207/99 Eur. Ct. H.R. (2001) (Dec. on admissibility).

Ocalan v. Turkey, App. No. 46221/99 Eur. Ct. H.R. (2000) (Dec. on admissibility).

Issa v. Turkey, App. No. 31821/96 Eur. Ct. H.R. (2000) (Dec. on admissibility).

Sale v. Haitian Centers Council, 509 U.S. 155 (1993).

3

Special U.S. Issues

ore than any other country, the United States has come to be
associated with issues of immigration and refugee protection. In the stirring words of Emma Lazarus's poem *The
New Colossus* that is inscribed on the base of the Statue of Liberty:

> *Give me your tired, your poor,*
> *Your huddled masses yearning to breathe free,*
> *The wretched refuse of your teeming shore.*
> *Send these, the homeless, tempest-tost to me,*
> *I lift my lamp beside the golden door!*

Despite the national mythology surrounding this issue, it is
important to note that there are, and always have been, two sides
to U.S. immigration/refugee policy. On the one hand, there is the
nation of immigrants, which is not only reflected in Lazarus's
poem, but more importantly in a reality that has brought count-
less millions to the United States. America has always seen itself
as a country of immigration. In fact, one of the charges set forth
in the Declaration of Independence in justifying the separation
from Great Britain was that King George III had unlawfully
restricted immigration: "He has endeavored to prevent the Population of these States; for that purpose obstructing the Laws for
Naturalization of Foreigners; refusing to pass others to encourage
their migrations hither, and raising the conditions of new Appro-
priations of Land." More than this, many of those who fled to
America over the course of the last three centuries have been people who would now be termed refugees—those fleeing from
political and religious persecution in their native lands.

83

On the other hand, as we will see in a moment, there has always been a deep anti-foreigner strain as well, which oftentimes has been obscured by the golden door imagery. To a certain extent, then, the treatment accorded Mexicans today mirrors that experienced by Germans, Irish, Chinese, Italians, and all (or nearly all) immigrant groups that have come to the United States.

A Historical Survey of U.S. Alien Admission Practices

Since there was no differentiation between immigrants and refugees for most of American history, we will spend some time examining the history of U.S. alien admission policy more generally. At the time of the first census in 1790, there were 3,227,000 people in this new country—all immigrants or descendants of immigrants. Despite this scarcity of people, Congress passed a series of acts that regulated naturalization. The first effort in 1790 was fairly liberal in scope, requiring only a two year period of residence and the renunciation of former allegiances before citizenship could be obtained. However, by 1795, largely in response to turmoil brought on by the French Revolution, the residency requirement was increased to five years. Three years later the residency requirement was raised to 14 years, and the new Alien Enemies Act and the Alien Friends Act gave the president the power to deport any alien whom he considered dangerous to the welfare of the nation. The expressed concern was that if the president did not have the ability to keep foreign undesirables out, the United States would be under the power of other sovereign countries. With the passing of political power in 1800 from the Federalists to the Republicans some of the national xenophobia abated. The Alien Friends Act was allowed to expire, and in 1802 a new Naturalization Act was passed that re-established the five year residency requirement for citizenship that in large part remains today.

Immigration was rather modest at the beginning of the republic. From the Revolutionary War to 1830, it is estimated that only 375,000 immigrants came to the new country. However, between 1830 and the start of the Civil War almost 4.5 million migrated here. Moreover, the composition of these immigrants began to change as there were more and more non-English—

primarily Germans and Irish. In response to this, a number of America First political parties came into existence, going under the banner of such colorful names as the Secret Order of the Star Spangled Banner or the Know-Nothing Party. What these groups all shared was a commitment to curb further immigration and to keep these new arrivals from participating in the country's political affairs. However, not all efforts followed democratic and lawful processes, as evidenced by the anti-immigrant riots that broke out in cities such as New York, Philadelphia, and Boston.

Yet immigration continued apace. From 1860 to 1880 about 2.5 million Europeans entered into this country during each of these decades, and this number then doubled to 5.25 million in the 1880s. Another 16 million immigrants entered during the next quarter century, with 1.25 million entering in 1907 alone—a number that has only been approached again in recent American history.

Despite these concerns with the American-ness of many of the new European arrivals, an even deeper fear related to immigration from Asia. From 1860 to 1880, Chinese immigration had increased from 40,000 to 100,000 as Chinese labor was welcomed to lay the railway lines of the transcontinental railway. However, with the completion of the line, followed by an economic depression in the 1870s, deep anti-Chinese sentiment began to grow. The fear of these newcomers was well captured in this 1878 report, An Address to the American People of the United States upon the Evils of Chinese Immigrants, by the California State Senate's Special Committee on Chinese Immigration, which described Chinese nationals as follows:

> They fail to comprehend our system of government; they perform no duties of citizenship. . . . they do not comprehend or appreciate our social ideas. . . . The great mass of the Chinese are not amenable to our laws. . . .

The Committee then concluded that "Chinese are inferior to any race God ever made." The general feeling, one even countenanced by the U.S. Supreme Court, was that the Chinese people were, at best, simply unassimilable—and at worse, nothing more than low-level criminals and prostitutes.

In 1882, the U.S. passed the Chinese Exclusion Act, representing the first racist, restictionist law in this country's history. This exclusion was to continue until 1943 at a time when China was an ally of the United States in World War II. In place of exclusion,

China was awarded a yearly quota of 105 admissions. The animosity toward Asians was not restricted to Chinese nationals. In 1907 the United States and Japan reached the Gentleman's Agreement that effectively ended Japanese immigration to the United States for decades. The terminology was used to help mask the virulent racism upon which the policy was based.

For followers of the nativist creed, these efforts did not go far enough—and they certainly did little to stem the tide of immigrants, now overwhelmingly from southern and eastern Europe. The 1.25 million immigrants in 1907 remains the highest one year total, and what also needs to be considered is that this occurred among a national population that was considerably smaller than it is today—representing one immigrant for every 60 persons in this country. These numbers, but also the origins of these newcomers, caught the attention of lawmakers in Washington and in response a special joint House-Senate committee (headed by Senator William Dillingham of Vermont) established a commission to study immigration. The Dillingham Commission produced a 42-volume report that confirmed what nativists had been claiming all along, namely, that the new immigrants were vastly inferior to those who had come to the United States before them. Proof of this proposition came mainly through science—eugenic science to be exact—which the Dillingham Commission relied on quite heavily for its findings and it conclusions. According to Edward Ross, one of the leading proponents of nativism, eugenics proved that Jews are "the polar opposite of our pioneer breed. Undersized and weak muscled, they shun bodily activity and are exceedingly sensitive to pain." In terms of Italians, another of the unpopular groups migrating to the United States at that time, Ross's studies showed that they "possess a distressing frequency of low foreheads, open mouths, weak chins, poor features, skewed faces, small or knobby crania, and backless heads." In addition, Italians "lack the power to take rational care of themselves" (Select Commission on Immigration and Refugee Policy 1981).

Based on the findings of the Dillingham Commission as well as public sentiment, Congress passed the Immigration Act of 1917, over U.S. President Woodrow Wilson's veto, which had four major provisions. The first was a literacy requirement. The second was an expanded list of deportable offenses that included men who entered the country for immoral purposes, chronic alcoholics, and those with one or more attacks of insanity. The third provision constituted a further geographic expansion excluding

Asiatic immigration. Interesting enough, however, an effort to exclude from immigration "all members of the African or black race" failed to win approval in the House of Representatives, although a similar measure passed the Senate. Finally, the 1917 Act expanded the country's ability to deport. In terms of this provision, Norm and Naomi Zucker explain how deportation can to be transformed:

> In the nineteenth and early twentieth centuries deportation was a bureaucratic mechanism used to return recently admitted aliens who should have been denied admission at the port of entry. Under the new act, aliens who preached revolution or sabotage could be deported at any time after entry. The act, and subsequent legislation, raised deportation from a simple administrative procedure to a public policy weapon, a potent instrument for enforcing social, cultural, and political conformity (Zucker and Zucker 1996, 15).

Restrictionism and isolationism reached new heights following World War I, as manifested in the congressional rejection of the Treaty of Versailles and the League of Nations. Beyond this, there was the Red Scare brought about by the Bolshevik Revolution in Russia, but also the fear of anarchism that resulted in the (in)famous trial against Ferdinando Sacco and Bartolomeo Vanzetti. One of the responses of the government were the so-called Palmer raids, carried out by U.S. Attorney General A. Mitchell Palmer against anarchists, communists, and all other groups that the government disapproved of and sought to remove from this country.

All of this led to further initiatives to close U.S. borders. In 1921 Congress passed what came to be called the National Origins Quota system, which established per country ceilings based on the 1910 census—when immigration from certain targeted countries was not as great. When this law did not fully satisfy nativist demands, the National Origins Quota Act of 1924 was passed, moving the base period back to 1890. As a result of these changes, the Italian quota was reduced from 42,000 to 4,000, the Polish quota from 31,000 to 6,000, and the Greek quota from 3,000 to 100.

Although World War II was fought against the Nazi German regime that was premised on the notion of racial superiority, in 1952 Congress passed the McCarran-Walter Act, over President

Truman's veto, which effectively kept in place an immigration quota system that gave strong preference to those from northern and western Europe. It was not until 1965 that Congress finally eliminated the practice of racial quotas—and for the first time instituted a category of admissions specifically for refugees, which we will return to in a moment.

Interestingly enough, given the national mythology concerning the admission of the "the tired, the poor, and the huddled masses yearning to breathe free," it was not until after World War II that the United States had anything even resembling a refugee policy as such. Certainly one of the cruelest instances of this inattention to people in great need was the incident involving the steamship S.S. *St. Louis*, which in 1939 sought to bring 900 Jewish children from Germany to the United States, but was turned away on the grounds that the German quota for that year had already been filled. The ship was eventually forced back to Europe, where the majority of its passengers were killed.

But it must also be said that the non-response to the plight of Germany's desperate Jews was mirrored throughout Europe. In 1938, an international conference at Évian-les-Bains, France (Évian Conference) sought to come up with solutions to this expanding crisis, but it did so only by promising that no country would be asked to accept additional immigrants. With respect to U.S. involvement in these proceedings, as Alan Dowty has written in his book *Closed Borders: The Contemporary Assault on Freedom of Movement*: "the principal aim in promoting the conference was precisely to head off any pressure to increase American quotas" (Dowty 1987, 92).

Unfortunately, the same obstructionist policies prevailed during the war itself. The historian David Wyman (1968) has used the term paper walls to describe the quiet, but deadly, manner by which administrative hurdles were erected and then used to prevent German Jews facing genocide in their home country from entering into the United States. Norm and Naomi Zucker quote U.S. Assistant Secretary of State Breckinridge Long, who was primarily responsible for refugee matters and a long time restrictionist:

> We can delay and effectively stop for a temporary period of indefinite length the number of immigrants into the United States. We could do this by simply advising our consuls to put every obstacle in the way and to require

additional evidence and to resort to various administrative devises which would postpone the granting of visas (Zucker and Zucker 1996, 21–22).

Delay, the U.S. State Department did. And as Wyman has pointed out, no exceptions were made, not even when an applicant faced immediate danger.

Some have argued that U.S. policy might have been different if the full extent of Nazi atrocities had been known during World War II. While it is debatable what was known and what was not known, and while it is also debatable whether U.S. policy would have changed one iota, what certainly is clear is that the same anti-Semitism that fueled opposition to increased Jewish immigration during the war was also evident even after the liberation of the concentration camps provided positive proof of Germany's genocidal goals.

Much has been made of the 1948 Displaced Persons Act (DP Act). Under the Act, approximately 400,000 refugees gained admission to the United States. The DP Act also began the process of differentiating between immigrants and refugees, and in this instance placing an emphasis on the admission of the latter over the former. However, what is perhaps the most noteworthy aspect of the DP Act is that a bill that ostensibly was aimed at providing protection to a group that had faced unimaginable horrors—and this is not even to mention the six million Jews who were exterminated—would be skewed in such a way so as to provide as little assistance as it could to these same people. In their book *Calculated Kindness: Refugees and America's Half-Open Door 1945–Present*, Gil Loescher and John Scanlan describe the workings of the DP Act in this manner:

> Thus the DP act that Congress passed was fraught with restrictions, and appeared purposely designed to favor groups other than surviving European Jews. . . . President Truman reluctantly signed the bill on June 25, 1948, but characterized it in an accompanying message as "form[ing] a pattern of discrimination and intolerance wholly inconsistent with the American sense of justice." The victims of that discrimination, he claimed, were Jewish displaced persons, more than 90 percent of whom would be denied the act's benefits. . . . No rationale, other than "abhorrent . . . intolerance," could explain

the wrongful exclu[sion] of almost all recent arrivals
(Loescher and Scanlan 1986, 21).

The Cold War, U.S. Foreign Policy, and Refugee Protection

Although nativist sentiments had prevailed during the war and
to a certain extent after it as well, much of this changed with the
advent of the Cold War, as refugee admissions from communist
states became one of the central tenets of U.S. refugee policy for
the next half century. As such, U.S. refugee policy became an
arm of U.S. foreign policy, and each refugee-escapee from a communist country was offered as further proof of the superiority of
the Western way of life.

Urged by Presidents Harry S. Truman and Dwight D. Eisen-
hower, Congress abandoned the numerical limits and quotas for
refugees from communist states, and even allocated specified
funding for the encouragement of departure (such as through
the Voice of America and Radio Free Europe) as well as for the
resettlement of these new heroes. The President's Escapee Program (PEP) began in 1952 and this was then followed by the Refugee Relief Act (RRA) a year later. The RRA authorized more than
200,000 non-quota visas for persons escaping from behind the
Iron Curtain (Zucker and Zucker 1996, 28).

Just as the RRA was about to expire, the Hungarian uprising
against Soviet-style rule broke out and approximately 200,000
freedom fighters fled to neighboring Austria, and from there
nearly 40,000 came to the United States. Some were given visas
under RRA, but others were simply paroled into the United
States—a source of admission for refugees-escapees that would
repeatedly be used in the ensuing years. Other Hungarians were
admitted under Refugee Escape Act (REA) and what was significant about this is that rather than having refugee admissions
apply against a country's immigration quota as it had in the past,
the REA created a separate category for refugee admissions. In
addition, the REA defined refugee-escapees as those fleeing communist lands, and this would remain the central core of American
refugee policy until 1980.

At the close of the decade there was to be another noteworthy
group fleeing from communist rule that would have a profound

effect on American refugee policy, but also U.S. politics, and this was the first wave of Cuban exiles arriving in the United States in 1959 after Fidel Castro came into power. Although there was always a steady steam of intermittent arrivals, the next large flow of Cubans came in the mid-1960s, and then again in 1980, which helped bring about passage of the Refugee Act of that year. It would not be inaccurate to say that for much of this time (and to a certain extent even in the present), Cubans had a refugee policy wholly on to themselves in the sense that Cuban nationals were almost automatically granted refugee status in the United States, while other groups—most notably Haitians who fled from another Caribbean country—were afforded much different treatment.

As mentioned earlier, the 1965 Immigration Act set aside 17,400 slots for refugee admissions. Perhaps the most telling feature of this new policy was that refugee admissions were purposely restricted to those fleeing from the Middle East (which was rarely ever invoked) or those from communist countries. However, what also has to be said is that the new law played only a peripheral role in terms of U.S. refugee policy. Rather, repeated waves of refugees fleeing from communist or former communist countries were simply and quickly paroled into the United States by authority of the Attorney General. After the 1980 Mariel boatlift, which resulted in the frantic admission of approximately 125,000 Cubans, Congress sought to regularize U.S. refugee flows by passage of the 1980 Refugee Act. The Refugee Act set a baseline of 50,000 and it also removed the ideological and geographical restrictions from the previous definition.

Notwithstanding these changes, for nearly two decades after this U.S. refugee policy remained virtually unchanged (Helton 1984). One aspect of U.S. refugee policy was the continuation of the Vietnam War—even decades after the fighting in this part of the world had ended. During the height of these practices, from 1975 to 1996, approximately 1.2 million Southeast Asians were admitted to the United States, with the largest group coming from Vietnam (700,000), followed by Laotians (250,000) and Cambodians (150,000).

Related to this, another aspect of U.S. refugee policy was devoted to the admission of refugees from the Soviet Union and then its successor the Russian Republic. Of course, the United States was always deeply interested in increased refugee admissions from its old adversary (or former adversary). As noted before, what better way of establishing the superiority of the West than by the existence of these courageous flights from totalitarian oppression? What prevented this from occurring for a long period of time were restrictions on emigration instituted by the Soviet government. However, when these restrictions were eventually loosened after the fall of the Berlin Wall and the institutionalization of *perestroika* in the (former) Soviet regime, what had been a trickle became a steam. To give some indication of those numbers, but also a tell-tale sign of U.S. refugee and foreign policy priorities, consider the year 1994. That year, the U.S. admitted 112,682 refugees and fully 43,000 of these were from the Russian Republic. What simply did not matter was that the Soviet Union ceased to exist, or that communism in that part of the world had no longer existed for half a decade. Apparently what also did not matter was that this same year, Rwanda experienced one of the worst episodes of genocide in human history, as 800,000 civilians were slaughtered in a matter of 100 days and even larger numbers desperately sought refuge in surrounding countries. That year— the same year that 43,000 Russian refugees came to the United States—all of 31 refugees from Rwanda were admitted to the United States. What also has to be noted is that 1994 was no aberration. Refugee admissions from Russia continued apace for a number of years, and it still remains one of the greatest sources of refugees for the United States. Likewise, refugee admissions from Rwanda remained virtually non-existent as well.

What this shows is not only the extent of the ideological bias in U.S. refugee admissions, even after the ideological exclusion had been removed from the law, but also the flip side, namely, the great difficulty that individuals from non-communist countries have had in gaining refugee status in the United States, no matter what levels of political violence and suffering. Perhaps no group suffered more or at least longer from this policy than Haitians, who repeatedly took to the seas in a desperate attempt to reach American shores. The United States did establish a special program for Haitians, but the Haitian interdiction program was not intended to provide assistance and protection to a group of people coming from the poorest country in the entire Western Hemisphere and arguably ruled by the most brutal dictatorship, at least in that part of the world. When the interdiction program began it was the policy of the U.S. government to provide asylum hearings for all those gathered up in the Atlantic Ocean. Up until the 1991 coup in Haiti, 22,716 Haitians had been stopped and interviewed on board U.S. Coast Guard cutters. However, of this number only 28 were allowed to proceed to the United States in order to pursue their claim for refugee status, while the rest were returned to Haiti. Mercifully, the pretense of fair and even-handed hearings was eventually stopped.

Yet, perhaps the worst manifestation of the other side of America's obsession with pursuing ideological ends through its refugee policy was with regard to Central America refugees throughout the entire decade of the 1980s. Notwithstanding the existence of brutal wars in both Guatemala (where some 200,000 civilians were killed) and El Salvador (where approximately 75,000 civilians were killed), year after year the United States rejected anywhere between 97 to 99 percent of the asylum claims filed by refugees from these two countries. In defense of this policy, Reagan administration officials repeatedly proclaimed that these asylum seekers were nothing but economic migrants seeking a better life in the United States. By way of proof, they would note that in order to get to the United States these migrants would have to pass through Mexico, a country where, at least according to the thinking of the Reagan administration, these individuals could have applied for refugee status.

Empirical research provides a much different story. William Stanley (1987) of the Massachusetts Institute of Technology conducted a study that showed that as political violence in El Salvador increased, so did apprehensions by the Immigration and Naturalization Service (INS) while, conversely, the numbers arriving at the U.S. border decreased substantially during those times when violence abated in that country. Stanley's conclusion was that political violence, and not economic circumstances, was the actual driving force behind Salvadoran migration patterns.

Similarly, Segundo Montes (1988) of Central American University in El Salvador conducted a study that used Salvadoran towns and villages as the unit of analysis. Similar to Stanley's findings, Montes data showed that the most violent provinces in El Salvador sent the largest proportions of their populations to the United States, while areas of the country that were relatively safe sent far fewer refugees to the United States. Like Stanley, Montes concluded that the rise and fall in asylum applicants in the United States could best be explained by violence, and not by poverty.

Yet, one reason why Salvadorans and Guatemalans were almost totally excluded from refugee protection in the United States was because of the enormous influence that the State Department played in refugee determinations. Under the asylum system that was employed at that time, each asylum application was sent to the State Department's Bureau of Human Rights and Humanitarian Affairs (BHRHA) for an advisory opinion. Not surprisingly, the opinions that came back to immigration officials strongly reflected the political stance of the Reagan administration. Perhaps what is more surprising was how enormously influential these opinions were in the asylum determination process itself. Of course, what further condemned the prospect of Salvadorans and Guatemalans was the deep seated fear that because of the geographical proximity to the United States, very large number of those people could actually arrive at the U.S. borders. What this led to was a non-admission policy directed at both of these groups, something that was confirmed by an internal INS study.

> Certain nationalities appear to benefit from presumptive status while others do not.
>   For example, for an El Salvadoran national to receive a favorable asylum advisory opinion, he or she must have a "classic textbook case." On the other hand, BHRHA sometimes recommends favorable action where the applicant cannot meet the individual well-founded fear of persecution test. This happened in December 1981 a week after martial law was declared in Poland. Seven Polish crewmen jumped ship and applied for asylum in Alaska. Even before seeing the asylum applications, a State Department official said, "We're going to approve them." All the applications, in the view of INS senior officials, were extremely weak. In one instance, the crewman said that the reason he feared returning to Poland was that he had once attended a Solidarity rally (he was one of the more than 100,000 participants at the rally). The crewman had never been a member of Solidarity, never participated in any political activity, etc. His claim was approved within forty-eight hours (INS 1982, 59).

Similarly, a General Accounting Office (GAO) study confirmed the degree to which nationality and ideology were the primary considerations driving U.S. refugee policy. For one thing, the GAO study compared asylum success rates for those who claimed to have been tortured. The success rate for Salvadorans was four percent, while it was 15 percent for those from Nicaragua (a country run by a group the Reagan administration considered communists), but fully 64 percent for Iranian claimants, and finally, an overwhelming 80 percent for Polish applicants who claimed to have been tortured (General Accounting Office 1987).

Although ideological considerations ruled U.S. refugee policy for nearly a half century, its role has now been diminished, although it continues to manifest itself in a number of ways. For one thing, Cubans no longer get a free pass. Rather, under agreements signed by the two countries in the mid-1990s, the United States now has implemented what has been described as a "wet foot, dry foot" policy. Individuals intercepted at sea are screened, and those found to have a well-founded fear of persecution are then resettled, but in some country other than the United States. This, of course, stands in marked contrast to previous policy whereby all Cubans were essentially guaranteed entry into the United States. However, Cubans who somehow manage to get to the United States are paroled in, and are eligible for adjustment of status under the Cuban Adjustment Act. Obviously, this dual-policy continues to provide an enormous incentive for Cubans to attempt to get to the United States and no other country receives similar treatment.

The lingering effect of ideological bias continues to manifest itself with regard to Russian refugees, although these numbers are less than a fraction of what they had been at the height of refugee flows in the early and mid-1990s. Under priority guidelines that will be discussed further on, certain groups of Russians are singled out as being of humanitarian concern to the United States—these are Jews, Evangelical Christians, and Ukrainians. Russia is still a dangerous country and certain groups are exposed to very high levels of political violence, particularly those in the civil war zone of Chechnya. Unfortunately, U.S. refugee policy is not set up to meet the protection needs of this group. Instead, the focus has been almost exclusively on those who, quite arguably, are really not refugees at all in the sense that they suffer from discrimination, but certainly not persecution.

Before turning to present practice, we will close this historical section by offering one last observation of U.S. policy—and this relates more to those who are absent (by and large) from the rolls of those arriving in the United States as refugees. Since late 2001, the United States has been fighting a war in Afghanistan and since the spring 2003 it has waged a war in Iraq. Both conflicts have had an enormous effect on refugee practices in both of these countries. Afghanistan has experienced all sides: both a massive influx of repatriated refugees, but sizable numbers of refugees fleeing the country as well. However, one country where these refugees are not fleeing to is the United States. For example, in 2008, the United States admitted all of 576 refugees from Afghanistan and the year before that 441. In terms of Iraq, it has been estimated that the war in that country has brought about the displacement of more than four million people, two million of whom have crossed national borders and are considered refugees. Given U.S. involvement in this war—which is an understatement of the highest order—one might expect the United States to shoulder a substantial amount of the load in providing refugee protection to these refugees. However, there were 298 Iraqi refugees admitted in 2003, 66 in 2004, 198 in 2005, 202 in 2006, and 1,608 in 2007. After a great deal of public criticism of these practices, in 2008 this number jumped to 13,823, which still represents a very small portion of the total Iraqi refugee population.

Current Refugee/Asylum Law and Practice in the United States

In this section we provide a closer analysis of U.S. refugee/asylum law and practice. As before, we begin with the definition of refugee, which, for the most part, mirrors that in the 1951 Refugee Convention, with a few exceptions. One minor difference is that while the Refugee Convention is only prospective in scope—the refugee applicant bases his or her claim on what might happen in the future, rather than what has already taken place in the past—under U.S. law an individual can base a claim on the future prospects of harm, but also on the basis of past harm, where the law provides a rebuttable presumption that those who have suffered past persecution will suffer future persecution as well. Another difference, one that has grown to be fairly significant, is that U.S. law does not demand that the refugee claimant be outside his or her country of nationality. In some years, in fact, upwards of 80 percent of those who are admitted as refugees under the Overseas Refugee Program (ORP) are individuals who have never left their country of origin, but instead, have applied for refugee status in country and awaited word of the status of their application from home. Of course, this raises the question (or at least should raise the question) whether it is accurate to describe this situation as one involving persecution.

The definition of refugee under the 1980 Refugee Act has been amended once and that was in 1996 when Congress sought to address claims based on China's one-child policy:

> For purposes of determination under this Act, a person who has been forced to abort a pregnancy or to undergo involuntary sterilization, or who has been persecuted for failure or refusal to undergo such a procedure or for other resistance to a coercive population control program, shall be deemed to have been persecuted on account of political opinion, and a person who has a well founded fear that he or she will be forced to undergo such a procedure or subject to persecution for such failure, refusal, or resistance, shall be deemed to have a well founded fear of persecution on account of political opinion.

Initially, the immigration act placed a ceiling of 1,000 per year on the number of persons who could receive protection on this basis. Those who applied after this yearly limit was reached were provided with a provisional grant of asylum. Within a decade there was a backlog of nearly 9,000 conditional grants, at which point Congress repealed the ceiling in 2005.

The 1980 Refugee Act establishes two procedures by which persons who meet the refugee definition can obtain such protection. The first set of procedures, referred to as the ORP, applies to refugees persons who are outside the United States (but who may be within their own country) who are then admitted to the United States as refugees, while the second set of procedures applies to persons seeking protection from within the United States or upon arrival at the country's borders. Although the term refugee does not change, the two programs will, at times, differ substantially.

Overseas Refugee Program

In a host of ways, the United States is unique with respect to alien admissions. One aspect of this is the relatively large influx of legal immigrants, with these numbers now routinely being in the vicinity of a million new arrivals each year. In addition, there is the undocumented population that in recent years has rivaled, and even surpassed, the number of those lawfully admitted. There is also the category of non-immigrants, people admitted for a limited period of time, but many of whom are ultimately able to regularize their status and remain in the country permanently.

In term of refugees specifically, although the United States cannot claim to be the only country that resettles refugees from outside the country (12 other Western states do as well), the ORP is unique both in terms of its size but also in terms of its the geographical scope. Table 3.1 provides data on refugee admissions from 1980 to 2008.

TABLE 3.1
Refugee Arrivals: Fiscal Years 1980 to 2008

Year	Number
1980	207,116
1981	159,252
1982	98,096
1983	61,218
1984	70,393
1985	67,704
1986	62,146
1987	64,528
1988	76,483
1989	107,070
1990	122,066
1991	113,389
1992	115,548
1993	114,181
1994	111,680
1995	98,973
1996	75,421
1997	69,653
1998	76,712
1999	85,076
2000	72,143
2001	68,925
2002	26,776
2003	28,304
2004	52,837
2005	53,738
2006	41,150
2007	48,218
2008	60,108

Note: Data series began following the Refugee Act of 1980. Excludes Amerasian immigrants except in fiscal years 1989 to 1991.
Source: U.S. Department of State, Bureau of Population, Refugees, and Migration (PRM), Worldwide Refugee Admissions Processing System (WRAPS), Fiscal Years 1980 to 2008.

As you can see in Table 3.1, the height of ORP admissions was 1980 when 207,116 refugees were brought to the United States. That number had decreased by more than two-thirds by 1986 (62,146), but refugee numbers increased again in the early 1990s, as the United States admitted tens of thousands of refugees from the (former) Soviet Union and from Vietnam. However, by 2001, refugee admission numbers had fallen to 68,925 and then following the September 11 attacks on the United States, only 26,776 refugees were admitted in 2002 and 28,304 in 2003. The numbers have increased since then, and in 2008, 60,108 were granted admission.

Table 3.2 provides data on refugee admissions for certain countries from 1999 to 2008. The countries selected represent both extremes of U.S. refugee admissions—those that are generally well represented (i.e., Bosnia, Iran, and Russia), as well as those that have not been well represented (i.e., Colombia, Democratic Republic of the Congo, and the Sudan), although the levels of political violence in those countries would indicate otherwise.

How are refugees selected? Each year, the President in consultation with Congress establishes the annual determination as to the number of refugees to be admitted that year under ORP as well as the how these slots are to be allocated worldwide by region of the world. Under the provisions of the Refugee Act, the numbers and the allocation are to reflect both humanitarian concerns as well as the national interest. In addition, the statute gives the President the authority to respond to "unforeseen emergency refugee" situations and provide additional slots for refugees of "special humanitarian concern" where "justified by grave humanitarian concerns or . . . otherwise in the national interest." Table 3.3 shows the work of this consultative process for the years 2006–2008.

Priorities for these categories are also established annually through the consultative process and individuals must come within a priority category in order to be considered for admission. As described by (Musalo et al. 2007, 76–76):

> Priority One is the only category not restricted by regional designation, but can include an individual in any nationality who has been identified by UNHCR or U.S. embassy personnel to be in need of resettlement for specified and compelling reasons.
> Two is comprised of groups of "Special Concern" to the United States, and generally includes specified

TABLE 3.2

Refugee Arrivals by Region and Country of Nationality: Fiscal Years 1999 to 2008

Country of Nationality	1999	2000	2001	2002	2003	2004	2005	2006	2007	2008
REGION										
Total	85,076	72,143	68,925	26,776	28,304	52,837	53,738	41,150	48,218	60,108
Africa	13,048	17,624	19,070	2,551	10,719	29,110	20,746	18,185	17,486	8,943
Asia	14,041	13,622	15,356	6,886	5,862	10,896	14,977	9,245	23,195	44,545
Europe	55,877	37,664	31,526	15,407	11,269	9,254	11,316	10,456	4,561	2,343
North America	D	3,233	2,968	1,924	305	2,998	6,368	3,145	2,922	4,177
Oceania	–	–	–	–	–	–	–	–	–	–
South America	D	–	5	8	149	579	331	119	54	100
COUNTRY										
Total	85,076	72,143	68,925	26,776	28,304	52,837	53,738	41,150	48,218	60,108
Afghanistan	365	1,709	2,930	1,683	1,453	959	902	651	441	576
Bhutan	–	–	–	–	–	–	–	D	–	5,320
Burma	295	637	543	128	203	1,056	1,447	1,612	13,896	18,139
Burundi	223	165	109	62	16	276	214	466	4,545	2,889
Central African Republic	D	–	D	–	D	24	–	23	15	56

Country										
China, People's Republic	D	D	12	9	9	3	13	21	27	50
Colombia	–	–	–	8	149	577	323	115	54	94
Congo, Democratic Republic	42	1,354	260	107	251	569	424	405	848	727
Cuba	2,018	3,184	2,944	1,919	305	2,980	6,360	3,143	2,922	4,177
Haiti	91	49	24	5	–	17	8	–	–	–
Iran	1,750	5,145	6,590	1,540	2,471	1,786	1,856	2,792	5,481	5,270
Iraq	1,955	3,158	2,473	472	298	66	198	202	1,608	13,823
Russia	4,386	3,723	4,454	2,105	1,394	1,446	5,982	6,003	1,773	426
Rwanda	153	345	94	47	47	176	183	112	202	108
Sudan	2,393	3,833	5,959	897	2,139	3,500	2,205	1,848	705	375
Ukraine	8,649	7,334	7,172	5,217	5,065	3,482	2,889	2,483	1,605	1,022
Vietnam	9,622	2,841	2,730	2,988	1,354	974	2,009	3,039	1,500	1,112

NA Not Available.

X-Not applicable.

D-Data withheld to limit disclosure.

—Represents zero.

Note: Excludes Amerasian Immigrants.

Source: U.S. Department of State, Bureau of Population, Refugees, and Migration (PRM), Worldwide Refugee Admissions Processing System (WRAPS).

TABLE 3.3
Refugee Admissions Ceilings: Fiscal Years 2006 to 2008

Region	Ceiling		
	2008	2007	2006
Total	80,000	70,000	70,000
Africa	16,000	20,000	20,000
East Asia	20,000	15,000	13,000
Europe/Central Asia	3,000	15,000	9,500
Latin America/Caribbean	3,000	5,000	5,000
Near East/South Asia	28,000	5,000	2,500
Unallocated Reserve	10,000	10,000	20,000

Source: U.S. Department of State, Proposed Refugee Admissions for FY 2008—Report to Congress.

categories within nationality groups. For example, in 2006, Priority Two included Cubans in certain categories, including former political prisoners, members of persecuted religious minorities, human rights activists, and those subjected to disproportionately or harsh discriminatory treatment because of their perceived or actual political or religious beliefs; citizens of the former Soviet Union who are Jewish, evangelical Christians, or members of the Ukrainian Catholic and Orthodox churches; certain categories of Vietnamese, including former re-education camp detainees or employees of the U.S. government who meet specified criteria; and specified ethnic or religious groups from Nepal, Burma, Tanzania, the former Soviet Union, and Iran.

Three includes family members of U.S. citizens, or other persons with specified legal status in the United States.

To be clear, individuals within in these priority categories are not guaranteed admission as refugees and they must also be approved in an interview that occurs outside the United States and conducted by a representative of the Department of Homeland Security's (DHS) Citizenship and Immigration Services, which makes this determination, one that is not subject to appeal or judicial review. In addition to the involvement of DHS, the U.S. State Department coordinates resettlement policy, including maintaining connections with nongovernmental organizations that assist newly arrived refugees, while the Department of Health and Human Services is responsible for financial, medical, and social services for the newly arrived refugees (Musalo et al. 2007, 76).

Criticisms of ORP

It is not easy to criticize a program that provides human rights protection to large numbers of people. It is estimated that since passage of the 1980 Refugee Act, the United States has admitted more than two million refugees through the ORP. In large part because of this humanitarian basis, refugee scholars are often reluctant to question the ORP more generally, or the priorities that it establishes more particularly. Rather, what seems to be at work is some notion that the admission of a refugee—perhaps any refugee—is a good thing that should not be seriously analyzed or questioned.

However, there is another way to think of U.S. refugee policy and it is to see admission slots as a kind of zero-sum game, where the admission of one refugee means that the chances of all other refugees are thereby diminished. More than this, and at the risk of sounding overly dramatic, the consequences for those who are not able to gain admission might well be severe. It is for this reason that we believe that there is something seriously and fundamentally wrong with a refugee protection system that admits 43,000 Russians, but only 31 Rwandans, at a time when the latter was experiencing massive levels of genocidal killing while the former was enjoying newfound freedoms.

Unfortunately, there are a host of other situations that are not much different from this. For example, over the course of the past decade arguably the single most violent country in the world has been the Democratic Republic of the Congo, where an estimated four million civilians have been killed. Based on this, one might expect a substantial number of refugee admissions. However, as shown in Table 3.2, throughout this entire period of time there has only been one year where more than 1,000 refugees were admitted from this country, while the norm has been to admit approximately 750 refugees a year.

Yet, this anemic response is reflective of U.S. refugee policy regarding Africa more generally. Although the greatest number of refugees in the world are from Africa (and have been for quite a period of time), the U.S. response to this entire continent has been underwhelming at best. It was not until 1992 that refugee admissions for the entire continent for one year reached 5,000, while admissions finally reached 10,000 in 1999. The next year, approximately 20,000 refugees were admitted to the United States—a fourfold increase in eight years, if you choose to look at it this way—and the numbers remained in this range for a few years, before falling substantially to 8,943 in 2008. The point is that these numbers represent but a small fraction of the total African refugee population (not to even mention the IDP population in Africa), a large portion of which has been warehoused in refugee camps for extensive periods of time. Of course, what this also means is that refugee protection has been shunted aside and left almost solely to a host of African states that are not well equipped to deal with the fiscal strains that go along with this, but which have also been negatively affected by the violence that sometimes accompanies fleeing refugees as well.

The last thing to note is that refugee admissions are almost never compared to the immigrant population coming to this country, which now averages nearly one million a year. As noted in the first part of this chapter, for much of U.S. history there was no distinction made between immigrants and refugees. Invariably, the term immigrant was used to describe all of those migrating to the United States, but what needs to be recognized is that many of these immigrants were what we would now term refugees. Or to state this more succinctly, huddled masses is another way of describing refugees. However, beginning in the post-World War II period a distinction between these two categories began to be made.

Yet, what is almost always ignored is the manner in which refugee admissions has long served as a kind of stepchild to U.S. immigration policy, although there is absolutely no reason why this has to be the case. Perhaps this was predestined when at the time that refugee admissions became permanent, this was accomplished as the seventh preference (which itself is revealing) of the 1965 Immigration Act (not the 1965 Immigration and Refugee Act). Since that time, refugee admissions have generally run in the vicinity of being one-tenth those admitted as normal flow immigrants, although in recent years the differential between the number of refugees and the number of immigrants admitted to the United States has gotten even larger. But this raises the question—or at least should raise the question—what is the optimal mix between refugees and immigrants?

Asylum

The second means by which individuals can gain refugee status in the United States is by being granted this status either at the country's borders at the time of arrival, or else after gaining entry into the United States. In terms of those already in the United States, there is a distinction made between affirmative applications and defensive applications—with the latter occurring once deportation proceedings have been instituted, while under the former an individual files for refugee status without a similar prompting by government officials. Note that unlike ORP, the system of asylum adjudications makes no provision for refugees who are of humanitarian or national concern to the United States.

In the 1970s, the number of asylum applications was in the range of 2,000 to 6,000 per year. However, shortly after the adoption of the 1980 Refugee Act, those numbers increased significantly, brought on by a confluence of political events. One was the Mariel boatlift, which brought approximately 125,000 Cuban refugees to the United States. Another was a sharp increase in the number of Haitians fleeing to the United States, who seemed to assume that the warm welcome given to Cuban nationals would be extended to them (it was not). And finally, the fall of the Shah of Iran and the ouster of Anastasio Somoza in Nicaragua resulted in greatly increased asylum applications from nationals of these two countries. In the 1980s, there were also an increasing number of asylum applications from El Salvador and Guatemala, although, as pointed out earlier, extraordinarily few were successful. However, litigation and special legislation eventually led to full legal status for most of the Nicaraguan, Guatemalan, Salvadoran, and Haitian asylum seekers of that era (Aleinikoff et al. 2008, 858).

In the latter part of the 1980s, the total numbers increased significantly, reaching 150,000 asylum claims a year. Congress responded with a series of reforms, which we will discuss in a moment. This, in turn, led to a substantial decrease in claims, which now average between 30,000 and 50,000. Table 3.4 presents data on countries with the largest number of asylum claims for the years 2006–2008.

One thing that is noteworthy is that as the number of asylum claims has decreased, the overall acceptance rate has generally increased, going from a low of 17 percent in 1996 to the situation at present where acceptance rates hover around 40 percent.

TABLE 3.4

All Asylees by Country of Nationality: Fiscal Years 2006 to 2008
(Ranked by 2008 Country of Nationality)

Country	2008		2007		2006	
	Number	Percent	Number	Percent	Number	Percent
Total	22,930	100.0	25,124	100.0	26,203	100.0
China	5,459	23.8	6,359	25.3	5,593	21.3
Colombia	1,646	7.2	2,177	8.7	2,961	11.3
Haiti	1,237	5.4	1,648	6.6	2,995	11.4
Venezuela	1,057	4.6	1,152	4.6	1,359	5.2
Iraq	1,002	4.4	671	2.7	370	1.4
Ethiopia	899	3.9	843	3.4	774	3.0
Indonesia	580	2.5	776	3.1	742	2.8
Russia	574	2.5	496	2.0	431	1.6
Guatemala	552	2.4	680	2.7	632	2.4
Nepal	497	2.2	413	1.6	376	1.4
All other countries, including unknown	9,427	41.1	9,909	39.4	9,970	38.0

Source: U.S. Department of Homeland Security, Refugee, Asylum, and Parole System (RAPS) and Executive Office for Immigration Review (EOIR) of the U.S. Department of Justice (DOJ).

1996 Changes to U.S. Asylum Law

In 1996, Congress made a number of substantive changes to U.S. asylum practices. One was the establishment of an expedited removal procedure for arriving aliens who are not in possession of valid travel documents, or who obtained their travel documents by fraud or misrepresentation. Under the new provisions of this act, immigration officials now have the authority to order such persons removed without the right to a hearing or to administrative or judicial review. However, additional administrative procedures will be given to all such persons who express a credible fear of persecution. For those not able to establish a credible fear, this individual can request a *de novo* review by an immigration judge. Those found to have such a fear are allowed to present their claims for refugee status or for other means of protection, such as that under the Torture Convention.

The 1996 law also bars an individual from filing for asylum unless he or she "demonstrates by clear and convincing evidence that the application has been filed within 1 year after the date of the alien's arrival in the United States." The only possible exception to this is if the applicant is able to demonstrate to the satisfaction of the Attorney General either the existence of changed circumstances which materially affect the applicant's eligibility for asylum or extraordinary circumstances relating to the delay in filing an application within the one year period. Note that there is no basis in the Refugee Convention for this one year ban, although other countries have instituted similar policies.

Prior to 1995, regulations authorized permission to work to all asylum seekers whose claims were not deemed frivolous (Aleinikoff et al. 2008, 852). In effect, nearly everyone who applied for asylum was thereby authorized to work in the United States. In 1995, new regulations were promulgated that postponed the issuance of work authorization until at least 180 days had elapsed—unless asylum had been granted before then. One of the immediate consequences of this was that the number of asylum applications decreased significantly. These regulatory provisions have now been incorporated into the governing statute. It should also be noted that the government generally completes the asylum proceedings within this period of time.

Asylum and Withholding of Deportation

One of the unique features of U.S. law is that there are two different statutory provisions dealing with individuals who seek to remain in this country due to a fear of being returned home: refugee status and withholding of deportation. The former should be familiar. The refugee claimant must prove that she has a well-founded fear of persecution on account of one of the five nexus factors. According to the Supreme Court in *INS v. Cardoza-Fonseca*, even if the standard is met it is up to the discretionary authority of the Attorney General to determine whether this refugee should be allowed to remain in the United States. In *Matter of Pula*, the Board of Immigration Appeals (BIA) set forth a totality of circumstances approach, and it presented a wide range of factors to be considered in determining whether to exercise this discretion:

> Among the factors which should be considered are whether the alien passed through any other countries or arrived in the United States directly from his country, whether orderly refugee procedures were in fact available to help him in any country he passed through, and whether he made any attempt to seek asylum before

coming to the United States. In addition, the length of time the alien remained in a third country, and his living conditions, safety, and potential for long-term residency there are also relevant. For example, an alien who faces imminent deportation back to the country where he fears persecution, may not have found a safe haven even though he has escaped to another country. Further, whether the alien has relatives legally in the United States or other personal ties to this country which motivated him to seek asylum here rather than elsewhere is another factor to consider. In this regard, the extent of the alien's ties to any other countries where he does not fear persecution should also be considered.

The BIA continues:

In addition to the circumstances and actions of the alien in his flight from the country where he fears persecution, general humanitarian considerations, such as an alien's tender age or poor health, may also be relevant in a discretionary determination. A situation of particular concern involves an alien who has established his statutory eligibility for asylum but cannot meet the higher burden required for withholding of deportation. Deportation to a country where the alien may be persecuted thus becomes a strong possibility. In such a case, the discretionary factors should be carefully evaluated in light of the unusually harsh consequences which he may befall an alien who has established a well-founded fear of persecution; the danger of persecution should generally outweigh all but the most egregious of adverse factors.

As noted in *Pula*, in addition to the refugee standard, there is also a provision in the Immigration and Nationality Act (Sec. 241 (b) (3)) for withholding of deportation.

The Attorney General shall not deport or return any alien . . . to a country if the Attorney General determines that such alien's life or freedom would be threatened in such country on account of race, religion, nationality, membership in a particular social group, or political opinion.

Prior to the Supreme Court's decision in *Cardoza-Fonseca*, these two standards were generally equated with one another. However, the Court ruled that there were important differences between the two. For one thing, the withholding statute creates a higher standard: the difference between "well-founded fear" and "would be threatened." However, along with this, withholding is mandatory, while an individual who only meets the refugee standard (but not the withholding standard) could be returned to her country of nationality at the Attorney General's discretion.

Beyond this, however, there are other important differences. For one thing, asylum leads to lawful permanent residence status and then citizenship if the alien decides to pursue this, while withholding only prevents the individual's return to a specified country in which his or her life or freedom would be threatened. In addition, a grant of asylum to an individual confers derivate status to that person's spouse or child, while a grant of withholding does not extend any benefit beyond the prohibition of removal to the person himself or herself (Musualo 2007, 86). Note, however, that many of these distinction between refugee and those eligible for withholding of deportation are oftentimes more theoretical than real. The primary reason for this is that if an individual is able to meet the higher withholding standard it would stand to reason that he or she would invariably also meet the lower refugee standard.

Disqualifications

Similar to the disqualifications for refugee status that exist under the 1951 Refugee Convention, U.S. law denies refugee status for those who are thought to be undeserving of such protection due to certain things that they have done—either in their home country or else after their arrival in the United States. The refugee definition provides: "The term 'refugee' does not include any person who ordered, incited, assisted, or otherwise participated in the persecution of any person on account of race, religion, nationality, membership in a particular social group, or political opinion." In addition, other provisions of the Immigration and Nationality Act (INA) further stipulate those who shall be denied refugee status: The first provision involves serious, nonpolitical crimes committed by the refugee seeker before arriving in the United States. The requirement that the crime be nonpolitical is in recognition that dictatorships will often make criminal of those who oppose the ruling regime. In terms of the serious component, it is generally agreed that what needs to be weighed against one another is the gravity of the persecution the individual would face if returned to his or her country of nationality against the seriousness of the crime committed.

The second category consists of crimes committed by the alien after arriving in the United States. Under the statutory framework, those noncitizens who have been convicted of particularly serious crimes are ineligible for relief under both asylum and withholding of deportation. Note that the bar applies to those who "having been convicted by a final judgment of a particularly serious crime, constitutes a danger to the community of the United States." Thus, the conviction alone will not suffice, but it must also be proven that this individual constitutes a present danger as well.

Finally, the deportation ground for the commission of aggravated felonies has come to play a central role not only for immigrants and non-immigrants alike, but also those seeking refugee status and/or withholding of deportation. The 1990 Act added language to the INA so that the commission of an aggravated felony is to be considered a particularly serious crime. Under present law, asylum remains barred for all aggravated felonies, but requires a threshold of a five year aggregate sentence in order to become ineligible for withholding of deportation (Aleinikoff et al. 2008, 938).

Detention

According to the UNHCR, the detention of asylum seekers is inherently undesirable, and this especially holds true for vulnerable groups including single women, children, unaccompanied minors, and those with special medial or psychological needs. Because of this, the agency is of the view that detention should only be resorted to in case of necessity. However, a number of states do not follow the *UNHCR Handbook* on this matter and the United States is one of those countries. From 1954 to 1982, the government followed a policy of paroling most undocumented persons seeking admission. However, in response to the arrival of large numbers of asylum seekers in the early 1980s, particularly Haitians and Cubans, the United States has now instituted a policy that releases persons much less frequently than they had in the past, and one in which detention has now become the norm (Musalo et al. 2007, 959).

Under current law, undocumented individuals (unless they committed certain crimes, are terrorists, or in expedited removal) may be paroled or released upon payment of a bond, which the Attorney General may grant for urgent humanitarian or significant public benefit reasons. According to government regulations, individuals can only be considered for parole if they "present neither a security risk nor a risk of absconding." What is also noteworthy is that the bond must be in the amount of at least $1,500. Prior to 1996, release decisions made by the government were subject to judicial review, but new amendments prohibit judicial review "of any action or decision by the Attorney General . . . regarding the detention or release of any alien or the grant, revocation, or denial of bond or parole." It is not unusual for asylum seekers to remain in detention for months, and even years (Musalo 2007, 960). And what should also be said is that most asylum seekers are being detained in the same prisons and detention centers that house some of the U.S.'s most hardened criminals. As Karen Musalo has pointed out, Gauziya Kassindja, who became famous because of her successful asylum application based on her fear of facing female genital mutilation, was detained for 16 months and subject to solitary confinement, punished for rising early to pray, repeatedly strip searched, and beaten and teargassed during a riot at one of the detention facilities where she was held (Musalo 1998, 369).

Temporary Protection

In Chapter 1, we briefly analyzed the practice of a number of European states that allow individuals who are not refugees under the 1951 Refugee Convention to remain. The term used to describe this practice is complementary protection. Similarly, the United States has experimented with certain temporary protection measures as well since passage of the 1980 Refugee Act. The first efforts were Deferred Enforced Departure (DED) and Extended Voluntary Departure (EVD). Under both of these programs, the Attorney General was able to exercise his/her discretion to allow citizens of designated countries to remain in the United States based on humanitarian considerations, particularly those relating to civil conflict. Due in large part to the absence of any governing standards, in 1990 Congress created a new temporary protection program known as Temporary Protected Status (TPS).

> TPS is blanket relief that may be granted under the following conditions: there is ongoing armed conflict

posing serious threat to personal safety; a foreign state requests TPS because it temporarily cannot handle the return of nationals due to environmental disaster; or there are extraordinary and temporary conditions in a foreign state that prevent aliens from returning, provided that granting TPS is consistent with U.S. national interests (Wasem and Ester 2008, 3).

To be clear, TPS only applies to foreign nationals who are already in the United States at the date of designation. Thus, it is not an invitation for foreign nationals to pick up and travel to the United States, nor is it intended as a way of helping to regularize a foreign national's immigration status. The Attorney General may grant TPS for an initial period of six to eighteen months, and then may extend this for another period of this same length. Nationals of designated states must register for TPS status in order to receive the statute's protection. If this procedure is followed, these individuals will be allowed to remain and to work in the United States during the time that TPS applies to their home country. In addition, they may not be detained on the basis of the immigration status and they may even travel abroad with permission. As of January 2010, the following countries listed in Table 3.5, along with a listing of the number of nationals of those countries, were designated for either TPS or DED status.

What remains unclear is why these particular countries have been selected for temporary protection status, but other states—some of which are suffering from much higher levels of political violence—are not included. For example, according to data from the Political Terror Scale (Gibney, Cornett, and Wood, 2008), which

TABLE 3.5
Countries Designated with TPS or DED Status

Burundi (27) TPS November 4, 1997—May 2, 2009 27
El Salvador (234,000) TPS March 2, 2001—March 9, 2009
Honduras (78,000) TPS December 30, 1998—January 5, 2009
Liberia (3600) DED October 1, 2007—March 31, 2009
Nicaragua (4000) TPS December 30, 1998—January 5, 2009
Somalia (300) TPS September 16, 1991—September 17, 2009
Sudan (500) TPS November 4, 1997—May 2, 2010
Haiti (100,000) TPS January 12, 2010 (18 months)

ranks countries according to their levels of political violence, the following countries were scored as a level 5 in 2008—representing the highest levels of political violence: Afghanistan, Chad, Colombia, Democratic Republic of Congo, Iraq, Palestinian Occupied Territories, Myanmar (Burma), Somalia, Sri Lanka, Sudan, and the United Arab Emirates (Gibney et al. 2009). Out of this group, only Somalia and the Sudan were designated for PTS/DED status.

Conclusion

There are two sides to immigration/refugee issues in the United States. There is the myth—but also the reality—of this being a nation of immigrants. On the other hand, co-existing alongside this has always been a nativist strain that has always questioned the American-ness of each new wave of immigrants. In terms of refugee protection in particular, once again there are two different versions to choose from. On the one hand, the United States has admitted more refugees than any other country in the world (by far). Since 1980, more than two million refugees have been admitted under the ORP, and this number does not include those granted refugee status by means of applying for asylum.

However, we have also seen how U.S. refugee policy has long been dominated by ideological and foreign policy considerations. Of course, this has long worked out well for Russians, Vietnamese, and Cubans who are desirous of living in the United States. However, what this has also meant is that refugees from non-communist countries have struggled mightily to gain refuge in this country.

References

Books, Articles, and Chapters

Aleinikoff, T. Alexander, David Martin, Hiroshi Motomura, and Maryellen Fullerton. 2008. *Immigration and Citizenship: Process and Policy* 6th ed. St. Paul, MN: Thompson/West.

Dowty, Alan. 1987. *Closed Borders: The Contemporary Assault on Freedom of Movement*. New Haven: CT: Yale University Press.

General Accounting Office. 1987. "Asylum: Approval Rates for Selected Applicants." Washington, DC: GAO.

Gibney, Mark, Linda Cornett, and Reed Wood. 2009. *The Political Terror Scale 1976–2008*. Last accessed on January 28, 2010, http://www.politicalterrorscale.org/.

Helton, Arthur. 1984. "Political Asylum under the 1980 Refugee Act: An Unfulfilled Promise." *University of Michigan Journal of Law Reform* 17: 243–264.

INS. June 1982. *Asylum Adjudications: An Evolving Concept for the Immigration and Naturalization Service*. Washington, DC.

Loescher, Gil, and John Scanlan. 1986. *Calculated Kindness: Refugees and America's Half-Open Door 1945–Present*. New York: Free Press.

Montes, Segundo. 1988. "Migration to the United States as an Index of the Intensifying Social and Political Crises in El Salvador." *Journal of Refugee Studies* 1: 107–126.

Musalo, Karen. 2007. "Protecting Victims of Gendered Persecution: Fear of Floodgates or Call to (Principled) Action?" *Virginia Journal of Social Policy* 14: 119–150.

Musalo, Karen, Jennifer Moore, and Richard A. Boswell. 2007. *Refugee Law and Policy: A Comparative and International Approach*, 3rd ed. Durham: Carolina Academic Press.

Select Commission on Immigration and Refugee Policy. 1981. *U.S. Immigration Policy and the National Interest*. Washington, DC: GPO.

Stanley, William. 1987. "Economic Migrants or Refugees from Violence? A Time Series Analysis of Salvadoran Migration to the U.S." *The Latin American Research Review* 22: 132–154.

Wasem, Rush Ellen, and Karma Ester. 2008. *Temporary Protected Status: Current Immigration Policy and Issues*. Congressional Research Service. Washington, DC: CRS.

Wyman, David. 1968. *Paper Walls: America and the Refugee Crisis 1938–1945*. Amherst, MA: University of Massachusetts Press.

Zucker, Norm, and Naomi Zucker. 1996. *Desperate Crossings: Seeking Refuge in America*. Armonk, NY: M.E. Sharpe.

Cases and Administrative Decisions

INS v. Cardoza-Fonseca, 480 U.S. 421 (1987)

Matter of Pula, 19 I. & N. Dec. 467 (BIA 1987)

4

Chronology

1914– Millions of people are displaced and made stateless in
1919 Europe and the Middle East as a result of World War I
and the breakup of the Hapsburg, Romanov, Ottoman,
and Hohenzollern empires.

1921 The League of Nations appoints Fridtjof Nansen as the
first high commissioner for refugees.

Over one million Russians become refugees as a result of
the collapse of czarist Russia, the Russian Civil War, the
Russo-Polish War, and the Soviet famine.

1922 The Graeco-Turkish War of 1922 displaces more than one
million people. Following the war, Nansen negotiates the
exchange of populations between Greece and Turkey,
and, later, between Greece and Bulgaria.

1930 Following the death of Nansen, the Nansen International
Office for Refugees is created.

1933 The Nazis come to power in Germany.

The Office of the High Commissioner for Refugees Coming from Germany is established outside of the League of
Nations framework. After Germany leaves the League,
the High Commissioner for Refugees comes under the
auspices of the League of Nations and remains so until
1938.

1933   The Convention Relating to the International Status of Ref-
(*cont.*)   ugees (covering Russian, Armenian, Turkish, Assyrian,
and Assyro-Chaldean refugees) is signed and ratified.

1935   The Nuremberg Laws, which discriminate against Jews,
are passed in Germany.

Conflict breaks out in Spain between Republicans and
Fascists. During the next several years, over 400,000
Spanish Republicans take refuge in France.

1938   In a night of violence, *Kristallnacht*, nearly 100 Jews are
murdered, and tens of thousands were arrested in
Germany.

U.S. President Franklin D. Roosevelt calls together an
international refugee conference at Évian-les-Bains concerning European Jews.

As a result of the conference at Évian-les-Bains, the Intergovernmental Committee of Refugees (IGCR) is established to discuss the fate of Jews with the German
government.

The Convention Concerning the Status of Refugees Coming from Germany is signed and ratified.

1939   The High Commissioner for Refugees under the Protection of the League of Nations is created, merging the
International Nansen Office with the High Commissioner for Refugees Coming from Germany.

World War II begins in Europe. Between 20–30 million
people will be displaced as a consequence of the war.

The Nazis begin deporting German Jews to Poland.

1940   The Nazis adopt the "Final Solution" (the systematic
extermination for the Jewish population) as state policy.
As a result, approximately six million Jews are murdered
as well as huge numbers of Gypsies, other minorities,
and political dissidents.

1943   The United Nations Relief and Rehabilitation Administration (UNRRA) is created to provide postwar reconstruction, but it becomes involved with relief for displaced persons and war victims and their repatriation. UNRRA repatriates millions of East Europeans and Soviet citizens, many of them forcibly.

The American Council for Voluntary Agencies in Foreign Service (ACVA) is established as the main umbrella organization for refugee voluntary agencies in the United States (it is now called InterAction).

1945   The United Nations is created following World War II to replace the League of Nations.

1946   The International Refugee Organization (IRO) is established. IRO resettles well over one million displaced persons overseas between 1946 and 1952.

1947   The partition of India unleashes the outflow of 14 million Hindus and Muslims from India and Pakistan.

1948   Conflict in Palestine and the creation of the state of Israel result in the expulsion and flight of over 700,000 Palestinians from their homeland.

The United Nations Relief and Works Agency for Palestine Refugees in the Near East (UNRWA) is created to provide assistance to displaced Palestinians.

The Universal Declaration of Human Rights (UDHR) is approved by the United Nations.

Conflict breaks out in Korea, where millions of people are displaced.

1950   The United Nations Korean Reconstruction Agency (UNKRA) is established to assist Korean refugees.

On December 14, Resolution 428 (V) of the UN General Assembly provides for the creation of the United Nations High Commissioner for Refugees (UNHCR). Resolution

1950   429 (V) calls for a conference of plenipotentiaries to draw
(*cont.*)   up a convention on refugees.

1951   UNHCR begins operating. At the time, there are roughly
1.5 million refugees in the world—mainly in Europe, but
also in Asia (Hong Kong and Macau) and in Latin
America.

On 28 July, the Convention Relating to the Status of Refugees is adopted in Geneva.

The Intergovernmental Committee for European Migration is established (now called International Organization for Migration, IOM).

1954   UNHCR is awarded the Nobel Peace Prize for the first
time.

1956   Due to the political crisis in Hungary, 200,000 refugees
flee to Austria and Yugoslavia.

An independence war in Algeria triggers an outward
flow into Tunisia and Morocco.

1957   UNHCR intervenes to assist Algerian refugees in
Morocco and Tunisia.

1958   Additional refugee flows take place in Africa, with
Uganda receiving people from Sudan and Rwanda.

1959   World Refugee Year is celebrated throughout the world.

The first large-scale flow of refugees from Cuba migrates
to the United States.

1960   The government of the Federal Republic of Germany
institutes an indemnification fund for victims of Nazism
and entrusts its administration to UNHCR.

1962   Burundi witnesses a mass influx of ethnic Tutsi from
Rwanda.

The International Council of Voluntary Agencies (ICVA) is created as the umbrella organization for many international and regional voluntary agencies working for refugees.

UNHCR helps to repatriate 260,000 Algerians from Morocco and Tunisia.

Ethnic Hutu of Burundi migrate to Rwanda. This will occur again twice before 1994.

1965   Immigration Act in the United States creates a seventh preference for refugees from the Middle East and/or communist countries.

1966   Refugees from Mozambique, fighting for independence, migrate to neighboring countries. Many will repatriate in 1975, when Mozambique becomes independent.

1967   The Protocol to the 1951 Convention Relating to the Status of Refugees is adopted in New York.

The United Nations makes its Declaration on Territorial Asylum.

1968   After the repression of the Prague Spring, 42,000 Czechs abroad do not return to their country.

1969   On September 10, the Organization for African Unity Convention governing the specific aspects of refugee problems in Africa is adopted in Addis Ababa.

1971   Nearly 10 million Bengalis from Eastern Pakistan take refuge in India.

1972   UNHCR launches special operations to repatriate and reintegrate over 200,000 refugees in southern Sudan as well as to assist hundreds of thousands of displaced persons.

The Bengalis taking refuge in India return home to the newly created state of Bangladesh.

1972   Thousands of Asians expelled from Uganda are resettled
(*cont.*)   abroad within a very short time.

Ethnic Hutus of Burundi migrate to Rwanda.

1973   Due to the political repression following the military
coup that overthrew Salvador Allende in Chile, a refugee
movement begins, resulting in some 200,000 Chileans
taking flight abroad.

A military take-over in Uruguay generates the flight of
about 200,000 Uruguayan refugees.

Approximately 160,000 Biharis are transferred from
Bangladesh to Pakistan. (Between 1977 and 1982 another
37,000 are moved.)

1974   Between 1974 and 1976, independence in Guinea-Bissau,
Mozambique, and Angola allows repatriation of hundreds
of thousands of refugees from neighboring countries.

In Cyprus, UNHCR launches a humanitarian program in
favor of those who have sought refuge on the other side
of the demarcation line. This includes 164,000 Greek
Cypriots from the north and 34,000 Turkish Cypriots
from the south.

1975   Between 1975 and 1980, about 350,000 Cambodians seek
asylum in Thailand, of which 310,000 are resettled in
third countries. (In 1993, as designated lead agency,
UNHCR repatriates approximately 370,000 border
Khmers and Cambodian refugees from Thailand, in the
context of an overall political settlement in their country.)

Tens of thousands of Saharawi move from Western
Sahara into Algeria.

In Argentina a military dictatorship emerges, which
drives 600,000 Argentine citizens into flight abroad.

The fall of Vietnam and Laos provokes the flight of
1.5 million Indochinese refugees into other countries in

Southeast Asia. More than 1.3 million of these people are eventually resettled in North America, Europe, and Oceania.

1977   Approximately 90,000 Muslim Filipinos seek refuge in Malaysia.

Angola receives 200,000 Zairians from the province of Katanga (now Shaba).

An outward flow of refugees from Equatorial Guinea move to Cameroon and Gabon. They will repatriate after a change of regime in their country.

About 200,000 Burmese of Bengali origin take refuge in Bangladesh.

The Conference to Review Draft Convention on Territorial Asylum fails.

1978   Movement from Laos to Thailand becomes a mass exodus. A number of Laotians also seek refuge in Vietnam.

The exodus of the boat people, who have been leaving Vietnam by sea since 1975, assumes dramatic dimension. Many drown or become victims of piracy.

The 200,000 Bengali Burmese displaced the previous year repatriate to Burma.

Afghan refugees begin to arrive in Pakistan and Iran. By 1990, five million Afghans leave their home country.

Approximately 130,000 Vietnamese of Chinese origin take refuge in China. By 1990, they will total 286,000.

Zairians, who in previous years sought refuge in neighboring countries, start returning to their home country.

Immigrants from all over the world rejected at European borders begin to ask for asylum, in addition to those

1978
(*cont.*)
arriving in Europe because of the political crises prevailing in Africa, the Middle East, and Latin America.

Central America begins to register outflows of population from Nicaragua, El Salvador, and Guatemala, and there are also many displaced persons within the countries themselves.

In the Caribbean area, many Haitians have already sought asylum in Dominican Republic, Venezuela, nearby islands, and the United States.

UNHCR launches an assistance program in the Horn of Africa for hundreds of thousands of Ethiopian refugees in the Sudan, Somalia, and Djibouti, as well as 500,000 internally displaced people in Ogaden.

An exodus of Ugandans moves into the Sudan.

1979
Following the Iranian Islamic Revolution, large numbers of Iranian asylum-seekers cross into neighboring countries. About 25,000 refugees approach the UNHCR in Pakistan and Turkey, request asylum, and the majority of those accepted are eventually resettled in Western countries.

The Conference on Indochinese Refugees meets in Geneva, and countries make pledges to resettle Vietnamese boat people.

The Pan-African Refugee Conference meets in Arusha, Tanzania, to determine ways to better assist and protect refugees.

1980
In repatriation efforts in Africa, 200,000 refugees return to Zimbabwe following independence, 190,000 to Zaire, and 50,000 to Angola.

Civil war in Chad again forces hundreds of thousands of people to take refuge in neighboring countries. They will repatriate in 1981–1982.

In March, the U.S. Congress passes the 1980 Refugee Act, the first comprehensive American legislation on refugee admission.

From April to September, 130,000 Cuban boat people arrive in Florida, causing a refugee emergency.

The United States admits a record 207,000 refugees this year.

1981   UNHCR is awarded the Nobel Peace Prize for the second time.

The International Conference on Assistance to Refugees in Africa (ICARA I) is held in Geneva to encourage donor states to increase their assistance to African host countries.

U.S. Haitian Interdiction program begins.

1982   The number of refugees in Central America, Mexico, and Panama increases considerably.

The United Nations Border Relief Operation is established to assist refugees on the Thai-Cambodian border until 1991.

Civil war in Sri Lanka causes an exodus of Tamils. By 1992, the numbers of Tamil refugees worldwide rises to almost half a million—200,000 asylum seekers in Europe and 230,000 in the Tamil populated regions of southern India.

The Refugee Studies Center, a part of the Oxford University Department of International Development, is founded. It will become a leading center for research and teaching about the causes and consequences of, and potential solutions to, forced migration.

1983   A mass influx from southern Sudan into Ethiopia begins; by 1990, this movement will have involved 400,000 Sudanese refugees.

A limited repatriation operation starts from Somalia to Ethiopia, and about 12,000 refugees return by 1990. A 1990 crisis in Somalia will force many more Ethiopian refugees to repatriate or to take refuge into Kenya.

1984 Papua New Guinea begins receiving refugees from the Indonesian province of Irian Jaya.

Salvadoran refugees—in limited numbers—begin to return home, mainly from Honduras. In 1990, almost all of them will have repatriated under the auspices of UNHCR.

On November 22, the Cartagena Declaration on International Protection of Refugees in Central America, Mexico, and Panama is adopted.

The second International Conference on Assistance to Refugees in Africa (ICARA II) meets in Geneva.

1985 The Sudan is in crisis as it receives an influx of tens of thousands of Ethiopians whose lives are menaced by war and famine.

1986 Between 1986 and 1989, approximately 320,000 Ugandans repatriate from the Sudan and Zaire.

Europe registers a considerable increase in asylum-seekers, with a growing percentage being non-European.

A mass exodus from Mozambique into neighboring countries begins. More than 900,000 of the one million refugees seek asylum in Malawi, an amount equaling 10 percent of its population.

Tens of thousands of Poles arrive in various countries of Western Europe.

1987 A Peace Plan for Central America (Esquipulas II) offers new opportunities for repatriation.

1988 About 60,000 Burundi nationals take refuge in Rwanda. They will be able to repatriate a few months later.

Ethiopia receives a mass influx of Somali refugees following armed conflict in Northwestern Somalia.

The International Conference on the Plight of Refugees, Returnees and Displaced Persons in Southern Africa meets in Oslo to effectuate a plan of action for the region.

The *Journal of Refugee Studies* is first published by Oxford Journals.

1989   Masses of East Germans flee to neighboring countries, particularly West Germany. In November, when it is clear that refugee flows cannot be contained, the Berlin Wall collapses and the post-Cold War era begins.

Hungary, which has received refugees from Romania, signs the 1951 Convention Relating to the Status of Refugees. Other East-European countries, such as Poland, begin to receive asylum-seekers and to consider adhesion to the Convention.

Following incidents in border areas, 75,000 refugees and displaced persons arrive in Senegal and Mauritania from Liberia.

In Geneva, the Conference on Southeast Asia adopts a Comprehensive Plan of Action to provide solutions— including refugee status determination and voluntary repatriation—for Vietnamese and Laotian refugees.

In Guatemala, the International Conference on Central American Refugees adopts a Plan of Action for Central American refugees, returnees, and displaced persons.

After many years in exile, 43,000 Namibians return to their home country from Angola and other countries.

The *International Journal of Refugee Law* is first published by Oxford Journals.

1990   Between 1990 and 1994, some 300,000 Colombians are forcibly displaced within their country as a result of

1990
(*cont.*) guerrilla war, counterinsurgency, and violence related to drug trafficking.

During the same period, at least 500,000 Peruvians are displaced as a result of continuing political violence between the military and the Shining Path guerrillas.

As a consequence of civil war in Somalia, the number of Somali refugees in Ethiopia reaches 375,000.

Due to civil war, 750,000 Liberians (32 percent of the entire population) take refuge in Guinea, Côte d'Ivoire, and Sierra Leone.

Approximately four million people are displaced in the 12 months following Iraq's August invasion of Kuwait. Between August and September, more than one million migrant workers and other foreign nationals flee from Iraq and Kuwait into Jordan and other neighboring countries, while 850,000 Yemenis living in Saudi Arabia return home.

The Cairo Declaration on Human Rights in Islam is adopted in August at the nineteenth Islamic Conference of Foreign Ministers in Cairo. It is generally seen as an Islamic response to the United Nations 1948 Universal Declaration of Human Rights.

1991 President Siad Barre of Somalia is ousted from office, and fighting breaks out between rival clans. Increasing numbers of Somalis flee into Kenya, Ethiopia, or the interior of Somalia.

Shortly after the Gulf War, armed conflict between the Iraqi government and Iraqi Kurds and Shiites provokes one of the largest and fastest refugee movements to this point. About 1.4 million people take refuge either in Iran or along the eastern border of Iraq. A huge international relief effort, Operation Provide Comfort, is mounted to aid the Kurds.

As fighting breaks out in Croatia, UNHCR begins to aid people displaced by war.

A military coup overthrows the first democratically elected president of Haiti, Jean-Bertrand Aristide. As repression spreads throughout the country over the next few months, more than 38,000 Haitians risk their lives at sea in an attempt to reach the United States.

The UN General Assembly creates the post of emergency relief coordinator to ensure more rapid and effective international responses to humanitarian emergencies.

1992 As conflict spreads to Bosnia and Herzegovina, UNHCR begins to distribute food aid to war victims. During the war, UNHCR assumes the lead role in organizing the UN relief effort in the former Yugoslavia.

The secretary-general of the United Nations creates the Department of Humanitarian Affairs, to be led by a new under secretary-general for humanitarian affairs.

Kenya is struck by one of the world's fastest-growing refugee emergencies, with an average of 900 refugees, mostly from Somalia, entering the country each day. By the end of the year, more than 400,000 refugees are in Kenya. In September, UNHCR launches a cross-border operation with the aim of stabilizing population movements inside Somalia.

During the first half of the year, nearly 100,000 Nepalese from Bhutan flee ethnic persecution and enter Nepal.

In a war between the government and opposition forces, up to half a million Tajiks are driven from their homes. About 356,000 of these remain in the southern part of the country of Tajikistan, while 60,000 refugees enter Afghanistan.

At the end of the year, the first of 28,000 U.S. troops arrive in Somalia in Operation Restore Hope to establish a more secure environment for humanitarian relief operations.

1993 In Togo, political unrest and government repression force more than 200,000 Togolese into Ghana and Benin.

1993   In Rwanda, peace negotiations between rebels and the
(*cont.*) government fail, leading to renewed fighting that displa-
       ces about 600,000 persons.

       In Zaire, an outbreak of politically instigated ethnic vio-
       lence forces an estimated 300,000 people from their
       homes by mid-year.

       In Mozambique, UNHCR begins a three-year repatria-
       tion program for about 1.5 million Mozambican refugees.
       The repatriation is the largest in the history of Africa.

       In Germany, the parliament passes a comprehensive asy-
       lum law that significantly restricts the previous unquali-
       fied right to apply for asylum in Germany.

       In the United States, the Supreme Court rules the
       international law prohibiting the forced return of refu-
       gees does not apply to a country that goes outside its bor-
       ders to apprehend and return refugees, upholding the
       U.S. policy of summarily returning all Haitian asylum-
       seekers seized by the U.S. Coast Guard on the high seas.

       The International Criminal Tribunal for the former Yugo-
       slavia (ICTY) is established as a United Nations court of
       law for the purpose of investigating and prosecuting
       war crimes committed during the conflicts in the Balkans.
       Its decisions set international legal precedents showing
       that an individual's political status does not offer protec-
       tion from prosecution.

       The conflict over Nagorno-Karabakh, a region inside
       Azerbaijan populated mainly by Armenians, causes the
       largest refugee movement in the former Soviet Union.
       By June, almost 200,000 Azeris have fled from Armenia
       to Azerbaijan, while some 300,000 Armenians have
       escaped in the opposite direction. Within Azerbaijan, an
       additional 300,000 people have been uprooted.

       In Burundi, 800,000 people are displaced as a result of an
       attempted *coup d'état* in October.

In preparation for the World Conference on Human Rights, ministers and representatives of Asian states create the Bangkok Declaration.

Germany amends its immigration laws so that those who have passed through "safe" third countries, including any European Union state, on their way to Germany could now be returned home, and it also streamlined its asylum determination process. The effect was immediate. While 322,600 asylum claims were filed in 1992, only 127,200 asylum applications were made in 1994.

1994   UNHCR assists four million people displaced by the conflict in the former Yugoslavia.

Israel and the Palestine Liberation Organization sign a Declaration of Principles, establishing the basis for a peace accord, which includes a provision for the return of the Palestinian refugees who fled from Gaza and the West Bank in 1967. The accord delays discussion of the return of Palestinian refugees who fled in 1948.

In Burma, the military government and UNHCR sign an agreement on repatriation of Burmese Rohingya refugees from Bangladesh.

After massive bloodletting in Rwanda, over 250,000 Rwandese, mostly Tutsis, flee to Tanzania in a 24-hour period in April.

As the Tutsi-led Rwanda Patriotic Front sweeps to victory in Rwanda, over one million Rwandese, mostly Hutus, take refuge in neighboring Zaire over a 48-hour period in July, causing a huge humanitarian crisis.

The United States rescinds its program of automatically returning all Haitian boat people to Haiti without an asylum hearing. Instead, the U.S. Coast Guard ships all Haitian asylum applicants it picks up at sea to the U.S. base at Guantanamo, Cuba, for asylum processing.

1994　Alarmed by a sudden surge in the number of Cubans
(*cont.*)　reaching Florida in August, the Clinton Administration
dramatically changes its policy of open entry for all
Cubans arriving in the United States. About 30,000
Cubans are picked up at sea and are taken to Guantanamo for processing. The administration agrees to admit
more the 20,000 Cubans a year as part of a deal in which
it won Fidel Castro's promise to stop the huge exodus
of Cuban boat people.

In November, the Security Council of the United Nations
creates the International Criminal Tribunal for Rwanda
(ICTR) to investigate and prosecute persons responsible
for the genocide committed during the year.

1995　The Abuja Agreement is signed, marking a third attempt
to end a six-year long civil war in Liberia during which
an estimated one million people have fled their country.

In Srebrenica, a UN protected "safe area" is breached
resulting in the summary execution of some 7,800 Bosnian
men and teenage boys; in addition, 25,000–30,000 Bosnians
are expelled from the area.

Naturalization becomes an option for 360,000 ethnic
Armenian refugees from Azerbaijan with Armenia's
enactment of a citizenship law.

Between 330 and 8,000 individuals are massacred by the
Rwandan Patriotic Army at the Kibeho camp for refugees
and internally displaced Rwandans.

During a two-month period, up to 400,000 Tamils flee
Jaffna and the surrounding areas as a result of the
ongoing civil war.

1996　Violence breaks out between Vietnamese boat people and
Filipino soldiers as the Philippine government attempts to
forcibly repatriate hundreds of Vietnamese asylum seekers.

During a period of heavy fighting between Israeli
Defense Forces and Hezbollah, Israeli Defense Forces

shelled a UN compound in Qana, killing 106 Lebanese and Palestinian civilians who had fled the fighting in other areas of Lebanon.

Around 200 Vietnamese boat people fled a detention center in Hong Kong after learning that they would be forcibly repatriated.

Ireland's Refugee Act, incorporating many of the international guarantees for the protection of refugees, becomes domestic law.

Following a 1992 peace accord and a national reconciliation ceremony, between 50,000 and 80,000 Malian refugees voluntarily repatriated during the year.

The United States' legislature passes the Illegal Immigration Reform and Immigrant Responsibility Act, making significant changes to existing United States immigration laws, and creating new obstacles to legal immigration.

1997 In Lebanon, 18 Palestinian refugees engaged in a hunger strike to protest planned UN budget cuts to the UNRWA, the agency which provides health, education, and relief services to Palestinian refugees.

Estonia adopts a national refugee law governing the processes for, and treatment of, refugees and asylum seekers.

European countries involuntarily return nearly 300 Tamil asylum seekers to Sri Lanka.

As fighting between Zairian rebels and government forces increases, 100,000 Rwandan Hutu refugees flee their UN camps for the jungles of eastern Zaire.

In December, over 200 Tutsi refugees from the Democratic Republic of the Congo are massacred by Hutu rebels at the Mudende refugee camp.

A military coup in Sierra Leone ousts the first democratically elected government after its being in office only

1997 one year. This event comes after a six-year civil war, which
(*cont.*) has resulted in at least 10,000 dead, 1 million refugees, and
another million individuals internally displaced.

1998 The U.S. Congress passes the Haitian Refugee Immigration Fairness Act, granting permanent U.S. residence for
eligible Haitian refugees.

Fighting between Cambodian government troops and
Khmer Rouge guerrillas drives over 30,000 Cambodians
to Thailand's border in only one day.

The Rome Statute, establishing the International Criminal
Court (ICC), is adopted at a diplomatic conference in
Rome. It will enter into force in 2002.

1999 The humanitarian crisis continues in and around
Chechnya, as 200,000 individuals have fled to the neighboring republic of Ingushetia and at least as many
remain displaced within Chechnya itself as the fighting
between the Russian military and Chechnyan fighters
continues.

NATO conducts an 11-week bombing campaign against
Yugoslavia to end the country's attempt to rid Kosovo of
its ethnic Albanian population. Approximately 90 percent
of Kosovo's population flees the region.

2000 In the worst single attack on UNHCR staff members, three
UNHCR workers are killed by militants in Atambua, West
Timor, highlighting the failure of Indonesian authorities to
protect humanitarian staff. The incident prompted the
evacuation of aid staff in the region.

Over 850,000 Albanians have fled the violence in Kosovo
since 1999.

The border war between Ethiopia and Eritrea continues.
A two-week bombing campaign by Ethiopia displaces
hundreds of thousands of Eritreans, with tens of thousands crossing borders into neighboring countries.

2001   Up to 100,000 East Timorese people continue to live in camps in Indonesian West Timor, 18 months after East Timor's independence.

After the terror attacks on September 11th, thousands of Afghans, fearing a retaliatory attack, attempt to flee their country. Most aid workers, including the World Food Programme, leave the country because of security concerns.

2002   The International Criminal Court, with the judicial power to end impunity for perpetrators of the most serious crimes of concern to the international community, is established.

Violence between Hindus and Muslims in the west Indian state of Gujarat worsens; over 100,000 individuals, mostly Muslims, take shelter in refugee camps.

2003   Renewed civil wars in Cote d'Ivoire and Liberia have forced over a million West Africans to leave their home countries in search of safety since 2002.

In Liberia, fighting between rebel forces attempting to overthrow President Charles Taylor and government troops intensifies. Most of the country's 3.3 million people are either sick or starving and a third are internally displaced, with 50,000–60,000 living in one camp outside of Monrovia.

At least 35 million people in the world are either refugees, asylum seekers, warehoused, or internally displaced.

The UN High Commissioner for Refugees, Ruud Lubbers, issues a statement cautioning that war in Iraq could result in over 600,000 people fleeing the country, creating a potential refugee crisis.

The "Coalition of the Willing" invade Iraq, resulting in massive human displacement.

The Canal Hotel bombing in Iraq results in the deaths of 22 people including UN Special Representative Sérgio

2003
(*cont.*) Vieira de Mello, refugee expert Arthur Helton, and more than 100 were wounded including refugee scholar Gil Loescher.

2004 In February, the northern Uganda based rebel group called the Lord's Resistance Army enters the Barlonyo camp for displaced persons in Uganda and massacres over 300 individuals.

Over 100,000 ethnic Nepalese of Bhutanese origin continue to live in seven refugee camps in eastern Nepal, having fled Bhutan in the 1990s after new citizenship laws targeting specific ethnic groups were implemented.

In August, armed combatants, many of whom are members of the Hutu rebel movement Forces for National Liberation, massacre at least 156 refugees at Gatumba camp in Burundi.

By the end of the year, Colombia's internal conflict had created up to three million internally displaced persons.

Fourteen Palestinians are killed when Israeli forces assault two densely populated refugee camps in Gaza.

In March, the ICC issues a warrant for the arrests of individuals accused of committing crimes against humanity in the Democratic Republic of the Congo.

2005 In July, the ICC issues arrest warrants for the leaders of the Lord's Resistance Army, a rebel group based in Uganda.

The director of the Institute for Environment and Human Security at the United Nations University in Bonn issued a report stating the rising sea levels, desertification, and shrinking freshwater supplies will create up to 50 million environmental refugees by the end of the decade.

2006 The crisis in Darfur, in which more than 200,000 civilians have been killed, spreads across the border into Chad, internally displacing 20,000 Chadians. There are currently over 200,000 Sudanese refugees in Chad.

The UN High Commissioner on Refugees visits China and publicly states that North Koreans are "persons of concern" and that forcibly repatriating them to North Korea without determining their status is in violation of the Refugee Convention. Depending on the source, between 10,000 and 300,000 North Koreans have fled to China.

2007   Over the course of three weeks, Iran forcibly repatriates 85,000 Afghan refugees, moving them across Afghanistan's southeastern border amid escalating violence between Taliban and coalition forces.

The influx of Iraqi refugees to Syria, an estimated 30,000 per month for a total population of nearly 1.4 million since 2003, puts a severe strain on Syrian society, overburdening social services and relief agencies.

Over two million Iraqis have fled into neighboring countries, but without residency permits, they have no ability to gain employment, and face severe impoverishment.

The continuing civil war in Somalia has led over half a million people to flee Mogadishu in three months.

2008   Nicaragua unanimously passes the Law for the Protection of Refugees, a piece of legislation affirming and clarifying their traditional openness to refugees, and incorporating the international guarantees for the protection of refugees.

In July, the Prosecutor for the ICC files formal charges against Sudanese President Omar al-Bashir of genocide, crimes against humanity, and war crimes. In 2009, the ICC issued a warrant for his arrest. He is the first sitting head of state indicted by the ICC.

The UNHCR and Google collaborate to create a new online mapping program, "Google Earth Outreach." The program will give non-profit organizations a new resource to use in making their work more visible to the public.

2009   Six years into the U.S. military intervention in Iraq, the refugee and displacement crisis continues to be one of

2009 the largest in the world, with two million Iraqis having
(*cont.*) fled to neighboring countries and nearly three million
more internally displaced within Iraq.

Nearly two million individuals have fled the violence in
Swat Valley in northern Pakistan.

Since the beginning of armed conflict in 2006, thousands
of refugees have fled to Kenya from Somalia every
month, with Dadaab in eastern Kenya hosting 280,000
refugees, triple its capacity.

Afghan refugees in Iran and Pakistan are under growing
pressure to leave, but Afghanistan, having endured
extensive infrastructure loss, is unable to cope with large
numbers of repatriating individuals. There are an estimated 2.7 million Afghans residing in Pakistan and Iran.

Two thousand Roma refugees continue to live in the
Konik refugee camp, located just outside of Montenegro,
more than 10 years after fleeing violence in Kosovo.

The United States Senate Committee on Foreign Relations
releases a report focusing on the mistreatment of Burmese
refugees, migrants, and asylum seekers in Malaysia.
Burmese who have fled the military junta in their home
country come to Malaysia to register with the UNHCR
for resettlement in a third country.

Colombia's internal conflict between government troops
and the rebel Revolutionary Armed Forces of Colombia
continues, causing further internal displacement, estimated at roughly four million individuals, and prompting about half a million Colombians to seek refuge in
neighboring countries.

2010 A devastating earthquake kills more than 111,000 Hai-
tians and leaves hundreds of thousands dispossessed.
In response, the Obama administration announces that
Haitians in the United States will receive Temporary Pro-
tected Status, but it vows to halt any efforts to flee to the
United States.

5

Biographical Sketches

Mahnaz Afkhami (1941–)

Mahnaz Afkhami was born into a traditional family in Kerman, Iran. As a young woman, she went to the United States to study. In 1967, after 13 years in the United States, she returned to Iran and taught literature at the National University. With her students, she founded the Association of University Women. In 1970 she became secretary general of the Women's Organization of Iran, and in 1975 became Iran's Cabinet Minister for Women's Affairs. During this time, women's rights in Iran improved significantly; laws were revised to ensure that women had equal access to child care and divorce, the minimum marriage age for girls was raised, and laws were passed that supported working women. However, after the 1979 Revolution, many of the laws that Afkhami and the Iranian women's movement had seen passed were overturned, her home and property were confiscated by the revolutionary government, and she was put on the death list, charged with "corruption on earth and warring with God." At the time the charges were brought against her, Afkhami was in New York working with the United Nations. She remains in exile in the United States. She is now the founder and president of Women's Learning Partnership for Rights, Development, and Peace (WLP), executive director of Foundation for Iranian Studies, and a co-chair of the Women Leaders Intercultural Forum. She has authored a number of books, including *Safe and Secure: Eliminating Violence Against Women and Girls in Muslim Societies.*

Sonya Aho (1966–)

Sonya Aho was born in Midyat, Turkey. She and her family fled from persecution when she was four years old; they were among the first Assyrian refugees to settle in Sweden in the 1970s. Throughout her adult life, Aho has used her experiences as a refugee to produce prize-winning journalism about her diasporic community. In 1990, she began a two-year documentary project that traced the Assyrian origins of the inhabitants of Södertälje, the Swedish city that is now home to over 15,000 of Sweden's 70,000-member Assyrian community. In 1989, her newspaper, *Länstidningen*, was awarded a prestigious Swedish journalism prize for its coverage of the Assyrian and other immigrant communities living in Sweden. Aho stresses the need to preserve her national identity and a cultural heritage that is at risk of disappearing. Since 1998, Aho has served as Chair of the women's section of the Ethnic Minorities Group of Sweden. She is currently writing a book that includes portraits of women from different cultural backgrounds and reflects varying experiences of immigration.

Madeleine Albright (1937–)

Madeleine Albright was born Marie Jana Korbelová, in Prague. She and her family were forced from their homeland twice due to political turmoil. When the Nazis invaded Czechoslovakia during World War II, the family fled to England. They returned to Prague when Albright's father, a diplomat, took a position with his government in the brief period between the liberation from the Germans and the communist coup of 1948. However, because of the communist takeover, the Korbelovas once again had to leave the country, immigrating to the United States when Albright was 11 years old. She earned her bachelor's degree in political science from Wellesley College in 1959, and later was awarded a masters (1968) and doctorate (1976) in public law and government from Columbia University. She was a research professor of International Affairs and director of Women in Foreign Service Program at Georgetown University's School of Foreign Service, taught undergraduate and graduate courses in international affairs and U.S. foreign policy, and was responsible for developing and implementing programs designed to enhance women's professional opportunities in international affairs. In 1993, U.S. President Bill Clinton named her the U.S. ambassador to the United Nations, and in 1996 named her Secretary of State. She was the first female secretary of state and the highest-ranking female in the history of U.S. government.

Isabel Allende (1942–)

Isabel Allende was born into a political family. Her father was the Chilean ambassador to Peru, and her uncle, from 1970–1973, was Chilean President Salvador Allende. After her father abandoned the family, her mother remarried a diplomat appointed to Bolivia and Beirut, Lebanon. The young Allende travelled with her family, attending schools in Chile, Bolivia, and Lebanon, with a period of time spent homeschooled as well. As a young woman, Allende worked for the UN Food and Agriculture Organization both in Santiago and in Europe; she also worked as a translator of novels from English to Spanish. In 1973, she went into exile after her uncle was overthrown in the military coup led by General Augusto Pinochet. At the time, she was receiving numerous death threats, and when she learned that her name was on a blacklist, she fled to Venezuela with her husband and two children. She worked as a journalist in Caracas and wrote her first novel, *The House of the Spirits* in 1981. She has since moved to the United States and written more than 15 novels. Allende visited Chile in 1990, after a 17 year absence.

Hannah Arendt (1906–1975)

Born in Hanover, Germany, the only child of middle-class Jewish parents, Hannah Arendt was encouraged to pursue academic and intellectual activities at a young age. As a university student in Germany, she studied with some of the most unorthodox scholars of her time, including Martin Heidegger, Karl Jaspers, and Edmund Husserl. She became politically active early, and was arrested and briefly imprisoned in 1933 for gathering evidence of growing Nazi anti-Semitism. After Hitler's rise to power, Arendt's apartment temporarily became a hiding place for fugitives as they fled Nazi persecution, but soon she fled to France with her mother and husband. There she worked for Jewish refugee organizations, but in 1940, she was taken to the intern-ment camp at Gurs, near the Pyrenees. She managed to escape before being taken to an extermination camp, moving to New York in 1941. During the war years, Arendt wrote a weekly political col-umn for a Jewish paper, *Aufbau*, and soon she began publishing articles in leading journals. Her first major work, *The Origins of Totalitarianism*, published in 1951, explored the connection between political fascism and political anti-Semitism, contending that modern totalitarianism was a new form of government that used fear to control society. She became a U.S. citizen the same year, and her later works led to her appointment as a professor at Princeton University, the first time a woman worked as a full time professor at that institution. In 1961, Arendt went to Jerusalem to attend the trial of Adolf Eichmann, a Nazi who had been accused of involvement in the murder of large numbers of Jews during World War II. She later wrote about the trial, first in *The New Yorker*, then as *Eichmann in Jerusalem: A Report on the Banality of Evil*. Her claims that evil actions are not necessarily the result of an evil desire were not well received, and her reputation suffered from the ensuing controversy. Arendt went on to teach at the University of Chicago and the University of California at Berkeley, and devoted her time as well as to her essays on political issues of the day. She was honored throughout her later life by a number of academic prizes, and her contributions to the study of political philosophy continue to be drawn upon.

Christine Arnothy (1930–)

Born in Budapest, Christine Arnothy is an acclaimed French author. During the battle of Budapest (occupied by the Germans and besieged by the Soviets) in 1945, she hid in her basement with her parents, keeping a daily journal in which she recorded the battle for the city. After her clandestine departure from Hungary with her parents, she moved first to Belgium and later settled in Paris. In 1954, her war journal, which she had titled *I am Fifteen and I Do Not Want to Die*, won the Grand Prix Vérité, an important French literary prize. It is considered one of the greatest autobio-graphical accounts of the Second World War.

Mathangi Maya Arulpragasam (a.k.a. M.I.A.) (1977–)

Mathangi Maya Arulpragasam was born in London into an ethnically Tamil family. Because of her father's desire to support the Tamil independence movement, the family moved to Sri Lanka when she was only six months old, and her father became politically active with a militant Tamil group. At first, the family lived on a relative's remote farm without electricity or running water. However, as the civil war escalated, it became unsafe for them to remain in Sri Lanka. Arulpragasam's mother moved with the three children to a small house in Madras, India, where the girls were finally able to attend school. Arulpragasam and her sister excelled as students, but as contact with their remaining family in Sri Lanka became limited and money grew tight, they often did not have enough to eat. She and her siblings became sick and they eventually moved back with family in Sri Lanka despite the danger posed by the conflict. Soon, however, the violence of the civil war peaked and Arulpragasam's mother began her attempts to flee the country with her young children. Soldiers bombed roads and escape routes, and often shot Tamils attempting to move across border areas. After a number of failed attempts, her mother fled the country with her children, moving briefly to India and then finally on to London. At 11 years old, living in Surrey, Arulpragasam first learned to speak English, and eventually won a place at London's Central Saint Martins College of Art & Design, where she studied fine art, film, and video. She began her career as an artist, and her first exhibit, of paintings depicting the Tamil movement, was nominated for the Turner prize and published in a monogram book. She later turned to music for expression, eventually adopting the alias M.I.A., and first gained notice in the music world in 2004 for two hit singles. She has since been nominated for two Grammy Awards and an Academy Award. She speaks publicly about the post-war situation in Sri Lanka and the effects of war on civilians. She has also actively participated in school-building projects in Liberia and spoken about the plight of former child soldiers.

Bertolt Brecht (1898–1956)

Bertolt Brecht was a German dramatist and poet who developed drama as a forum for leftist causes. His books and plays were banned in Germany beginning in the 1930s because of his leftist views, and he went into exile, living variously in Denmark, Finland, and Russia, and finally moving to the United States in 1941. During the war years, Brecht expressed his opposition to Nazism and Fascism in some of his most famous plays, including *Life of Galileo, Mother Courage and her Children,* and *Fear and Misery of the Third Reich.* However, he was not successful as a playwright in Hollywood, with only one script titled *Hangmen Also Die!* finding partial acceptance. In 1947, Brecht was accused of harboring communist and anti-American sentiment, and was required to give testimony before the House Un-American Activities Committee. He subsequently left the United States and went to Switzerland. He finally returned to Berlin in 1949, becoming the most popular contemporary poet in both East and West Germany. Brecht was awarded the Stalin Peace Prize in 1954 for his work.

Nadia Comaneci (1961–)

Nadia Comaneci was born in Onesti, a factory town in the mountains of Romania. An extremely active child, she had a habit of jumping on her family's couches until they broke. When Comaneci was six, Béla Károlyi, a gymnastics coach from a local sports school, came to her school to recruit potential gymnasts. Her love of gymnastics was apparent at this early age and soon after, she began training at his gym. She trained six days a week, four hours per day, and after only one year of training, she was ready to begin competing. At only seven years old, she placed 13th her first year competing in the Romanian National Junior Gymnastics Championships. She returned to the same competition the next year and won first place. In 1971, Comaneci became a member of the Romanian Gymnastics Team and over the next five years won gold medals in national and international championships. In 1976, she competed in the Montreal Olympics, where she won eight perfect 10s, the first person ever to do so. The Romanian government awarded her the Hero of Socialist Labor because of the Olympic performance. It was the highest honor in Romania, and she was the youngest woman ever to receive it. In 1981, her former teacher, Károlyi, and his wife defected from Romania. The Romanian government feared that because of his influence, she might defect also, and they would not allow her to leave the country except as a coach of the Romanian team at the 1984 Olympics. In 1989, she defected to the United States in the middle of the night, leaving everything including her family, behind. In 2000, she became the first athlete to speak in the United Nations to launch the International Year of Volunteers, and actively works for charity organizations around the world. She built a clinic for Romanian homeless children and orphans in 2006, the Nadia Comaneci Children's Clinic.

Zohra Daoud (1954–)

In 1972, Zohra Daoud was the first and only woman to be crowned Miss Afghanistan. Born into a life of privilege, Daoud entered the competition out of personal interest, seeing it as an opportunity for herself and the other young Afghan women to promote higher education and academic achievement. She won because of her intelligent responses during the question and answer session. Daoud spent the first months after the competition promoting literacy and distributing supplies throughout the underdeveloped country. She later became the host of a television quiz show and hosted shows on Radio Afghanistan; she also earned a degree in French Literature from Kabul University. However, after the Soviet invasion in 1979, Daoud left Afghanistan with her family, staying briefly in Germany before immigrating to the United States. She co-founded the Afghan International Association for Professionals to assist in the reconstruction of Afghanistan and works with the organization Women for Afghan Women.

Leandro Despouy (1947–)

Leandro Despouy is an Argentinean lawyer who defended political refugees from across Latin America, including Uruguayans, Bolivians, Brazilians, and Chileans. Soon he began receiving death threats, first from neighboring countries and then from inside Argentina. A bomb was planted at his office, and his working partner was kidnapped and killed. Despouy realized that he had to leave his country, and after a period of months in hiding and moving clandestinely from country to country, he arrived in France. Once there, he campaigned for international recognition of the human rights abuses in Argentina and on behalf of the tortured and the missing. Working with other Latin American refugees, Despouy founded an agency to promote solidarity in the exile community. Despouy returned to Argentina at the beginning of 1984, after the democratic elections in the country. He is currently an ambassador for Argentina, working as Special Representative for International Human Rights for the United Nations. Despouy was one of the five authors of a recent report on human rights abuses committed against the extrajudicial prisoners the United States detains at its naval base at Guantanamo Bay, Cuba.

Emmanuel Dongala (1941–)

Emmanuel Dongala is a doctor of physics, a professor of chemistry, as well as one of the finest writers in the history of the Republic of the Congo. He studied science in France and the United States, where he received his doctorate in Physics. He returned home to lecture in chemistry at the University of Brazzaville and was later appointed Dean. As an author, in 1973 he published *Un Fusil dans la Main (A Gun in Hand)*, which won him the Ladislas-Dormandi prize. With his novel, *The Fire of Origin*, published in Spanish in 1982, he gained the attention of international literary circles. For that novel, Dongala won the Grand Prix Litteraire de l'Afique Noire and the Prix Charles-Oulmont, awarded by the Fondation Française. In honor of his literary achievements, Dongala was appointed Chevalier des Arts et des Lettres by the French Ministry of Culture. During the civil war of the mid-1990s, Dongala and his family applied for asylum at the French embassy in Brazzaville, but were unsuccessful. However, in 1997, they were able to move to the United States, due in part to the influence of writers and other individuals in American literary circles. Dongala was awarded a Guggenheim fellowship in 1999, and now writes for newspapers and magazines in the United States.

Ariel Dorfman (1942–)

Born to parents of Eastern European heritage who fled to Argentina as the Nazis took power, Ariel Dorfman's life has been defined by the experience of exile. He was born in Buenos Aries, where his father had become a prominent professor at the Universidad Nacional de la Plata, but the family moved to New York for safety when Dorfman was two years old. His father had written a letter protesting the military regime's takeover of the university and had subsequently been threatened with a trial and deportation. Dorfman's father then took a post at the United Nations, but in the mid-1950s, as the United States succumbed to McCarthyism, he, along with other suspected communists, were forced to leave their jobs. They went to Santiago, where Dorfman spent the next 19 years. As a young man, he became involved in politics, and as a student at the University of Chile, he was elected president of the Independent Allendista Students. He later wrote *How to Read Donald Duck*, a best-selling book examining Disney cartoons as an instrument of the spread of U.S. cultural imperialism, and took posts as a professor of Literature at the University of Chile, and eventually, as cultural advisor to President Salvador Allende's chief of staff. After the 1973 coup, Dorfman went into exile in the United States, and has since written extensively about Chile, political oppression and terror, and human rights. He is a member of L'Academie Universelle Des Cultures, in Paris, and the American Academy of Arts and Sciences; his books have been internationally acclaimed and translated into more than 40 languages. He is now a professor of literature and Latin American Studies at Duke University and divides his time between the United States and Chile.

Jaroslav Drobny (1921–2001)

Jaroslav Drobny was born in Prague, the son of a grounds man at the Prague Lawn Tennis Club. As a boy, Jaroslav learned to string rackets and was a ball boy beginning at the age of five. He soon began playing tennis, and by the time he was a teenager, he was considered one of his country's most promising young athletes in both tennis and ice hockey. He first went to Wimbledon as a 16-year-old in 1938, losing to Argentinean

Alejo Russell. He returned the next year, representing Bohemia Moravia, the one part of his home country that had not been annexed by the Nazis and lost again. During World War II, Drobny worked in a munitions factory to avoid being sent to a work camp in Germany. After the war, he returned to sports, pursuing both ice hockey and tennis, and in 1948 won a silver medal for ice hockey at the St. Moritz winter Olympics. The same year, a Moscow-led coup removed the elected Czechoslovak leader Eduard Benes, an event that eventually led to his defection from Czechoslovakia. In 1949, Drobny reached his first Wimbledon final but lost. He was severely criticized by the communist-controlled newspapers in Czechoslovakia, and was ordered to return home. Instead, Drobny defected with another teammate during a Swiss tournament in Gstaad. He traveled on a passport provided by the Egyptian government, and began the best part of his career. He was in the world's top ten for ten successive years from 1949, winning the French title in 1951 and 1952, and the Italian in 1950, 1951, and 1953. Drobny was a Wimbledon finalist in 1952, finally winning Wimbledon on his third attempt in 1954. Drobny retired in 1959 and became a British citizen in 1960. He was inducted into the International Tennis Hall of Fame in 1983.

Albert Einstein (1879–1955)

Albert Einstein was a theoretical physicist who is often regarded as the creator of modern physics. He was born in Germany, and was educated in Germany, Italy, and Switzerland. In 1901 he gained his diploma, but, unable to find a teaching position, took a position as a technical assistant in the Swiss Patent Office. He obtained his doctor's degree in physics in 1905 and held various teaching posts in Berne, Zurich, Prague, and Berlin. In 1933, he renounced his German citizenship for political reasons and immigrated to the United States. There he took a position as a professor of Theoretical Physics at Princeton University. After World War II, Einstein was a leading figure in the World Government Movement and was offered the presidency of the State of Israel, which he declined. He lived in Princeton until his death in 1955. His most important works include *Special Theory of Relativity* and *The Evolution of Physics*. Einstein was awarded the Nobel Prize in Physics in 1921.

Nawal El Saadawi (1931–)

Born in Egypt, Nawal El Saadawi was the second of nine children. Her father, a civil servant, was relatively progressive and wanted all of his children to get a university education. El Saadawi attended the University of Cairo and graduated in 1955 with a degree in psychiatry. In 1965, she published a novel, *Memoirs of a Female Physician*, and in 1972, she published her first non-fiction book, *Women and Sex*, which caused her to lose her job as director of health education for the Ministry of Health and as chief editor of its journal. In 1977, she published *The Hidden Face of Eve*, in which she recalls her own experience of undergoing female circumcision at the age of six. The book was banned in Egypt. In 1981, she was arrested on the orders of President Anwar El Sadat under the Law for the Protection of Values from Shame. Released the following year, following Sadat's assassination, she founded the Arab Women's Solidarity Association (AWSA). It was the first legal, independent feminist organization in Egypt. However, the Hosni Mubarak government forced AWSA to close down in 1991. El Saadawi took the Egyptian government to court, but lost the case. Following these events, El Saadawi was on a death list of Islamic groups and lived with bodyguards. She decided that same year to accept a job at Duke University in North Carolina, where she taught until 1996. She has since moved back to Egypt.

Philip Emeagwali (1954–)

Philip Emeagwali was born in Nigeria, one of nine children, and showed early promise in school, even though he often had to work to help support his family. In 1966, the Biafran civil war broke out and Emeagwali and his family were forced to flee from their home and live for nearly three years in a refugee camp. In 1974, Emeagwali was able to go to the United States on a scholarship, and 15 years later he graduated with degrees in mathematics, engineering, and computer science. In 1989, he won the prestigious Gordon Bell Prize for solving a problem that had been classified by the U.S. government as one of the 20 most difficult computing problems ever. His invention is widely used in programming and building the world's most powerful supercomputers. Former President Clinton has called him "one of the great minds of the information age."

Enrico Fermi (1901–1954)

Enrico Fermi showed an early aptitude for mathematics and physics and gained his doctor's degree in physics in 1922, at the age of 21. In 1926, Fermi discovered the statistical laws, now known as the Fermi-Dirac statistics, which govern the behavior of certain types of particles. He was elected professor of theoretical physics at the University of Rome in 1927, a post he held until 1938, when he immigrated to the United States to escape Benito Mussolini's fascist dictatorship. Fermi is best known for discovery of nuclear fission and the production of elements lying beyond what was until then the Periodic Table. He was one of the leaders of the team of physicists on the Manhattan Project for the development of nuclear energy and the atomic bomb. Fermi was awarded the Nobel Prize in Physics in 1938.

Tenzin Gyatso (1935–)

His Holiness the 14th Dalai Lama, Tenzin Gyatso, is both the head of state and the spiritual leader of Tibet. He was born to a farming family in a small town located in northeastern Tibet. At the age of two, he was recognized as the reincarnation of the 13th Dalai Lama, Thubten Gyatso. His Holiness began his monastic education at the age of six. In 1950, His Holiness was called upon to assume full political power after China's invasion of Tibet in 1949. In 1954, he went to Beijing for peace talks with Mao Zedong and other Chinese leaders, including Deng Xiaoping and Zhou Enlai. However, in 1959, with the Chinese military occupation of Tibet, His Holiness was forced to escape into exile. Since then he has been living in Dharamsala, northern India, the seat of the Tibetan political administration in exile. His Holiness was awarded the Nobel Peace Prize in 1989.

Thich Nhat Hanh (1926–)

Thich Nhat Hanh is a Vietnamese Buddhist monk who joined the monkhood in 1942 and founded the School of Youth for Social Services in Saigon in the early 1960s. The organization, a corps of Buddhist peace-workers, rebuilt bombed villages, set up schools, and established medical centers. He was banned from returning to Vietnam after he travelled to the United States and Europe in 1966. He was nominated for the Nobel Peace Prize in 1967 by Martin Luther King, Jr., and spent years making the case for an end to the Vietnam War to federal and Pentagon officials. Hanh founded Plum Village, a Buddhist community in exile, in France in 1982. He continues to work to alleviate the suffering of refugees and political prisoners throughout the Third World. In 2005, Hanh returned to Vietnam after a series of negotiations allowed him to teach and publish some of his books in Vietnamese and to travel the country briefly. He lives in Plum Village, where he leads meditation retreats. Hanh was awarded the Courage of Conscience award in 1991.

Jóse Ramos Horta (1949–)

Jóse Ramos Horta was born in Dili, East Timor. He worked as a journalist from 1969–1974, during which time he was exiled to Mozambique by the Portuguese authorities for two years because of his involvement in politics. He later co-founded the Revolutionary Front for an Independent East Timor, and as the Portuguese withdrew in 1974, he was appointed Minister for External Affairs and Information in the first transitional government of the Democratic Republic of East Timor. However, in 1975, while Horta was travelling abroad, Indonesia invaded and annexed the territory. Horta spent the next 23 years in exile, defending the right of the people of East Timor to self-determination. He was the leading international representative for the East Timorese cause, and formulated a three-phase peace plan that became the foundation for UN negotiations with Indonesia. In 1996, Horta was jointly awarded the Nobel Peace Prize along with Bishop Carlos Belo. After a UN supervised referendum in 1999, East Timor voted for independence, and in May 2002, East Timor became an independent country (Timor-Leste), with Horta as Foreign Minister.

Michaëlle Jean (1957–)

Michaëlle Jean was born in Port-au-Prince, Haiti. At the age of 11, she and her family fled the Haiti to escape the regime of François Duvalier and settled in Montreal. During her educational career,

Jean worked in a women's shelter, an experience which inspired her to work for the establishment of a network of shelters for women and children across Canada. She also worked for an organization dedicated to assisting immigrants gain entry to Canada. After having a career as a well-known journalist and broadcaster in Quebec, Jean became the first black and only the third woman to hold the post of governor-general of Canada in 2005. She is fluent in five languages—French, English, Italian, Spanish, and Haitian Creole—and remains a social activist for women and children at risk of domestic violence.

Wassily Kandinsky (1866–1944)

One of the founding fathers of abstract painting, Wassily Kandinsky was born in Moscow, the son of a tea merchant. Kandinsky was drawn to the artistic and the creative when he was young, writing poetry, drawing, and playing the piano and the cello. However, as a young man Kandinsky studied law, economics, and ethnography at the University of Moscow, eventually accepting a position on the university's law faculty in 1893. It was not until 1896, when he was 30 years old, that he decided to become an artist. He was greatly influenced by the French Impressionist painters, especially Claude Monet, appreciating that the subject of the painting played an inferior role to the colors used. His earliest paintings, which were based on folk art, demonstrate this fascination with color rather than form, and even as his work became more complex, the focus remained with color. In 1910, Kandinsky produced his first abstract watercolor, in which all aspects of subject representation have disappeared, and continued perfecting his art over the following years. During the Russian Revolution, Kandinsky held important posts at the Commissariat of Popular Culture and at the Academy in Moscow, later receiving a professorial appointment at the University of Moscow. However, near the end of 1921, the Soviet attitude toward art changed, and to continue his work, Kandinsky had to leave Russia. He became a German citizen in 1928, holding major exhibitions in Berlin and Paris. Because of Nazi persecution Kandinsky emigrated to France in 1934 and continued working even during the period of German occupation until his death.

Fazil Kawani (1959–)

Fazil Kawani, an Iraqi Kurd, has had to flee his country twice. In 1974, as fighting between the Iraqi authorities and the Kurdish movement began, he and his family escaped, settling in a refugee camp in Iran. Within a year, the Kurdish movement collapsed and lost international support and he, as well as nearly one million other Kurdish refugees, returned home. Although there was an amnesty issued by Saddam Hussein at the time of the refugees' return, within one year, arrests and disappearances of Kurdish people began and Hussein started a campaign aimed at the destruction of Kurdish villages. Kawani, then still a student, was active in the human rights movement. He became a target of the government because of his open criticism of the security forces, and in order to survive he had to leave Iraq for a second time. Kawani applied for asylum in the United Kingdom in 1987, and was recognized as a refugee in 1989. In 1993, after earning a degree in civil engineering, he became the coordinator of the Kurdish Cultural Center. Currently, Kawani is working as the communications director at the Refugee Council in London.

Mebrahtom Keflezighi (1975–)

Mebrahtom Keflezighi is a U.S. athlete who specializes in long distance running, especially marathons. He and his family were refugees from Eritrea who moved to Italy in 1985 to escape the civil war. They moved to the United States in 1987 and Keflezighi became a naturalized citizen of the United States in 1998, the same year he graduated from University of California, Los Angeles, with a degree in business communications. He won the silver medal in the men's marathon in the 2004 Summer Olympics in Athens.

Akbar Khurasani (1961–)

Akbar Khurasani was born in a small village located in the mountains of Uruzgan province, Afghanistan. When he was 15, he moved to Kabul and was drafted into the army. However, during his military service, Khurasani began attending art classes with a tutor from Moscow, and painting became his passion. He displayed an exceptional talent early, and was, in 1986, given the opportunity to study at the Ukrainian Academy of Arts. Before he could finish his education, the Taliban took over Afghanistan, preventing him from returning home. In 1999, the UNHCR opened a social center for refugees in Kiev, and Khurasani taught art there to both local and refugee children. After living in the Ukraine for 16 years, Khurasani was granted citizenship in 2003. His paintings can be found in collections worldwide, and in 2000, he presented his paintings at an International Art Festival in Kiev.

Walter Lam (1954–)

Walter Lam was born and raised in northern Uganda. After graduating from high school, he fled to Kenya to escape political persecution. While in Kenya, he attended Egerton University and graduated with a degree in agricultural engineering. He returned to Uganda in 1981 where he worked with the government in various management positions. He was forced out of the country again in 1986 and moved to the United States. In 1989, he founded the Alliance for African Assistance, an organization that helps refugees that are fleeing persecution to settle in the United States by providing the basic assistance needed to start a new life. The Alliance began to assist Africans, but is now providing assistance to refugees from all over the world.

Raphael Lemkin (1901–1959)

Raphael Lemkin was born in Poland and studied philology and law at Lwow and Heidelberg Universities. He was a prominent international jurist in pre-war Poland, and in 1933, he came before the Legal Council of the League of Nations with a proposal to outlaw acts of "Barbarism and vandalism." When the Nazis invaded Poland in 1939, Lemkin joined the resistance, but fled to Sweden after being injured. Lemkin was the first academic to study Nazism from the standpoint of jurisprudence. He identified Adolf Hitler's intention, and labeled it genocide, a hybrid word consisting of the Greek prefix *genos*, meaning race, and the Latin suffix *cide*, meaning killing. In 1941, he moved to the United States, and in 1945 was appointed a consultant on international law to the Judge Advocate of the U.S. Army; he also served as legal advisor to the U.S. Chief Prosecutor at Nuremberg. At international legal meetings, he began to outline ideas for a change in international law. On December 9, 1948, the UN General Assembly adopted the Convention on the Prevention and Punishment of the Crime of Genocide unanimously. Lemkin was twice nominated for the Nobel Peace Prize, in 1950 and 1952.

Miriam Makeba (1932–2008)

Sixties icon and singer Miriam Makeba was born in South Africa, the daughter of a housekeeper and a Shell clerk. Makeba discovered music early in her life, realizing that it was something that could lift her out of the poverty and despair that surrounded her. Her career began in the early 1950s as a vocalist for the Manhattan Brothers. She then appeared in an anti-apartheid documentary called *Come Back Africa*, a movie that made her famous, but also caused the South African government to revoke her citizenship. Makeba's uncles were killed in the Sharpeville Massacre, and her mother died soon afterwards, but she was prohibited from entering South Africa to attend the funerals. In 1963, she spoke to the United Nations about apartheid; later in her life, during her exile in Guinea, she would become a Guinean delegate to the UN General Assembly. Her song "Pata Pata" launched her recording career, and she was toured worldwide. However, in 1968, when she married black social justice activist Stokely Carmichael, her U.S. concerts were cancelled and her recording contract broken. She found herself simultaneously exiled from her home country and from many Western countries for her anti-apartheid and civil rights activism. She was able to return to South Africa in 1990, at the end of the apartheid regime, after 30 years of exile. Soon after, she began a charity project to raise money for the protection of women in South Africa. Often referred to as Mama Africa because of her lifelong commitment to her homeland, Makeba received a number of awards, both for her music and for her activism. She was the first black African woman to receive a Grammy Award; she was also given the Dag Hammarskjöld Peace Prize in 1986 for her peace efforts. Makeba died in Italy, after a concert given to support writer Roberto Saviano in his stand against organized crime.

Tatyana Mamonova (1943–)

Tatyana Mamonova is considered the founder of the Russian Women's Movement. She was exiled from Russia in 1980 for editing and publishing an underground journal containing the first collection of Soviet feminist writings. She was awarded the U.S. World Heroine Prize for her work as an international women's leader. During the 1990s, Mamonova founded, edited, and began publishing *Women and Earth*, an international and bilingual Russian-English eco-feminist almanac. It is a continuation of her original underground journal.

Predrag Matvejevic (1932–)

Predrag Matvejevic was born in the ethnically mixed town of Mostar in the former Yugoslavia, the son of a Croatian mother and a Russian father. He studied philology and humanities at Zagreb and Sarajevo universities, going on to study comparative literature at the University of Paris. In 1968, when Matvejevic was a Professor of French at the University of Zagreb, he was prohibited from speaking at a student demonstration because of his involvement in a circle known as the School of Korcula, a culturally mixed group of intellectuals that continually called for "socialism with a human face." The school, and its journal, *Praxis*, were banned in Yugoslavia after 1974. In 1974, Matvejevic wrote an open letter asking Yugoslavia's President Josip Tito to step down, one of dozens of open letters he wrote from the 1970s on. He publicly supported the causes of many political dissidents, actions that led to his expulsion from the Communist League. One year before the outbreak of war in Yugoslavia, Matvejevic wrote another open letter, this time to Slobodan Milošević, asking him to resign. In the letter, Matvejevic claimed that the only other option for Milosevic was suicide. When the war began, Matvejevic chose to leave, a situation he calls "midway between asylum and exile," living variously in France and Italy. He currently serves as president of the International Committee for the Mediterranean Centre, vice-president of International Pen, and co-founder of the Sarajevo Association based in Paris and Rome. He teaches Slavic languages at the Sapienza University of Rome, and has published over 20 books.

Thabo Mbeki (1942–)

Born in South Africa to parents who were both teachers and activists, Thabo Mbeki joined the African National Congress (ANC) in 1956 as a 14-year-old student. In 1959, as a result of a strike, his school was closed down and Mbeki continued his studies at home, eventually enrolling in a correspondence course with University of London. After the ANC was banned, Mbeki continued his activism underground in Pretoria and Witwatersrand. It was at this time that Mbeki's father, along with Nelson Mandela, was imprisoned for his activities with the ANC, and, facing a similar fate, Mbeki left the country to continue his work in exile. He played a critical role in building up the youth and student sections of ANC, the underground movement in general, and coordinated the movement's propaganda campaign in London. In 1989, Mbeki became head of the ANC's International Affairs Department. He returned to South Africa in 1990, after a 28-year exile, when he was elected as the first deputy president of the new Government of National Unity. Mbeki succeeded Mandela as president of South Africa when he was inaugurated in 1999.

Golda Meir (1898–1978)

Golda Meir was born in Kiev to a lower-middle-class family. When she was eight years old, her family moved to the United States because of the pogroms against Jews taking place in Russia at that time. Meir later recalled that her childhood terror of anti-Semitic violence strongly influenced her commitment to the establishment of Israel as a safe and secure Jewish state. She married in 1917 and moved with her husband to Palestine in 1921. By 1928, she was the secretary of the Working Women's Council in Palestine and in 1929 was chosen to be a delegate to the World Zionist Organization. In 1940, she became the head of the political department of Histadruth trade union. Her official political career began in 1948 when she was elected to be a member of Israel's Provisional Council of State and served as the Israeli ambassador to Soviet Union. She was chosen to be the foreign minister in 1956, and despite poor health, she became Prime Minister of Israel in 1969. Meir was Israel's first female head of state and the third woman in the world to hold that position.

Makau Mutua (1958–)

Makau Mutua was born in Kenya, the second of seven children. An excellent student, he attended the University of Nairobi Law School, where he became the secretary general of the Students Union. He was arrested and detained for organizing students against one-party rule, official corruption, and human rights violations in Kenya. He was subsequently expelled from the University of Nairobi during his second year in law school, and left the country in 1981. He went to Tanzania, where he applied for, and was granted, UN refugee status. With the financial assistance provided for him by the UN refugee agency, he was able to attend the University of Dar-Es-Salaam. In 1982, he survived an attempted kidnapping by security forces. He left Tanzania and moved to the United States, where he attended Harvard Law School. Mutua is now a professor of law at the State University of New York at Buffalo School of Law. He is also the director of Human Rights Center, and is co-founder and chair of the Nairobi-based Kenya Human Rights Commission. He has written extensively on human rights, international law, and African politics.

Martina Navratilova (1956–)

Martina Navratilova received her first tennis lesson at age six and played her first tournament at age eight. She won the Czechoslovakian Women's singles title in 1972 at the age of 16, beginning a career that dominated women's tennis from 1975 to 1994. She was the number one player in communist Czechoslovakia from 1972 until her defection at the U.S. Open in 1975; she would become a U.S. citizen in 1981. She had been told by sports federation authorities in Czechoslovakia that she needed to return to school in her homeland and make tennis secondary because she was becoming too Americanized. She made the decision to defect when they indicated to her that they would begin to restrict her travel. Until her return to Czechoslovakia as a U.S. citizen in 1986, when she led the American team to a Federation Cup victory, she was considered a non-person, her name and results never appearing in Czechoslovakian newspapers. From 1975 until she retired from tennis in 1994, she was consistently in the top 10 worldwide, and by her retirement she had won 167 titles, more than any other player, male or female, in the history of tennis. These included nine Wimbledon, two French Open, three Australian Open, and four U.S. Open championships. She was inducted into the Tennis Hall of Fame in 2000, and is considered one of the greatest tennis players in the history of the sport. Navratilova is also renowned for being one of the first athletes to acknowledge being homosexual.

Le Thanh Nhon (1940–2002)

Le Thanh Nhon was one of the first modern sculptors of Vietnam, who was noted for his ability to combine the cultural heritage of Eastern and Western art in his work. Nhon was a top graduate of Saigon's School of Fine Arts in 1964, and became internationally known at an early age, participating in the Paris Biennale in 1963 when he was only 23. He became a lecturer in fine arts at Saigon University, Saigon College of Fine Arts, and The Imperial Capital of Hue College of Fine Arts. In 1975, when the government changed in Saigon, he gathered his family and fled by boat. He and his family were given asylum in Australia, and Nhon became a tram driver and a spray painter to support his wife and four children. However, he continued his art as well, and won a prize at the Asian Arts Exhibition and Competition in 1976. He fashioned a career in Melbourne as a sculptor, painter, book illustrator, and lecturer at the Royal Melbourne Institute of Technology until his death in 2002.

Rudolf Nureyev (1938–1993)

Rudolf Nureyev was a Soviet ballet dancer, director, and choreographer, who is often best remembered for his versatility and determination, as well as his work with dancer Margot Fonteyn. His father held a post as a political education officer in the Red Army, and his mother was travelling to meet him when Nureyev was born on the Trans-Siberian train. He was the youngest of four children, and the only boy, growing up in the Soviet Union during the Second World War. Nureyev saw a ballet for the first time at the age of six, and decided then that he wanted to be a dancer. After considerable difficulty owing to his family's poverty, he was accepted as a student of the outstanding teacher Alexander

Pushkin at the Leningrad Choreographic School. After his graduation, he accepted a position with the Kirov Ballet Company. When the company went on tour to Paris in 1961, Nureyev seized an opportunity to escape from Soviet security at the Le Bourget airport and subsequently defected. He resided in Paris until his death in 1993, having only returned to the Soviet Union once in 1989 to visit his mother.

Edward Said (1935–2003)

Edward Said was born into a Palestinian Christian family in East Jerusalem. He was 13 when he and his family were forced to leave Palestine and settle in Cairo. In 1951, he moved to the United States, eventually obtaining his Ph.D. from Harvard. In 1963 he took a faculty position at Columbia as a professor of English and Comparative Literature. After the 1967 Arab-Israeli war, Said became the main representative for the cause of Palestinian independence in the United States. As a result of his high profile on this issue, he was vilified as the professor of terror, his office at Columbia was set on fire, and he and his family received death threats. His books were banned in countries like Kuwait, Jordan, and Saudi Arabia and in Palestine in 1996. His two most prominent books are *Orientalism* (1978) and *Culture and Imperialism* (1993). Said was a member of the Palestine National Council, where he incurred the wrath of nationalists because he advocated coexistence between Israeli Jews and Palestinian Arabs. After resigning from the Council in the early 1990s, he called for a bi-national state as a solution to the Israel-Palestine issue. Said's autobiography, *Out of Place: A Memoir*, was published in 1999.

Nolvia Dominguez Skjetne (1948–)

Nolvia Dominguez Skjetne was born in Chile, and as a young adult was highly active in left-wing politics. In 1973, Augusto Pinochet led a military coup that overthrew Salvador Allende, the first Marxist to be elected President by popular vote in the country's history. After the coup, Skjetne was fired from her job because of her leftist political involvement; her husband, a member of the workers' union, was executed. She spent several subsequent years in Chile, fighting against the military regime and working to protect and defend human rights. However, in 1980, she was arrested and detained by the Chilean intelligence service. After her release, she fled Chile with her 10-year-old son, applying for refugee status in Norway, which she was granted by the end of the year. She continued to campaign for human rights and for the leftist movement in Chile. In the early 1980s, Skjetne became one of the leaders of the Association of Latin American Exiles in Oslo, helping Norwegian lawyers to work effectively with Chileans. She also founded the Norwegian branch of the Committee for Defending People's Rights. Skjetne was the first female immigrant to be elected to the Oslo City Council in 1990, and she remains highly involved with Norwegian and Chilean politics.

Aleksandr Solzhenitsyn (1918–2008)

Aleksandr Solzhenitsyn wrote that even as a child, he knew he wanted to be an author. However, he was unable to attend a school where he could get a good literary education, so instead he studied mathematics at Rostov University. He was finally able to obtain some literary education in the late 1930s and early 1940s and began writing. In 1945, Solzhenitsyn wrote a letter to a friend criticizing Joseph Stalin; as a result he spent eight years in prison and labor camps and three years in enforced exile. He was rehabilitated and allowed to return to Russia in 1956 where he began to write again. He became a vocal opponent of the repressive Soviet regime after Nikita Khrushchev's fall from power in 1964. The authorities would not allow him to publish his work legally, so he published illegally in Russia and abroad. He was awarded the Nobel Prize for literature in 1970. In 1974, after the international publication of *The Gulag Archipelago*, he was arrested and charged with treason. He was exiled the day after his sentencing and resided in the United States until his return to Russia in 1994.

George Soros (1930–)

Born in Budapest, George Soros survived the Nazi seizure of Hungary and the 1945 battle of Budapest. In 1946, as the Soviet Union was taking control of the country, Soros defected and immigrated to England. He graduated in 1952 from the London

School of Economics, and obtained an entry-level position with an investment bank. In 1956, Soros moved to the United States. In 1967, he helped establish an offshore investment fund; and in 1973, he set up a private investment firm that eventually evolved into the Quantum Fund, one of the first hedge funds, through which he accumulated a massive fortune. A global financier and philanthropist, Soros is the founder and chairman of a network of foundations that promote the creation of open, democratic societies based upon the rule of law, market economies, transparent and accountable governance, freedom of the press, and respect for human rights. Soros has received honorary degrees from the New School for Social Research, Oxford University, the Budapest University of Technology and Economics, and Yale University.

Loung Ung (1970–)

Loung Ung is a survivor of the killing fields of Cambodia, where roughly 1.7 million Cambodians died at the hands of Pol Pot and the Khmer Rouge regime. Ung was born in Phnom Penh to a middle-class family, but at the age of five, she and her family were forced out of the city in a mass evacuation to the countryside. By 1978, the Khmer Rouge had killed her parents and two of her siblings. Ung was forced to train as a child soldier. In 1980, she and her brother escaped to Thailand, and spent five months in a refugee camp before being sponsored to immigrate to the United States. Ung now works for justice and reconciliation in her homeland as a human rights activist and featured speaker on Cambodia, child soldiers, refugees, and landmines. She has authored several books, including *First They Killed My Father: a Daughter of Cambodia Remembers*, which was a recipient of the 2001 Asian/Pacific American Librarians' Association award for Excellence in Adult Non-fiction Literature.

Alek Wek (1977–)

Alek Wek, one of the most famous African supermodels, was born in Sudan, the seventh of what would be nine children. In 1991, Wek and her family fled the civil war in Sudan and received refugee status in Britain. She was discovered by a talent agent at a street fair in London at the age of 18, and has since been awarded for her modeling achievements with the Best New Model award, Model of the Decade award, and the Venus de la Mode award (1997). Outside of the fashion world, Wek has served on the advisory board for the U.S. Committee for Refugees Advisory Council. In 2007, she released an autobiography entitled *Alek: From Sudanese Refugee to International Supermodel*, documenting her journey from a childhood of poverty in Sudan to the catwalks of Europe.

Gao Xingjian (1940–)

Gao Xingjian is a writer of prose and a dramatist. He was born in Jiangxi province in eastern China. He received his basic education in the schools of the People's Republic and took a degree in French in 1962 at the Beijing Foreign Studies University. However, during the Cultural Revolution he was sent to a re-education camp where he spent 10 years. In 1979, he was finally allowed to publish his work and to travel abroad. During the period from 1980–1987, he published four books as well as short stories, essays, and dramas in literary magazines in China. A number of his dramas were produced at the Theater of Popular Art in Beijing, some of which were successes, although several were condemned. One, *Bus Stop*, was described as the most pernicious piece of writing since the foundation of the People's Republic. In 1986, his play *The Other Shore* was banned and in 1987, he left China and settled in Paris as a political refugee. Xingjian won the Nobel Prize for Literature in 2000.

6

Data and Documents

This chapter is divided into two sections. The first section consists of four refugee treaties: the 1951 Refugee Convention, the 1967 Protocol, the Organization of African Union Convention, and the Cartagena Declaration. In addition, the Torture Convention is also reproduced. All have been referred to in the text. The second part of the chapter consists of data for the analysis of asylum abuse that is taken up in Chapter 2. What the data track are the non-European asylum applicants who have made claims in select Western states for three time periods over three decades: 2008/1998/1988, along with the Political Terror Scale (PTS) score (U.S. State Department) for these states for that year.

International and Regional Treaties
Convention Relating to the Status of Refugees
Adopted on 28 July 1951 by the United Nations Conference of Plenipotentiaries on the Status of Refugees and Stateless Persons convened under General Assembly resolution 429 (V) of 14 December 1950. Entry into force: 22 April 1954, in accordance with article 43

Preamble

The High Contracting Parties,

Considering that the Charter of the United Nations and the Universal Declaration of Human Rights approved on 10 December 1948 by the General Assembly have affirmed the principle that human beings shall enjoy fundamental rights and freedoms without discrimination,

163

Considering that the United Nations has, on various occasions, manifested its profound concern for refugees and endeavoured to assure refugees the widest possible exercise of these fundamental rights and freedoms,

Considering that it is desirable to revise and consolidate previous international agreements relating to the status of refugees and to extend the scope of and the protection accorded by such instruments by means of a new agreement,

Considering that the grant of asylum may place unduly heavy burdens on certain countries, and that a satisfactory solution of a problem of which the United Nations has recognized the international scope and nature cannot therefore be achieved without international co-operation,

Expressing the wish that all States, recognizing the social and humanitarian nature of the problem of refugees, will do everything within their power to prevent this problem from becoming a cause of tension between States,

Noting that the United Nations High Commissioner for Refugees is charged with the task of supervising international conventions providing for the protection of refugees, and recognizing that the effective co-ordination of measures taken to deal with this problem will depend upon the co-operation of States with the High Commissioner,

Have agreed as follows:

Chapter I

GENERAL PROVISIONS

Article 1. Definition of the term "refugee"

A. For the purposes of the present Convention, the term "refugee" shall apply to any person who:

(1) Has been considered a refugee under the Arrangements of 12 May 1926 and 30 June 1928 or under the Conventions of 28 October 1933 and 10 February 1938, the Protocol of 14 September 1939 or the Constitution of the International Refugee Organization;

Decisions of non-eligibility taken by the International Refugee Organization during the period of its activities shall not prevent the status of refugee being accorded to persons who fulfil the conditions of paragraph 2 of this section;

(2) As a result of events occurring before 1 January 1951 and owing to well-founded fear of being persecuted for reasons of race, religion, nationality, membership of a particular social group or political opinion, is outside the country of his nationality and is unable or, owing to such fear, is unwilling to avail himself of the

protection of that country; or who, not having a nationality and being outside the country of his former habitual residence as a result of such events, is unable or, owing to such fear, is unwilling to return to it.

In the case of a person who has more than one nationality, the term "the country of his nationality" shall mean each of the countries of which he is a national, and a person shall not be deemed to be lacking the protection of the country of his nationality if, without any valid reason based on well-founded fear, he has not availed himself of the protection of one of the countries of which he is a national.

B. (1) For the purposes of this Convention, the words "events occurring before 1 January 1951" in article 1, section A, shall be understood to mean either (a) "events occurring in Europe before 1 January 1951"; or (b) "events occurring in Europe or elsewhere before 1 January 1951"; and each Contracting State shall make a declaration at the time of signature, ratification or accession, specifying which of these meanings it applies for the purpose of its obligations under this Convention.

(2) Any Contracting State which has adopted alternative (a) may at any time extend its obligations by adopting alternative (b) by means of a notification addressed to the Secretary-General of the United Nations.

C. This Convention shall cease to apply to any person falling under the terms of section A if:

(1) He has voluntarily re-availed himself of the protection of the country of his nationality; or

(2) Having lost his nationality, he has voluntarily reacquired it; or

(3) He has acquired a new nationality, and enjoys the protection of the country of his new nationality; or

(4) He has voluntarily re-established himself in the country which he left or outside which he remained owing to fear of persecution; or

(5) He can no longer, because the circumstances in connection with which he has been recognized as a refugee have ceased to exist, continue to refuse to avail himself of the protection of the country of his nationality;

Provided that this paragraph shall not apply to a refugee falling under section A (1) of this article who is able to invoke compelling reasons arising out of previous persecution for refusing to avail himself of the protection of the country of nationality;

(6) Being a person who has no nationality he is, because the circumstances in connection with which he has been recognized as a refugee have ceased to exist, able to return to the country of his former habitual residence;

Provided that this paragraph shall not apply to a refugee falling under section A (1) of this article who is able to invoke compelling reasons arising out of previous persecution for refusing to return to the country of his former habitual residence.

D. This Convention shall not apply to persons who are at present receiving from organs or agencies of the United Nations other than the United Nations High Commissioner for Refugees protection or assistance.

When such protection or assistance has ceased for any reason, without the position of such persons being definitively settled in accordance with the relevant resolutions adopted by the General Assembly of the United Nations, these persons shall ipso facto be entitled to the benefits of this Convention.

E. This Convention shall not apply to a person who is recognized by the competent authorities of the country in which he has taken residence as having the rights and obligations which are attached to the possession of the nationality of that country.

F. The provisions of this Convention shall not apply to any person with respect to whom there are serious reasons for considering that:

(a) He has committed a crime against peace, a war crime, or a crime against humanity, as defined in the international instruments drawn up to make provision in respect of such crimes;

(b) He has committed a serious non-political crime outside the country of refuge prior to his admission to that country as a refugee;

(c) He has been guilty of acts contrary to the purposes and principles of the United Nations.

Article 2. General obligations

Every refugee has duties to the country in which he finds himself, which require in particular that he conform to its laws and regulations as well as to measures taken for the maintenance of public order.

Article 3. Non-discrimination

The Contracting States shall apply the provisions of this Convention to refugees without discrimination as to race, religion or country of origin.

Article 4. Religion

The Contracting States shall accord to refugees within their territories treatment at least as favourable as that accorded to their nationals with respect to freedom to practice their religion and freedom as regards the religious education of their children.

Article 5. Rights granted apart from this Convention

Nothing in this Convention shall be deemed to impair any rights and benefits granted by a Contracting State to refugees apart from this Convention.

Article 6. The term "in the same circumstances"

For the purposes of this Convention, the term "in the same circumstances" implies that any requirements (including requirements as to length and conditions of sojourn or residence) which the particular individual would have to fulfil for the enjoyment of the right in question, if he were not a refugee, must be fulfilled by him, with the exception of requirements which by their nature a refugee is incapable of fulfilling.

Article 7. Exemption from reciprocity

1. Except where this Convention contains more favourable provisions, a Contracting State shall accord to refugees the same treatment as is accorded to aliens generally.

2. After a period of three years' residence, all refugees shall enjoy exemption from legislative reciprocity in the territory of the Contracting States.

3. Each Contracting State shall continue to accord to refugees the rights and benefits to which they were already entitled, in the absence of reciprocity, at the date of entry into force of this Convention for that State.

4. The Contracting States shall consider favourably the possibility of according to refugees, in the absence of reciprocity, rights and benefits beyond those to which they are entitled according to paragraphs 2 and 3, and to extending exemption from reciprocity to refugees who do not fulfil the conditions provided for in paragraphs 2 and 3.

5. The provisions of paragraphs 2 and 3 apply both to the rights and benefits referred to in articles 13, 18, 19, 21 and 22 of this Convention and to rights and benefits for which this Convention does not provide.

Article 8. Exemption from exceptional measures

With regard to exceptional measures which may be taken against the person, property or interests of nationals of a foreign State, the Contracting States shall not apply such measures to a refugee who is formally a national of the said State solely on account of such nationality. Contracting States which, under their legislation, are prevented from applying the general principle expressed in this article, shall, in appropriate cases, grant exemptions in favour of such refugees.

Article 9. Provisional measures

Nothing in this Convention shall prevent a Contracting State, in time of war or other grave and exceptional circumstances, from taking provisionally measures which it considers to be essential to the national security in the case of a particular person, pending a determination by the Contracting State that that person is in fact a refugee and that the continuance of such measures is necessary in his case in the interests of national security.

Article 10. Continuity of residence

1. Where a refugee has been forcibly displaced during the Second World War and removed to the territory of a Contracting State, and is resident there, the period of such enforced sojourn shall be considered to have been lawful residence within that territory.

2. Where a refugee has been forcibly displaced during the Second World War from the territory of a Contracting State and has, prior to the date of entry into force of this Convention, returned there for the purpose of taking up residence, the period of residence before and after such enforced displacement shall be regarded as one uninterrupted period for any purposes for which uninterrupted residence is required.

Article 11. Refugee seamen

In the case of refugees regularly serving as crew members on board a ship flying the flag of a Contracting State, that State shall give sympathetic consideration to their establishment on its territory and the issue of travel documents to them or their temporary admission to its territory particularly with a view to facilitating their establishment in another country.

Chapter II

JURIDICAL STATUS

Article 12. Personal status

1. The personal status of a refugee shall be governed by the law of the country of his domicile or, if he has no domicile, by the law of the country of his residence.

2. Rights previously acquired by a refugee and dependent on personal status, more particularly rights attaching to marriage, shall be respected by a Contracting State, subject to compliance, if this be necessary, with the formalities required by the law of that State, provided that the right in question is one which would have been recognized by the law of that State had he not become a refugee.

Article 13. Movable and immovable property

The Contracting States shall accord to a refugee treatment as favourable as possible and, in any event, not less favourable than that accorded to aliens generally in the same circumstances, as regards the acquisition of movable and immovable property and other rights pertaining thereto, and to leases and other contracts relating to movable and immovable property.

Article 14. Artistic rights and industrial property

In respect of the protection of industrial property, such as inventions, designs or models, trade marks, trade names, and of rights in literary, artistic and scientific works, a refugee shall be accorded in the country in which he has his habitual residence the same protection as is accorded to nationals of that country. In the territory of any other Contracting States, he shall be accorded the same protection as is accorded in that territory to nationals of the country in which he has his habitual residence.

Article 15. Right of association

As regards non-political and non-profit-making associations and trade unions the Contracting States shall accord to refugees lawfully staying in their territory the most favourable treatment accorded to nationals of a foreign country, in the same circumstances.

Article 16. Access to courts

1. A refugee shall have free access to the courts of law on the territory of all Contracting States.

2. A refugee shall enjoy in the Contracting State in which he has his habitual residence the same treatment as a national in matters pertaining to access to the courts, including legal assistance and exemption from cautio judicatum solvi.

3. A refugee shall be accorded in the matters referred to in paragraph 2 in countries other than that in which he has his habitual residence the treatment granted to a national of the country of his habitual residence.

Chapter III

GAINFUL EMPLOYMENT

Article 17. Wage-earning employment

1. The Contracting States shall accord to refugees lawfully staying in their territory the most favourable treatment accorded to nationals of a foreign country in the same circumstances, as regards the right to engage in wage-earning employment.

2. In any case, restrictive measures imposed on aliens or the employment of aliens for the protection of the national labour market shall not be applied to a refugee who was already exempt from them at the date of entry into force of this Convention for the Contracting State concerned, or who fulfils one of the following conditions:

(a) He has completed three years' residence in the country;

(b) He has a spouse possessing the nationality of the country of residence. A refugee may not invoke the benefit of this provision if he has abandoned his spouse;

(c) He has one or more children possessing the nationality of the country of residence.

3. The Contracting States shall give sympathetic consideration to assimilating the rights of all refugees with regard to wage-earning employment to those of nationals, and in particular of those refugees who have entered their territory pursuant to programmes of labour recruitment or under immigration schemes.

Article 18. Self-employment

The Contracting States shall accord to a refugee lawfully in their territory treatment as favourable as possible and, in any event, not less favourable than that accorded to aliens generally in the same circumstances, as regards the right to engage on his own account in agriculture, industry, handicrafts and commerce and to establish commercial and industrial companies.

Article 19. Liberal professions

1. Each Contracting State shall accord to refugees lawfully staying in their territory who hold diplomas recognized by the competent authorities of that State, and who are desirous of practising a liberal profession, treatment as favourable as possible and, in any event, not less favourable than that accorded to aliens generally in the same circumstances.

2. The Contracting States shall use their best endeavours consistently with their laws and constitutions to secure the settlement of such refugees in the territories, other than the metropolitan territory, for whose international relations they are responsible.

Chapter IV

WELFARE

Article 20. Rationing

Where a rationing system exists, which applies to the population at large and regulates the general distribution of products in short supply, refugees shall be accorded the same treatment as nationals.

Article 21. Housing

As regards housing, the Contracting States, in so far as the matter is regulated by laws or regulations or is subject to the control of public authorities, shall accord to refugees lawfully staying in their territory treatment as favourable as possible and, in any event, not less favourable than that accorded to aliens generally in the same circumstances.

Article 22. Public education

1. The Contracting States shall accord to refugees the same treatment as is accorded to nationals with respect to elementary education.

2. The Contracting States shall accord to refugees treatment as favourable as possible, and, in any event, not less favourable than that accorded to aliens generally in the same circumstances, with respect to education other than elementary education and, in particular, as regards access to studies, the recognition of foreign school certificates, diplomas and degrees, the remission of fees and charges and the award of scholarships.

Article 23. Public relief

The Contracting States shall accord to refugees lawfully staying in their territory the same treatment with respect to public relief and assistance as is accorded to their nationals.

Article 24. Labour legislation and social security

1. The Contracting States shall accord to refugees lawfully staying in their territory the same treatment as is accorded to nationals in respect of the following matters;

(a) In so far as such matters are governed by laws or regulations or are subject to the control of administrative authorities: remuneration, including family allowances where these form part of remuneration, hours of work, overtime arrangements, holidays with pay, restrictions on work, minimum age of employment, apprenticeship and training, women's work and the work of young persons, and the enjoyment of the benefits of collective bargaining;

(b) Social security (legal provisions in respect of employment injury, occupational diseases, maternity, sickness, disability, old age, death, unemployment, family responsibilities and any other contingency which, according to national laws or regulations, is covered by a social security scheme), subject to the following limitations:

(i) There may be appropriate arrangements for the maintenance of acquired rights and rights in course of acquisition;

(ii) National laws or regulations of the country of residence may prescribe special arrangements concerning benefits or portions of benefits which are payable wholly out of public funds, and concerning allowances paid to persons who do not fulfil the contribution conditions prescribed for the award of a normal pension.

2. The right to compensation for the death of a refugee resulting from employment injury or from occupational disease shall not be affected by the fact that the residence of the beneficiary is outside the territory of the Contracting State.

3. The Contracting States shall extend to refugees the benefits of agreements concluded between them, or which may be concluded between them in the future, concerning the maintenance of acquired rights and rights in the process of acquisition in regard to social security, subject only to the conditions which apply to nationals of the States signatory to the agreements in question.

4. The Contracting States will give sympathetic consideration to extending to refugees so far as possible the benefits of similar agreements which may at any time be in force between such Contracting States and non-contracting States.

Chapter V

ADMINISTRATIVE MEASURES

Article 25. Administrative assistance

1. When the exercise of a right by a refugee would normally require the assistance of authorities of a foreign country to whom he cannot have recourse, the Contracting States in whose territory he is residing shall arrange that such assistance be afforded to him by their own authorities or by an international authority.

2. The authority or authorities mentioned in paragraph 1 shall deliver or cause to be delivered under their supervision to refugees such documents or certifications as would normally be delivered to aliens by or through their national authorities.

3. Documents or certifications so delivered shall stand in the stead of the official instruments delivered to aliens by or through their national authorities, and shall be given credence in the absence of proof to the contrary.

4. Subject to such exceptional treatment as may be granted to indigent persons, fees may be charged for the services mentioned herein, but such fees shall be moderate and commensurate with those charged to nationals for similar services.

5. The provisions of this article shall be without prejudice to articles 27 and 28.

Article 26. Freedom of movement

Each Contracting State shall accord to refugees lawfully in its territory the right to choose their place of residence and to move freely within its territory subject to any regulations applicable to aliens generally in the same circumstances.

Article 27. Identity papers

The Contracting States shall issue identity papers to any refugee in their territory who does not possess a valid travel document.

Article 28. Travel documents

1. The Contracting States shall issue to refugees lawfully staying in their territory travel documents for the purpose of travel outside their territory, unless compelling reasons of national security or public order otherwise require, and the provisions of the Schedule to this Convention shall apply with respect to such documents. The Contracting States may issue such a travel document to any other refugee in their territory; they shall in particular give sympathetic consideration to the issue of such a travel document to refugees in their territory who are unable to obtain a travel document from the country of their lawful residence.

2. Travel documents issued to refugees under previous international agreements by Parties thereto shall be recognized and treated by the Contracting States in the same way as if they had been issued pursuant to this article.

Article 29. Fiscal charges

1. The Contracting States shall not impose upon refugees duties, charges or taxes, of any description whatsoever, other or higher than those which are or may be levied on their nationals in similar situations.

2. Nothing in the above paragraph shall prevent the application to refugees of the laws and regulations concerning charges in respect of the issue to aliens of administrative documents including identity papers.

Article 30. Transfer of assets

1. A Contracting State shall, in conformity with its laws and regulations, permit refugees to transfer assets which they have brought into its

territory, to another country where they have been admitted for the purposes of resettlement.

2. A Contracting State shall give sympathetic consideration to the application of refugees for permission to transfer assets wherever they may be and which are necessary for their resettlement in another country to which they have been admitted.

Article 31. Refugees unlawfully in the country of refuge

1. The Contracting States shall not impose penalties, on account of their illegal entry or presence, on refugees who, coming directly from a territory where their life or freedom was threatened in the sense of article 1, enter or are present in their territory without authorization, provided they present themselves without delay to the authorities and show good cause for their illegal entry or presence.

2. The Contracting States shall not apply to the movements of such refugees restrictions other than those which are necessary and such restrictions shall only be applied until their status in the country is regularized or they obtain admission into another country. The Contracting States shall allow such refugees a reasonable period and all the necessary facilities to obtain admission into another country.

Article 32. Expulsion

1. The Contracting States shall not expel a refugee lawfully in their territory save on grounds of national security or public order.

2. The expulsion of such a refugee shall be only in pursuance of a decision reached in accordance with due process of law. Except where compelling reasons of national security otherwise require, the refugee shall be allowed to submit evidence to clear himself, and to appeal to and be represented for the purpose before competent authority or a person or persons specially designated by the competent authority.

3. The Contracting States shall allow such a refugee a reasonable period within which to seek legal admission into another country. The Contracting States reserve the right to apply during that period such internal measures as they may deem necessary.

Article 33. Prohibition of expulsion or return ("refoulement")

1. No Contracting State shall expel or return ("refouler") a refugee in any manner whatsoever to the frontiers of territories where his life or freedom would be threatened on account of his race, religion, nationality, membership of a particular social group or political opinion.

2. The benefit of the present provision may not, however, be claimed by a refugee whom there are reasonable grounds for regarding as a danger

to the security of the country in which he is, or who, having been convicted by a final judgment of a particularly serious crime, constitutes a danger to the community of that country.

Article 34. Naturalization

The Contracting States shall as far as possible facilitate the assimilation and naturalization of refugees. They shall in particular make every effort to expedite naturalization proceedings and to reduce as far as possible the charges and costs of such proceedings.

Chapter VI

EXECUTORY AND TRANSITORY PROVISIONS

Article 35. Co-operation of the national authorities with the United Nations

1. The Contracting States undertake to co-operate with the Office of the United Nations High Commissioner for Refugees, or any other agency of the United Nations which may succeed it, in the exercise of its functions, and shall in particular facilitate its duty of supervising the application of the provisions of this Convention.

2. In order to enable the Office of the High Commissioner or any other agency of the United Nations which may succeed it, to make reports to the competent organs of the United Nations, the Contracting States undertake to provide them in the appropriate form with information and statistical data requested concerning:

(a) The condition of refugees,

(b) The implementation of this Convention, and

(c) Laws, regulations and decrees which are, or may hereafter be, in force relating to refugees.

Article 36. Information on national legislation

The Contracting States shall communicate to the Secretary-General of the United Nations the laws and regulations which they may adopt to ensure the application of this Convention.

Article 37. Relation to previous conventions

Without prejudice to article 28, paragraph 2, of this Convention, this Convention replaces, as between Parties to it, the Arrangements of 5 July 1922, 31 May 1924, 12 May 1926, 30 June 1928 and 30 July 1935, the Conventions of 28 October 1933 and 10 February 1938, the Protocol of 14 September 1939 and the Agreement of 15 October 1946.

Chapter VII

FINAL CLAUSES

Article 38. Settlement of disputes

Any dispute between Parties to this Convention relating to its interpretation or application, which cannot be settled by other means, shall be referred to the International Court of Justice at the request of any one of the parties to the dispute.

Article 39. Signature, ratification and accession

1. This Convention shall be opened for signature at Geneva on 28 July 1951 and shall thereafter be deposited with the Secretary-General of the United Nations. It shall be open for signature at the European Office of the United Nations from 28 July to 31 August 1951 and shall be re-opened for signature at the Headquarters of the United Nations from 17 September 1951 to 31 December 1952.

2. This Convention shall be open for signature on behalf of all States Members of the United Nations, and also on behalf of any other State invited to attend the Conference of Plenipotentiaries on the Status of Refugees and Stateless Persons or to which an invitation to sign will have been addressed by the General Assembly. It shall be ratified and the instruments of ratification shall be deposited with the Secretary-General of the United Nations.

3. This Convention shall be open from 28 July 1951 for accession by the States referred to in paragraph 2 of this article. Accession shall be effected by the deposit of an instrument of accession with the Secretary-General of the United Nations.

Article 40. Territorial application clause

1. Any State may, at the time of signature, ratification or accession, declare that this Convention shall extend to all or any of the territories for the international relations of which it is responsible. Such a declaration shall take effect when the Convention enters into force for the State concerned.

2. At any time thereafter any such extension shall be made by notification addressed to the Secretary-General of the United Nations and shall take effect as from the ninetieth day after the day of receipt by the Secretary-General of the United Nations of this notification, or as from the date of entry into force of the Convention for the State concerned, whichever is the later.

3. With respect to those territories to which this Convention is not extended at the time of signature, ratification or accession, each State

concerned shall consider the possibility of taking the necessary steps in order to extend the application of this Convention to such territories, subject, where necessary for constitutional reasons, to the consent of the Governments of such territories.

Article 41. Federal clause

In the case of a Federal or non-unitary State, the following provisions shall apply:

(a) With respect to those articles of this Convention that come within the legislative jurisdiction of the federal legislative authority, the obligations of the Federal Government shall to this extent be the same as those of parties which are not Federal States;

(b) With respect to those articles of this Convention that come within the legislative jurisdiction of constituent States, provinces or cantons which are not, under the constitutional system of the Federation, bound to take legislative action, the Federal Government shall bring such articles with a favourable recommendation to the notice of the appropriate authorities of States, provinces or cantons at the earliest possible moment;

(c) A Federal State Party to this Convention shall, at the request of any other Contracting State transmitted through the Secretary-General of the United Nations, supply a statement of the law and practice of the Federation and its constituent units in regard to any particular provision of the Convention showing the extent to which effect has been given to that provision by legislative or other action.

Article 42. Reservations

1. At the time of signature, ratification or accession, any State may make reservations to articles of the Convention other than to articles 1, 3, 4, 16 (1), 33, 36–46 inclusive.

2. Any State making a reservation in accordance with paragraph 1 of this article may at any time withdraw the reservation by a communication to that effect addressed to the Secretary-General of the United Nations.

Article 43. Entry into force

1. This Convention shall come into force on the ninetieth day following the day of deposit of the sixth instrument of ratification or accession.

2. For each State ratifying or acceding to the Convention after the deposit of the sixth instrument of ratification or accession, the Convention shall enter into force on the ninetieth day following the

date of deposit by such State of its instrument of ratification or accession.

Article 44. Denunciation

1. Any Contracting State may denounce this Convention at any time by a notification addressed to the Secretary-General of the United Nations.

2. Such denunciation shall take effect for the Contracting State concerned one year from the date upon which it is received by the Secretary-General of the United Nations.

3. Any State which has made a declaration or notification under article 40 may, at any time thereafter, by a notification to the Secretary-General of the United Nations, declare that the Convention shall cease to extend to such territory one year after the date of receipt of the notification by the Secretary-General.

Article 45. Revision

1. Any Contracting State may request revision of this Convention at any time by a notification addressed to the Secretary-General of the United Nations.

2. The General Assembly of the United Nations shall recommend the steps, if any, to be taken in respect of such request.

Article 46. Notifications by the Secretary-General of the United Nations

The Secretary-General of the United Nations shall inform all Members of the United Nations and non-member States referred to in article 39:

(a) Of declarations and notifications in accordance with section B of article 1;

(b) Of signatures, ratifications and accessions in accordance with article 39;

(c) Of declarations and notifications in accordance with article 40;

(d) Of reservations and withdrawals in accordance with article 42;

(e) Of the date on which this Convention will come into force in accordance with article 43;

(f) Of denunciations and notifications in accordance with article 44;

(g) Of requests for revision in accordance with article 45.

In faith whereof the undersigned, duly authorized, have signed this Convention on behalf of their respective Governments.

Done at Geneva, this twenty-eighth day of July, one thousand nine hundred and fifty-one, in a single copy, of which the English and French texts are equally authentic and which shall remain deposited in the archives of the United Nations, and certified true copies of which shall be delivered to all Members of the United Nations and to the non-member States referred to in article 39.

Protocol Relating to the Status of Refugees

606 U.N.T.S. 267, *entered into force* Oct. 4, 1967.

The Protocol was taken note of with approval by the Economic and Social Council in resolution 1186 (XLI) of 18 November 1966 and was taken note of by the General Assembly in resolution 2198 (XXI) of 16 December 1966. In the same resolution the General Assembly requested the Secretary-General to transmit the text of the Protocol to the States mentioned in article 5 thereof, with a view to enabling them to accede to the Protocol

ENTRY INTO FORCE: 4 October 1967, in accordance with article 8

The States Parties to the present Protocol,

Considering that the Convention relating to the Status of Refugees done at Geneva on 28 July 1951 (hereinafter referred to as the Convention) covers only those persons who have become refugees as a result of events occurring before 1 January 1951,

Considering that new refugee situations have arisen since the Convention was adopted and that the refugees concerned may therefore not fall within the scope of the Convention,

Considering that it is desirable that equal status should be enjoyed by all refugees covered by the definition in the Convention irrespective of the dateline 1 January 1951,

Have agreed as follows:

Article 1. General provision

1. The States Parties to the present Protocol undertake to apply articles 2 to 34 inclusive of the Convention to refugees as hereinafter defined.

2. For the purpose of the present Protocol, the term "refugee" shall, except as regards the application of paragraph 3 of this article, mean any person within the definition of article I of the Convention as if the words "As a result of events occurring before 1 January 1951 and ..." and the words "... as a result of such events", in article 1 A (2) were omitted.

3. The present Protocol shall be applied by the States Parties hereto without any geographic limitation, save that existing declarations made by States already Parties to the Convention in accordance with article 1 B (I) (a) of the Convention, shall, unless extended under article 1 B (2) thereof, apply also under the present Protocol.

*Article 2. Co-operation of the national authorities
with the United Nations*

1. The States Parties to the present Protocol undertake to co-operate with the Office of the United Nations High Commissioner for Refugees, or any other agency of the United Nations which may succeed it, in the exercise of its functions, and shall in particular facilitate its duty of supervising the application of the provisions of the present Protocol.

2. In order to enable the Office of the High Commissioner or any other agency of the United Nations which may succeed it, to make reports to the competent organs of the United Nations, the States Parties to the present Protocol undertake to provide them with the information and statistical data requested, in the appropriate form, concerning:

(a) The condition of refugees;

(b) The implementation of the present Protocol;

(c) Laws, regulations and decrees which are, or may hereafter be, in force relating to refugees.

Article 3. Information on national legislation

The States Parties to the present Protocol shall communicate to the Secretary-General of the United Nations the laws and regulations which they may adopt to ensure the application of the present Protocol.

Article 4. Settlement of disputes

Any dispute between States Parties to the present Protocol which relates to its interpretation or application and which cannot be settled by other means shall be referred to the International Court of Justice at the request of any one of the parties to the dispute.

Article 5. Accession

The present Protocol shall be open for accession on behalf of all States Parties to the Convention and of any other State Member of the United Nations or member of any of the specialized agencies or to which an invitation to accede may have been addressed by the General Assembly of the United Nations. Accession shall be effected by the deposit of an instrument of accession with the Secretary-General of the United Nations.

Article 6. Federal clause

In the case of a Federal or non-unitary State, the following provisions shall apply:

(a) With respect to those articles of the Convention to be applied in accordance with article I, paragraph 1, of the present Protocol that come within the legislative jurisdiction of the federal legislative authority, the obligations of the Federal Government shall to this extent be the same as those of States Parties which are not Federal States;

(b) With respect to those articles of the Convention to be applied in accordance with article I, paragraph 1, of the present Protocol that come within the legislative jurisdiction of constituent States, provinces or cantons which are not, under the constitutional system of the Federation, bound to take legislative action, the Federal Government shall bring such articles with a favourable recommendation to the notice of the appropriate authorities of States, provinces or cantons at the earliest possible moment;

(c) A Federal State Party to the present Protocol shall, at the request of any other State Party hereto transmitted through the Secretary-General of the United Nations, supply a statement of the law and practice of the Federation and its constituent units in regard to any particular provision of the Convention to be applied in accordance with article I, paragraph 1, of the present Protocol, showing the extent to which effect has been given to that provision by legislative or other action.

Article 7. Reservations and declarations

1. At the time of accession, any State may make reservations in respect of article IV of the present Protocol and in respect of the application in accordance with article I of the present Protocol of any provisions of the Convention other than those contained in articles 1, 3, 4, 16(1) and 33 thereof, provided that in the case of a State Party to the Convention reservations made under this article shall not extend to refugees in respect of whom the Convention applies.

2. Reservations made by States Parties to the Convention in accordance with article 42 thereof shall, unless withdrawn, be applicable in relation to their obligations under the present Protocol.

3. Any State making a reservation in accordance with paragraph 1 of this article may at any time withdraw such reservation by a communication to that effect addressed to the Secretary-General of the United Nations.

4. Declarations made under article 40, paragraphs 1 and 2, of the Convention by a State Party thereto which accedes to the present Protocol shall be deemed to apply in respect of the present Protocol, unless upon accession a notification to the contrary is addressed by the State Party concerned to the Secretary-General of the United Nations. The provisions of article 40, paragraphs 2 and 3, and of article 44, paragraph 3, of the Convention shall be deemed to apply muratis mutandis to the present Protocol.

Article 8. Entry into Protocol

1. The present Protocol shall come into force on the day of deposit of the sixth instrument of accession.

2. For each State acceding to the Protocol after the deposit of the sixth instrument of accession, the Protocol shall come into force on the date of deposit by such State of its instrument of accession.

Article 9. Denunciation

1. Any State Party hereto may denounce this Protocol at any time by a notification addressed to the Secretary-General of the United Nations.

2. Such denunciation shall take effect for the State Party concerned one year from the date on which it is received by the Secretary-General of the United Nations.

Article 10. Notifications by the Secretary-General of the United Nations

The Secretary-General of the United Nations shall inform the States referred to in article V above of the date of entry into force, accessions, reservations and withdrawals of reservations to and denunciations of the present Protocol, and of declarations and notifications relating hereto.

Article 11. Deposit in the archives of the Secretariat of the United Nations

A copy of the present Protocol, of which the Chinese, English, French, Russian and Spanish texts are equally authentic, signed by the President of the General Assembly and by the Secretary-General of the United Nations, shall be deposited in the archives of the Secretariat of the United Nations. The Secretary-General will transmit certified copies thereof to all States Members of the United Nations and to the other States referred to in article 5 above.

Organization of African Unity, Convention Governing the Specific Aspects of Refugee Problems in Africa

Adopted on 10 September 1969 by the Assembly of Heads of State and Government. Entered into force on 20 June 1974.

Preamble

We, the Heads of State and Government, assembled in the city of Addis Ababa,

1. **Noting with concern** the constantly increasing numbers of refugees in Africa and desirous of finding ways and means of alleviating their misery and suffering as well as providing them with a better life and future,

2. **Recognizing** the need for an essentially humanitarian approach towards solving the problems of refugees,

3. **Aware**, however, that refugee problems are a source of friction among many Member States, and desirous of eliminating the source of such discord,

4. **Anxious** to make a distinction between a refugee who seeks a peaceful and normal life and a person fleeing his country for the sole purpose of fomenting subversion from outside,

5. **Determined** that the activities of such subversive elements should be discouraged, in accordance with the Declaration on the Problems of Subversion and Resolution on the Problem of Refugees adopted at Accra in 1965,

6. **Bearing** in mind that the Charter of the United Nations and the Universal Declaration of Human Rights have affirmed the principle that human beings shall enjoy fundamental rights and freedoms without discrimination,

7. **Recalling** Resolution 2312 (XXII) of 14 December 1967 of the United Nations General Assembly, relating to the Declaration on Territorial Asylum,

8. **Convinced** that all the problems of our continent must be solved in the spirit of the Charter of the Organization of African Unity and in the African context,

9. **Recognizing** that the United Nations Convention of 28 July 1951, as modified by the Protocol of 31 January 1967, constitutes the basic and universal instrument relating to the status of refugees and reflects the deep concern of States for refugees and their desire to establish common standards for their treatment,

10. **Recalling** Resolutions 26 and 104 of the OAU Assemblies of Heads of State and Government, calling upon Member States of the Organization who had not already done so to accede to the United Nations Convention of 1951 and to the Protocol of 1967 relating to the Status of Refugees, and meanwhile to apply their provisions to refugees in Africa,

11. **Convinced** that the efficiency of the measures recommended by the present Convention to solve the problem of refugees in Africa necessitates close and continuous collaboration between the Organization of African Unity and the Office of the United Nations High Commissioner for Refugees,

Have agreed as follows:

Article 1. Definition of the term "Refugee"

1. For the purposes of this Convention, the term "refugee" shall mean every person who, owing to well-founded fear of being persecuted for

reasons of race, religion, nationality, membership of a particular social group or political opinion, is outside the country of his nationality and is unable or, owing to such fear, is unwilling to avail himself of the protection of that country, or who, not having a nationality and being outside the country of his former habitual residence as a result of such events, is unable or, owing to such fear, is unwilling to return to it.

2. The term "refugee" shall also apply to every person who, owing to external aggression, occupation, foreign domination or events seriously disturbing public order in either part or the whole of his country of origin or nationality, is compelled to leave his place of habitual residence in order to seek refuge in another place outside his country of origin or nationality.

3. In the case of a person who has several nationalities, the term "a country of which he is a national" shall mean each of the countries of which he is a national, and a person shall not be deemed to be lacking the protection of the country of which he is a national if, without any valid reason based on well-founded fear, he has not availed himself of the protection of one of the countries of which he is a national.

4. This Convention shall cease to apply to any refugee if:

(a) he has voluntarily re-availed himself of the protection of the country of his nationality, or

(b) having lost his nationality, he has voluntarily reacquired it, or

(c) he has acquired a new nationality, and enjoys the protection of the country of his new nationality, or

(d) he has voluntarily re-established himself in the country which he left or outside which he remained owing to fear of persecution, or

(e) he can no longer, because the circumstances in connection with which he was recognized as a refugee have ceased to exist, continue to refuse to avail himself of the protection of the country of his nationality, or

(f) he has committed a serious non-political crime outside his country of refuge after his admission to that country as a refugee, or

(g) he has seriously infringed the purposes and objectives of this Convention.

5. The provisions of this Convention shall not apply to any person with respect to whom the country of asylum has serious reasons for considering that:

(a) he has committed a crime against peace, a war crime, or a crime against humanity, as defined in the international instruments drawn up to make provision in respect of such crimes,

(b) he committed a serious non-political crime outside the country of refuge prior to his admission to that country as a refugee,

(c) he has been guilty of acts contrary to the purposes and principles of the Organization of African Unity,

(d) he has been guilty of acts contrary to the purposes and principles of the United Nations.

6. For the purposes of this Convention, the Contracting State of asylum shall determine whether an applicant is a refugee.

Article 2. Asylum

1. Member States of the OAU shall use their best endeavours consistent with their respective legislation to receive refugees and to secure the settlement of those refugees who, for well-founded reasons, are unable or unwilling to return to their country of origin or nationality.

2. The granting of asylum to refugees is a peaceful and humanitarian act and shall not be regarded as an unfriendly act by any Member State.

3. No person shall be subjected by a Member State to measures such as rejection at the frontier, return or expulsion, which would compel him to return to or remain in a territory where his life, physical integrity or liberty would be threatened for the reasons set out in Article I, paragraphs 1 and 2.

4. Where a Member State finds difficulty in continuing to grant asylum to refugees, such Member State may appeal directly to other Member States and through the OAU, and such other Member States shall in the spirit of African solidarity and international co-operation take appropriate measures to lighten the burden of the Member State granting asylum.

5. Where a refugee has not received the right to reside in any country of asylum, he may be granted temporary residence in any country of asylum in which he first presented himself as a refugee pending arrangement for his re-settlement in accordance with the preceding paragraph.

6. For reasons of security, countries of asylum shall, as far as possible, settle refugees at a reasonable distance from the frontier of their country of origin.

Article 3. Prohibition of Subversive Activities

1. Every refugee has duties to the country in which he finds himself, which require in particular that he conforms with its laws and regulations as well as with measures taken for the maintenance of public order. He shall also abstain from any subversive activities against any Member State of the OAU.

2. Signatory States undertake to prohibit refugees residing in their respective territories from attacking any State Member of the OAU, by

any activity likely to cause tension between Member States, and in particular by use of arms, through the press, or by radio.

Article 4. Non-discrimination

Member States undertake to apply the provisions of this Convention to all refugees without discrimination as to race, religion, nationality, membership of a particular social group or political opinions.

Article 5. Voluntary Repatriation

1. The essentially voluntary character of repatriation shall be respected in all cases and no refugee shall be repatriated against his will.

2. The country of asylum, in collaboration with the country of origin, shall make adequate arrangements for the safe return of refugees who request repatriation.

3. The country of origin, on receiving back refugees, shall facilitate their re-settlement and grant them the full rights and privileges of nationals of the country, and subject them to the same obligations.

4. Refugees who voluntarily return to their country shall in no way be penalized for having left it for any of the reasons giving rise to refugee situations. Whenever necessary, an appeal shall be made through national information media and through the Administrative Secretary-General of the OAU, inviting refugees to return home and giving assurance that the new circumstances prevailing in their country of origin will enable them to return without risk and to take up a normal and peaceful life without fear of being disturbed or punished, and that the text of such appeal should be given to refugees and clearly explained to them by their country of asylum.

5. Refugees who freely decide to return to their homeland, as a result of such assurances or on their own initiative, shall be given every possible assistance by the country of asylum, the country of origin, voluntary agencies and international and intergovernmental organizations, to facilitate their return.

Article 6. Travel Documents

1. Subject to Article III, Member States shall issue to refugees lawfully staying in their territories travel documents in accordance with the United Nations Convention relating to the Status of Refugees and the Schedule and Annex thereto, for the purpose of travel outside their territory, unless compelling reasons of national security or public order otherwise require. Member States may issue such a travel document to any other refugee in their territory.

2. Where an African country of second asylum accepts a refugee from a country of first asylum, the country of first asylum may be dispensed from issuing a document with a return clause.

3. Travel documents issued to refugees under previous international agreements by State Parties thereto shall be recognized and treated by Member States in the same way as if they had been issued to refugees pursuant to this Article.

Article 7. Co-Operation of the National Authorities with the Organization of African Unity

In order to enable the Administrative Secretary-General of the Organization of African Unity to make reports to the competent organs of the Organization of African Unity, Member States undertake to provide the Secretariat in the appropriate form with information and statistical data requested concerning:

(a) the condition of refugees,

(b) the implementation of this Convention, and

(c) laws, regulations and decrees which are, or may hereafter in force relating to refugees.

Article 8. Co-Operation with the Office of the United Nations High Commissioner For Refugees

1. Member States shall co-operate with the Office of the United Nations High Commissioner for Refugees.

2. The Present Convention shall be the effective regional complement in Africa of the 1951 United Nations Convention on the Status of Refugees.

Article 9. Settlement of Disputes

Any dispute between States signatories to this Convention relating to its interpretation or application, which cannot be settled by other means, shall be referred to the Commission for Mediation, Conciliation and Arbitration of the Organization of African Unity, at the request of any one of the Parties to the dispute.

Article 10. Signature and Ratification

1. This Convention is open for signature and accession by all Member States of the Organization of African Unity and shall be ratified by signatory States in accordance with their respective constitutional

processes. The instruments of ratification shall be deposited with the Administrative Secretary-General of the Organization of African Unity.

2. The original instrument, done if possible in African languages, and in English and French, all texts being equally authentic, shall be deposited with the Administrative Secretary-General of the Organization of African Unity.

3. Any independent African State, Member of the Organization of African Unity, may at any time notify the Administrative Secretary-General of the Organization of African Unity of its accession to this Convention.

Article 11. Entry into Force

This Convention shall come into force upon deposit of instruments of ratification by one-third of the Member States of the Organization of African Unity.

Article 12. Amendment

This Convention may be amended or revised if any Member State makes a written request to the Administrative Secretary-General to that effect, provided, however, that the proposed amendment shall not be submitted to the Assembly of Heads of State and Government for consideration until all Member States have been duly notified of it and a period of one year has elapsed. Such an amendment shall not be effective unless approved by at least two-thirds of the Member States Parties to the present Convention.

Article 13. Denunciation

1. Any Member State Party to this Convention may denounce its provisions by a written notification to the Administrative Secretary-General.

2. At the end of one year from the date of such notification, if not withdrawn, the Convention shall cease to apply with respect to the denouncing State.

Article 14. Registration with the United Nations

Upon entry into force of this Convention, the Administrative Secretary-General of the OAU shall register it with the Secretary-General of the United Nations, in accordance with Article 102 of the Charter of the United Nations.

Article 15. Notifications by the Administrative Secretary-General of the Organization of African Unity

The Administrative Secretary-General of the Organization of African Unity shall inform all Members of the Organization:

(a) of signatures, ratifications and accessions in accordance with Article X;

(b) of entry into force, in accordance with Article XI;

(c) of requests for amendments submitted under the terms of Article XII;

(d) of denunciations, in accordance with Article XIII.

IN WITNESS WHEREOF WE, the Heads of African State and Government, have signed this Convention.

Cartagena Declaration on Refugees

Adopted at a colloquium entitled "Coloquio Sobre la Proteccíon Internacional de los Refugiados en Américan Central, México y Panamá: Problemas Jurídicos y Humanitarios" held at Cartagena, Colombia from 19–22 November 1984

Having acknowledged with appreciation the commitments with regard to refugees included in the Contadora Act on Peace and Co-operation in Central America, the bases of which the Colloquium fully shares and which are reproduced below:

(a) "To carry out, if they have not yet done so, the constitutional procedures for accession to the 1951 Convention and the 1967 Protocol relating to the Status of Refugees."

(b) "To adopt the terminology established in the Convention and Protocol referred to in the foregoing paragraph with a view to distinguishing refugees from other categories of migrants."

(c) "To establish the internal machinery necessary for the implementation, upon accession, of the provisions of the Convention and Protocol referred to above."

(d) "To ensure the establishment of machinery for consultation between the Central American countries and representatives of the Government offices responsible for dealing with the problem of refugees in each State."

(e) "To support the work performed by the United Nations High Commissioner for Refugees (UNHCR) in Central America and to establish direct co-ordination machinery to facilitate the fulfillment of his mandate."

(f) "To ensure that any repatriation of refugees is voluntary, and is declared to be so on an individual basis, and is carried out with the co-operation of UNHCR."

(g) "To ensure the establishment of tripartite commissions, composed of representatives of the State of origin, of the receiving State and of UNHCR with a view to facilitating the repatriation of refugees."

(h) "To reinforce programmes for protection of and assistance to refugees, particularly in the areas of health, education, labour and safety."

(i) "To ensure that programmes and projects are set up with a view to ensuring the self-sufficiency of refugees."

(j) "To train the officials responsible in each State for protection of and assistance to refugees, with the co-operation of UNHCR and other international agencies."

(k) "To request immediate assistance from the international community for Central American refugees, to be provided either directly, through bilateral or multilateral agreements, or through UNHCR and other organizations and agencies."

(l) "To identify, with the co-operation of UNHCR, other countries which might receive Central American refugees. In no case shall a refugee be transferred to a third country against his will."

(m) "To ensure that the Governments of the area make the necessary efforts to eradicate the causes of the refugee problem."

(n) "To ensure that, once agreement has been reached on the bases for voluntary and individual repatriation, with full guarantees for the refugees, the receiving countries permit official delegations of the country of origin, accompanied by representatives of UNHCR and the receiving country, to visit the refugee camps."

(o) "To ensure that the receiving countries facilitate, in co-ordination with UNHCR, the departure procedure for refugees in instances of voluntary and individual repatriation."

(p) "To institute appropriate measures in the receiving countries to prevent the participation of refugees in activities directed against the country of origin, while at all times respecting the human rights of the refugees."

III

The Colloquium adopted the following conclusions:

1. To promote within the countries of the region the adoption of national laws and regulations facilitating the application of the Convention and the Protocol and, if necessary, establishing internal procedures and mechanisms for the protection of refugees. In addition, to ensure that the national laws and regulations adopted reflect the principles and criteria of the Convention and the Protocol, thus fostering the necessary process of systematic harmonization of national legislation on refugees.

2. To ensure that ratification of or accession to the 1951 Convention and the 1967 Protocol by States which have not yet taken these steps is unaccompanied by reservations limiting the scope of those instruments, and to invite countries having formulated such reservations to consider withdrawing them as soon as possible.

3. To reiterate that, in view of the experience gained from the massive flows of refugees in the Central American area, it is necessary to consider enlarging the concept of a refugee, bearing in mind, as far as appropriate and in the light of the situation prevailing in the region, the precedent of the OAU Convention (article 1, paragraph 2) and the doctrine employed in the reports of the Inter-American Commission on Human Rights. Hence the definition or concept of a refugee to be recommended for use in the region is one which, in addition to containing the elements of the 1951 Convention and the 1967 Protocol, includes among refugees persons who have fled their country because their lives, safety or freedom have been threatened by generalized violence, foreign aggression, internal conflicts, massive violation of human rights or other circumstances which have seriously disturbed public order.

4. To confirm the peaceful, non-political and exclusively humanitarian nature of grant of asylum or recognition of the status of refugee and to underline the importance of the internationally accepted principle that nothing in either shall be interpreted as an unfriendly act towards the country of origin of refugees.

5. To reiterate the importance and meaning of the principle of non-refoulement (including the prohibition of rejection at the frontier) as a corner-stone of the international protection of refugees. This principle is imperative in regard to refugees and in the present state of international law should be acknowledged and observed as a rule of jus cogens.

6. To reiterate to countries of asylum that refugee camps and settlements located in frontier areas should be set up inland at a reasonable distance from the frontier with a view to improving the protection afforded to refugees, safeguarding their human rights and implementing projects aimed at their self-sufficiency and integration into the host society.

7. To express its concern at the problem raised by military attacks on refugee camps and settlements which have occurred in different parts of the world and to propose to the Governments of the Central American countries, Mexico and Panama that they lend their support to the measures on this matter which have been proposed by the High Commissioner to the UNHCR Executive Committee.

8. To ensure that the countries of the region establish a minimum standard of treatment for refugees, on the basis of the provisions of the 1951 Convention and 1967 Protocol and of the American Convention on

Human Rights, taking into consideration the conclusions of the UNHCR Executive Committee, particularly No. 22 on the Protection of Asylum Seekers in Situations of Large-Scale Influx.

9. To express its concern at the situation of displaced persons within their own countries. In this connection, the Colloquium calls on national authorities and the competent international organizations to offer protection and assistance to those persons and to help relieve the hardship which many of them face.

10. To call on States parties to the 1969 American Convention on Human Rights to apply this instrument in dealing with asilados and refugees who are in their territories.

11. To make a study, in countries in the area which have a large number of refugees, of the possibilities of integrating them into the productive life of the country by allocating to the creation or generation of employment the resources made available by the international community through UNHCR, thus making it possible for refugees to enjoy their economic, social and cultural rights.

12. To reiterate the voluntary and individual character of repatriation of refugees and the need for it to be carried out under conditions of absolute safety, preferably to the place of residence of the refugee in his country of origin.

13. To acknowledge that reunification of families constitutes a fundamental principle in regard to refugees and one which should be the basis for the regime of humanitarian treatment in the country of asylum, as well as for facilities granted in cases of voluntary repatriation.

14. To urge non-governmental, international and national organizations to continue their worthy task, co-ordinating their activities with UNHCR and the national authorities of the country of asylum, in accordance with the guidelines laid down by the authorities in question.

15. To promote greater use of the competent organizations of the inter-American system, in particular the Inter-American Commission on Human Rights, with a view to enhancing the international protection of asilados and refugees. Accordingly, for the performance of this task, the Colloquium considers that the close co-ordination and co-operation existing between the Commission and UNHCR should be strengthened.

16. To acknowledge the importance of the OAS/UNHCR Programme of Cooperation and the activities so far carried out and to propose that the next stage should focus on the problem raised by massive refugee flows in Central America, Mexico and Panama.

17. To ensure that in the countries of Central America and the Contadora Group the international norms and national legislation relating to the protection of refugees, and of human rights in general, are disseminated

at all possible levels. In particular, the Colloquium believes it especially important that such dissemination should be undertaken with the valuable co-operation of the appropriate universities and centres of higher education.

IV

The Cartagena Colloquium therefore Recommends:

That the commitments with regard to refugees included in the Contadora Act should constitute norms for the 10 States participating in the Colloquium and be unfailingly and scrupulously observed in determining the conduct to be adopted in regard to refugees in the Central American area.

That the conclusions reached by the Colloquium (III) should receive adequate attention in the search for solutions to the grave problems raised by the present massive flows of refugees in Central America, Mexico and Panama.

That a volume should be published containing the working document and the proposals and reports, as well as the conclusions and recommendations of the Colloquium and other pertinent documents, and that the Colombian Government, UNHCR and the competent bodies of OAS should be requested to take the necessary steps to secure the widest possible circulation of the volume in question. That the present document should be proclaimed the "Cartagena Declaration on Refugees".

That the United Nations High Commissioner for Refugees should be requested to transmit the contents of the present declaration officially to the heads of State of the Central American countries, of Belize and of the countries forming the Contadora Group.

Finally, the Colloquium expressed its deep appreciation to the Colombian authorities, and in particular to the President of the Republic, Mr. Belisario Betancur, the Minister for Foreign Affairs, Mr. Augusto Ramírez Ocampo, and the United Nations High Commissioner for Refugees, Mr. Poul Hartling, who honoured the Colloquium with their presence, as well as to the University of Cartagena de Indias and the Regional Centre for Third World Studies for their initiative and for the realization of this important event. The Colloquium expressed its special recognition of the support and hospitality offered by the authorities of the Department of Bolivar and the City of Cartagena. It also thanked the people of Cartagena, rightly known as the "Heroic City", for their warm welcome.

In conclusion, the Colloquium recorded its acknowledgement of the generous tradition of asylum and refuge practised by the Colombian people and authorities.

Cartagena de Indias, 22 November 1984

Convention Against Torture and Other Cruel, Inhuman or Degrading Treatment or Punishment

Adopted, without a vote, by the United Nations General Assembly on December 10, 1984. Opened for signature on February 4, 1985. Entered into force June 26, 1987

The States Parties to this Convention,

Considering that, in accordance with the principles proclaimed in the Charter of the United Nations, recognition of the equal and inalienable rights of all members of the human family is the foundation of freedom, justice and peace in the world,

Recognizing that those rights derive from the inherent dignity of the human person,

Considering the obligation of States under the Charter, in particular Article 55, to promote universal respect for, and observance of, human rights and fundamental freedoms,

Having regard to article 5 of the Universal Declaration of Human Rights and article 7 of the International Covenant on Civil and Political Rights, both of which provide that no one may be subjected to torture or to cruel, inhuman or degrading treatment or punishment,

Having regard also to the Declaration on the Protection of All Persons from Being Subjected to Torture and Other Cruel, Inhuman or Degrading Treatment or Punishment, adopted by the General Assembly on 9 December 1975 (resolution 3452 (XXX)),

Desiring to make more effective the struggle against torture and other cruel, inhuman or degrading treatment or punishment throughout the world,

Have agreed as follows:

Part I

Article 1

1. For the purposes of this Convention, torture means any act by which severe pain or suffering, whether physical or mental, is intentionally inflicted on a person for such purposes as obtaining from him or a third person information or a confession, punishing him for an act he or a third person has committed or is suspected of having committed, or intimidating or coercing him or a third person, or for any reason based on discrimination of any kind, when such pain or suffering is inflicted by or at the instigation of or with the consent or acquiescence of a public official

or other person acting in an official capacity. It does not include pain or suffering arising only from, inherent in or incidental to lawful sanctions.

2. This article is without prejudice to any international instrument or national legislation which does or may contain provisions of wider application.

Article 2

(1) Each State Party shall take effective legislative, administrative, judicial or other measures to prevent acts of torture in any territory under its jurisdiction.

(2) No exceptional circumstances whatsoever, whether a state of war or a threat or war, internal political instability or any other public emergency, may be invoked as a justification of torture.

(3) An order from a superior officer or a public authority may not be invoked as a justification of torture.

Article 3

1. No State Party shall expel, return ("refouler") or extradite a person to another State where there are substantial grounds for believing that he would be in danger of being subjected to torture.

2. For the purpose of determining whether there are such grounds, the competent authorities shall take into account all relevant considerations including, where applicable, the existence in the State concerned of a consistent pattern of gross, flagrant or mass violations of human rights.

Article 4

1. Each State Party shall ensure that all acts of torture are offences under its criminal law. The same shall apply to an attempt to commit torture and to an act by any person which constitutes complicity or participation in torture.

2. Each State Party shall make these offences punishable by appropriate penalties which take into account their grave nature.

Article 5

1. Each State Party shall take such measures as may be necessary to establish its jurisdiction over the offences referred to in article 4 in the following cases:

(1) When the offences are committed in any territory under its jurisdiction or on board a ship or aircraft registered in that State;

(2) When the alleged offender is a national of that State;

(3) When the victim was a national of that State if that State considers it appropriate.

2. Each State Party shall likewise take such measures as may be necessary to establish its jurisdiction over such offences in cases where the alleged offender is present in any territory under its jurisdiction and it does not extradite him pursuant to article 8 to any of the States mentioned in Paragraph 1 of this article.

3. This Convention does not exclude any criminal jurisdiction exercised in accordance with internal law.

Article 6

1. Upon being satisfied, after an examination of information available to it, that the circumstances so warrant, any State Party in whose territory a person alleged to have committed any offence referred to in article 4 is present, shall take him into custody or take other legal measures to ensure his presence. The custody and other legal measures shall be as provided in the law of that State but may be continued only for such time as is necessary to enable any criminal or extradition proceedings to be instituted.

2. Such State shall immediately make a preliminary inquiry into the facts.

3. Any person in custody pursuant to paragraph 1 of this article shall be assisted in communicating immediately with the nearest appropriate representative of the State of which he is a national, or, if he is a stateless person, to the representative of the State where he usually resides.

4. When a State, pursuant to this article, has taken a person into custody, it shall immediately notify the States referred to in article 5, paragraph 1, of the fact that such person is in custody and of the circumstances which warrant his detention. The State which makes the preliminary inquiry contemplated in paragraph 2 of this article shall promptly report its findings to the said State and shall indicate whether it intends to exercise jurisdiction.

Article 7

1. The State Party in territory under whose jurisdiction a person alleged to have committed any offence referred to in article 4 is found, shall in the cases contemplated in article 5, if it does not extradite him, submit the case to its competent authorities for the purpose of prosecution.

2. These authorities shall take their decision in the same manner as in the case of any ordinary offence of a serious nature under the law of that State. In the cases referred to in article 5, paragraph 2, the standards of evidence required for prosecution and conviction shall in no way be less stringent than those which apply in the cases referred to in article 5, paragraph 1.

3. Any person regarding whom proceedings are brought in connection with any of the offences referred to in article 4 shall be guaranteed fair treatment at all stages of the proceedings.

Article 8

1. The offences referred to in article 4 shall be deemed to be included as extraditable offences in any extradition treaty existing between States Parties. States Parties undertake to include such offences as extraditable offences in every extradition treaty to be concluded between them.

2. If a State Party which makes extradition conditional on the existence of a treaty receives a request for extradition from another State Party with which it has no extradition treaty, it may consider this Convention as the legal basis for extradition in respect of such offenses. Extradition shall be subject to the other conditions provided by the law of the requested State.

3. States Parties which do not make extradition conditional on the existence of a treaty shall recognize such offences as extraditable offences between themselves subject to the conditions provided by the law of the requested state.

4. Such offences shall be treated, for the purpose of extradition between States Parties, as if they had been committed not only in the place in which they occurred but also in the territories of the States required to establish their jurisdiction in accordance with article 5, paragraph 1.

Article 9

1. States Parties shall afford one another the greatest measure of assistance in connection with civil proceedings brought in respect of any of the offences referred to in article 4, including the supply of all evidence at their disposal necessary for the proceedings.

2. States Parties shall carry out their obligations under paragraph 1 of this article in conformity with any treaties on mutual judicial assistance that may exist between them.

Article 10

1. Each State Party shall ensure that education and information regarding the prohibition against torture are fully included in the training of law enforcement personnel, civil or military, medical personnel, public officials and other persons who may be involved in the custody, interrogation or treatment of any individual subjected to any form of arrest, detention or imprisonment.

2. Each State Party shall include this prohibition in the rules or instructions issued in regard to the duties and functions of any such persons.

Article 11

Each State Party shall keep under systematic review interrogation rules, instructions, methods and practices as well as arrangements for the custody and treatment of persons subjected to any form of arrest, detention or imprisonment in any territory under its jurisdiction, with a view to preventing any cases of torture.

Article 12

Each State Party shall ensure that its competent authorities proceed to a prompt and impartial investigation, wherever there is reasonable ground to believe that an act of torture has been committed in any territory under its jurisdiction.

Article 13

Each State Party shall ensure that any individual who alleges he has been subjected to torture in any territory under its jurisdiction has the right to complain to, and to have his case promptly and impartially examined by, its competent authorities. Steps shall be taken to ensure that the complainant and witnesses are protected against all ill-treatment or intimidation as a consequence of his complaint or any evidence given.

Article 14

1. Each State Party shall ensure in its legal system that the victim of an act of torture obtains redress and has an enforceable right to fair and adequate compensation including the means for as full rehabilitation as possible. In the event of the death of the victim as a result of an act of torture, his dependents shall be entitled to compensation.

2. Nothing in this article shall affect any right of the victim or other person to compensation which may exist under national law.

Article 15

Each State Party shall ensure that any statement which is established to have been made as a result of torture shall not be invoked as evidence in any proceedings, except against a person accused of torture as evidence that the statement was made.

Article 16

1. Each State Party shall undertake to prevent in any territory under its jurisdiction other acts of cruel, inhuman or degrading treatment or punishment which do not amount to torture as defined in article 1, when such acts are committed by or at the instigation of or with the consent or acquiescence of a public official or other person acting in an official capacity. In particular, the obligations contained in articles 10, 11, 12 and 13 shall apply with the substitution for references to torture or references to other forms of cruel, inhuman or degrading treatment or punishment.

2. The provisions of this Convention are without prejudice to the provisions of any other international instrument or national law which prohibit cruel, inhuman or degrading treatment or punishment or which relate to extradition or expulsion.

Data on Asylum Applicants for Selected Western States 2008, 1998, and 1988

TABLE 6.1
Asylum Applicants in Selected Western Countries, 2008/1998/1988

2008
United States

Top Ten Countries of Origin	Population	State PTS Score
China	9,831	4
El Salvador	2,789	3
Mexico	2,713	3
Haiti	2,078	3
Guatemala	1,853	3
Ethiopia	1,168	4
Colombia	910	4
Indonesia	894	3
Honduras	893	3
Iraq	809	5
Total Number of Asylum Applications	37,597	
% from PTS 5	5.9	
% from PTS 4	50.4	
% from PTS 3	38.4	
% from PTS 2	4	
% from PTS 1	0.1	
% from other/unscored	1.1	

United Kingdom

Top Ten Countries of Origin	Population	State PTS Score
Zimbabwe	4,330	5
Afghanistan	3,730	5
Iran	2,585	4
Eritrea	2,345	4
Iraq	2,030	5
Pakistan	2,010	4
Sri Lanka	1,840	5
Somalia	1,575	5
China	1,490	4
Nigeria	970	4

TABLE 6.1 (Continued)

	Total Number of Asylum Applications	30,065	
	% from PTS 5	48.2	
	% from PTS 4	40.8	
	% from PTS 3	7.5	
	% from PTS 2	2.2	
	% from PTS 1	0	
	% from other/unscored	1.3	

Sweden

Top Ten Countries of Origin	Population	State PTS Score
Iraq	6,083	5
Somalia	3,361	5
Russia	933	4
Eritrea	857	4
Iran	799	4
Mongolia	791	3
Afghanistan	784	5
Uzbekistan	741	3
Libya	646	3
Syria	551	4

Total Number of Asylum Applications	21,146	
% from PTS 5	49.3	
% from PTS 4	22.5	
% from PTS 3	18.1	
% from PTS 2	2.8	
% from PTS 1	0	
% from other/unscored	7.2	

The Netherlands

Top Ten Countries of Origin	Population	State PTS Score
Iraq	5,027	5
Somalia	3,842	5
China	563	4
Afghanistan	395	5
Iran	322	4
Eritrea	236	4
Sri Lanka	216	5
Guinea	154	3
Sierra Leone	129	2
Mongolia	103	3

Total Number of Asylum Applications	13,092	
% from PTS 5	73.3	
% from PTS 4	16.3	

(continued)

TABLE 6.1 (Continued)

% from PTS 3	6
% from PTS 2	1.5
% from PTS 1	0
% from other/unscored	2.9

Italy

Top Ten Countries of Origin	Population	State PTS Score
Nigeria	5,673	4
Somalia	4,864	5
Eritrea	2,934	4
Ghana	1,815	3
Afghanistan	1,732	5
Bangladesh	1,684	4
Ivory Coast	1,653	4
Pakistan	1,143	4
Iraq	758	5
Burkina Faso	646	3
Total Number of Asylum Applications	29,884	
% from PTS 5	27.8	
% from PTS 4	50.2	
% from PTS 3	18.2	
% from PTS 2	2.3	
% from PTS 1	0	
% from other/unscored	1.4	

Germany

Top Ten Countries of Origin	Population	State PTS Score
Iraq	6,836	5
Turkey	1,408	4
Viet Nam	1,042	3
Iran	815	4
Syria	775	4
Afghanistan	657	5
Nigeria	561	4
Lebanon	525	3
India	485	4
Sri Lanka	468	5
Total Number of Asylum Applications	19,822	
% from PTS 5	42.8	
% from PTS 4	34.1	
% from PTS 3	18.6	
% from PTS 2	1.1	
% from PTS 1	0	
% from other/unscored	3.4	

TABLE 6.1 (Continued)

France

Top Ten Countries of Origin	Population	State PTS Score
Russia	3,595	4
Mali	2,670	2
D.R. Congo	2,543	5
Sri Lanka	2,322	5
Turkey	2,198	4
Guinea	1,270	3
Bangladesh	1,249	4
Comoros	1,105	3
Algeria	978	3
Haiti	930	3
Total Number of Asylum Applications	29,043	
% from PTS 5	22.6	
% from PTS 4	36.8	
% from PTS 3	26.2	
% from PTS 2	13.3	
% from PTS 1	0	
% from other/unscored	1.1	

Denmark

Top Ten Countries of Origin	Population	State PTS Score
Iraq	543	5
Afghanistan	418	5
Iran	196	4
Russia	183	4
Syria	105	4
West Bank/Gaza Strip	91	5
Somalia	58	5
Sri Lanka	53	5
Turkey	39	4
Algeria	38	3
Total Number of Asylum Applications	2,124	
% from PTS 5	56	
% from PTS 4	34.6	
% from PTS 3	6.5	
% from PTS 2	2.2	
% from PTS 1	0	
% from other/unscored	0.6	

(*continued*)

TABLE 6.1 (Continued)

Canada

Top Ten Countries of Origin	Population	State PTS Score
Mexico	8,070	3
Haiti	4,935	3
Colombia	3,130	4
China	1,710	4
Sri Lanka	1,010	5
United States	970	n/a
Nigeria	765	4
El Salvador	585	3
India	560	4
Somalia	505	5
Total Number of Asylum Applications	32,310	
% from PTS 5	11.3	
% from PTS 4	29	
% from PTS 3	49.3	
% from PTS 2	6.9	
% from PTS 1	0.2	
% from other/unscored	3.2	

Australia

Top Ten Countries of Origin	Population	State PTS Score
China	1,230	4
Sri Lanka	420	5
India	375	4
Indonesia	240	3
Malaysia	240	2
Pakistan	220	4
Zimbabwe	215	5
Iraq	200	5
Iran	160	4
South Korea	135	2
Total Number of Asylum Applications	4,685	
% from PTS 5	20.8	
% from PTS 4	54.9	
% from PTS 3	12.8	
% from PTS 2	10.6	
% from PTS 1	0.4	
% from other/unscored	0.5	

TABLE 6.1 (Continued)

1998
United States

Top Ten Countries of Origin	Population	State PTS Score
Mexico	4,460	3
El Salvador	3,553	2
China	3,074	4
Haiti	2,676	3
Guatemala	2,526	3
Somalia	2,268	3
India	1,764	4
Russia	1,073	5
Ethiopia	868	4
Mauritania	765	2
Total Number of Asylum Applications	32,529	
% from PTS 5	11.2	
% from PTS 4	24.5	
% from PTS 3	48.4	
% from PTS 2	14.7	
% from PTS 1	0.4	
% from other/unscored	0.7	

United Kingdom

Top Ten Countries of Origin	Population	State PTS Score
Somalia	4,685	3
Sri Lanka	3,505	4
Russia	2,820	5
Afghanistan	2,395	5
Turkey	2,015	4
Pakistan	1,975	4
China	1,925	4
Nigeria	1,380	4
Iraq	1,295	5
Algeria	1,260	5
Total Number of Asylum Applications	35,180	
% from PTS 5	28.7	
% from PTS 4	36.5	
% from PTS 3	19.8	
% from PTS 2	0.1	
% from PTS 1	0	
% from other/unscored	14	

(continued)

TABLE 6.1 (Continued)

Sweden

Top Ten Countries of Origin	Population	State PTS Score
Iraq	3,843	5
Iran	613	3
Afghanistan	330	5
Colombia	303	5
Turkey	280	4
Russia	229	5
Somalia	228	3
Syria	226	3
Lebanon	125	3
Pakistan	122	4
Total Number of Asylum Applications	7,545	
% from PTS 5	64.3	
% from PTS 4	10	
% from PTS 3	19	
% from PTS 2	2.5	
% from PTS 1	0	
% from other/unscored	4.1	

The Netherlands

Top Ten Countries of Origin	Population	State PTS Score
Iraq	8,300	5
Afghanistan	7,118	5
Somalia	2,775	3
Sudan	1,875	5
Iran	1,679	3
Azerbaijan	1,268	2
Turkey	1,222	4
Sri Lanka	1,049	4
China	919	4
Syria	828	3
Total Number of Asylum Applications	34,966	
% from PTS 5	60.5	
% from PTS 4	13.9	
% from PTS 3	18.4	
% from PTS 2	4.8	
% from PTS 1	0	
% from other/unscored	2.4	

TABLE 6.1 (Continued)

Italy

Top Ten Countries of Origin	Population	State PTS Score
Iraq	3,362	5
Turkey	1,790	4
D.R. Congo	149	5
Sierra Leone	134	5
Iran	69	3
Sri Lanka	65	4
Afghanistan	63	5
Algeria	63	5
Pakistan	60	4
Ethiopia	52	4
Total Number of Asylum Applications	6,119	
% from PTS 5	63.4	
% from PTS 4	33.6	
% from PTS 3	2.7	
% from PTS 2	0.3	
% from PTS 1	0	
% from other/unscored	0	

Germany

Top Ten Countries of Origin	Population	State PTS Score
Turkey	11,754	4
Iraq	7,435	5
Afghanistan	3,768	5
Viet Nam	2,991	2
Iran	2,955	3
Sri Lanka	1,982	4
Georgia	1,979	3
Syria	1,753	3
Algeria	1,572	5
Azerbaijan	1,566	2
Total Number of Asylum Applications	56,832	
% from PTS 5	29.6	
% from PTS 4	36.4	
% from PTS 3	19.3	
% from PTS 2	10.8	
% from PTS 1	0	
% from other/unscored	3.8	

(continued)

TABLE 6.1 (Continued)

France

Top Ten Countries of Origin	Population	State PTS Score
China	2,076	4
Sri Lanka	1,832	4
D.R. Congo	1,778	5
Turkey	1,621	4
Algeria	920	5
Pakistan	813	4
Cambodia	563	4
Bangladesh	555	4
Mauritania	542	2
India	463	4
Total Number of Asylum Applications	16,447	
%from PTS 5	28.9	
% from PTS 4	51.2	
% from PTS 3	8.7	
% from PTS 2	10.2	
% from PTS 1	0.1	
% from other/unscored	0.8	

Denmark

Top Ten Countries of Origin	Population	State PTS Score
Iraq	2,007	5
Somalia	662	3
Afghanistan	332	5
India	172	4
Iran	170	3
Sri Lanka	142	4
Pakistan	73	4
Turkey	72	4
Burundi	60	5
Russia	60	5
Total Number of Asylum Applications	4,857	
% from PTS 5	52.2	
% from PTS 4	11.9	
% from PTS 3	21.2	
% from PTS 2	2.3	
% from PTS 1	0	
% from other/unscored	12.3	

TABLE 6.1 (Continued)

Canada

Top Ten Countries of Origin	Population	State PTS Score
Sri Lanka	2,634	4
Pakistan	1,607	4
China	1,420	4
Mexico	1,158	3
India	1,157	4
Iran	880	3
Algeria	813	5
D.R. Congo	744	5
Russia	666	5
Somalia	653	3
Total Number of Asylum Applications	20,691	
% from PTS 5	19.7	
% from PTS 4	46.6	
% from PTS 3	26.2	
% from PTS 2	4.8	
% from PTS 1	2.2	
% from other/unscored	0.3	

Australia

Top Ten Countries of Origin	Population	State PTS Score
Indonesia	1,895	4
China	1,091	4
Sri Lanka	464	4
Philippines	455	3
India	328	4
Thailand	247	2
Iraq	238	5
Colombia	201	5
Iran	169	3
Bangladesh	161	4
Total Number of Asylum Applications	8,003	
% from PTS 5	9	
% from PTS 4	54.6	
% from PTS 3	13.5	
% from PTS 2	4.5	
% from PTS 1	1.5	
% from other/unscored	16.7	

(continued)

TABLE 6.1 (Continued)

1988
United States

Top Ten Countries of Origin	Population	State PTS Score
El Salvador	27,048	4
Nicaragua	16,170	4
Guatemala	6,384	4
Iran	1,742	5
Cuba	1,683	3
Ethiopia	900	5
Honduras	524	3
Haiti	314	3
Lebanon	262	n/a
China	205	3
Total Number of Asylum Applications	57,110	
% from PTS 5	5	
% from PTS 4	87.4	
% from PTS 3	5.4	
% from PTS 2	0.1	
% from PTS 1	0	
% from other/unscored	2.1	

United Kingdom

Top Ten Countries of Origin	Population	State PTS Score
Uganda	415	4
Sri Lanka	400	5
Iran	395	5
Turkey	335	3
Pakistan	330	3
Somalia	305	4
India	295	4
Ethiopia	225	5
Ghana	170	2
Iraq	165	5
Total Number of Asylum Applications	3,980	
% from PTS 5	30.3	
% from PTS 4	27.5	
% from PTS 3	20.7	
% from PTS 2	4.6	
% from PTS 1	0	
% from other/unscored	16.8	

TABLE 6.1 (Continued)

Sweden

Top Ten Countries of Origin	Population	State PTS Score
Iran	5,022	5
Chile	3,384	4
Iraq	1,147	5
Ethiopia	1,090	5
Turkey	869	3
Lebanon	760	n/a
Syria	363	4
Bangladesh	258	3
Somalia	160	4
Algeria	145	3
Total Number of Asylum Applications	16,453	
% from PTS 5	44.6	
% from PTS 4	23.9	
% from PTS 3	8.9	
% from PTS 2	0.8	
% from PTS 1	0	
% from other/unscored	21.7	

The Netherlands

Top Ten Countries of Origin	Population	State PTS Score
Ghana	920	2
Ethiopia	682	5
Iran	641	5
India	489	4
D.R. Congo	448	3
Sri Lanka	404	5
Somalia	395	4
Turkey	381	3
Lebanon	239	n/a
Pakistan	227	3
Total Number of Asylum Applications	6,542	
% from PTS 5	30.8	
% from PTS 4	18.5	
% from PTS 3	27.3	
% from PTS 2	17.5	
% from PTS 1	1.3	
% from other/unscored	4.6	

(continued)

TABLE 6.1 (Continued)

Italy

Top Ten Countries of Origin	Population	State PTS Score
Ethiopia	327	5
Iran	306	5
Somalia	129	4
Iraq	84	5
Angola	65	4
Lebanon	45	n/a
Turkey	37	3
Sri Lanka	37	5
Sudan	24	5
Syria	19	4
Total Number of Asylum Applications	1,235	
% from PTS 5	63.3	
% from PTS 4	21.5	
% from PTS 3	8.9	
% from PTS 2	2.1	
% from PTS 1	0.4	
% from other/unscored	3.8	

Germany

Top Ten Countries of Origin	Population	State PTS Score
Turkey	14,873	3
Iran	7,867	5
Lebanon	4,233	n/a
Sri Lanka	3,383	5
Pakistan	2,390	3
West Bank/Gaza Strip	1,705	4
India	1,590	4
Afghanistan	1,462	5
Ghana	1,304	2
D.R. Congo	1,192	3
Total Number of Asylum Applications	46,649	
% from PTS 5	29.5	
% from PTS 4	11.4	
% from PTS 3	43.2	
% from PTS 2	5.4	
% from PTS 1	1	
% from other/unscored	9.5	

TABLE 6.1 (Continued)

France

Top Ten Countries of Origin	Population	State PTS Score
Turkey	6,735	3
D.R. Congo	4,255	3
Mali	2,703	2
Angola	1,876	4
Viet Nam	1,670	3
Sri Lanka	1,498	5
Haiti	1,456	3
Cambodia	1,416	4
Laos	1,377	3
Ghana	1,240	2
Total Number of Asylum Applications	32,203	
% from PTS 5	6.8	
% from PTS 4	13.8	
% from PTS 3	53.6	
% from PTS 2	21.5	
% from PTS 1	3.7	
% from other/unscored	0.6	

Denmark

Top Ten Countries of Origin	Population	State PTS Score
West Bank/Gaza Strip	3,356	4
Lebanon	2,725	n/a
Iran	1,417	5
Sri Lanka	680	5
Iraq	588	5
Afghanistan	272	5
Turkey	121	3
Viet Nam	92	3
Somalia	89	4
Syria	86	4
Total Number of Asylum Applications	10,162	
% from PTS 5	30	
% from PTS 4	35.6	
% from PTS 3	3.2	
% from PTS 2	0.8	
% from PTS 1	0	
% from other/unscored	30.2	

(continued)

TABLE 6.1 (Continued)

Canada			
	Top Ten Countries of Origin	Population	State PTS Score
	n/a	n/a	n/a
	Total Number of Asylum Applications	48,000	
Australia			
	Top Ten Countries of Origin	Population	State PTS Score
	n/a	n/a	n/a
	Total Number of Asylum Applications	n/a	

Asylum seekers from these European countries are excluded from this spreadsheet (44 countries).
Albania, Andorra, Armenia, Austria, Belarus, Belgium, Bosnia/Herzegovina, Bulgaria, Croatia, Cyprus, Czech Republic, Denmark, Estonia, Finland, France, Germany, Greece, Hungary, Iceland, Italy, Ireland, Latvia, Liechtenstein, Lithuania, Luxembourg, Malta, Macedonia, Moldova, Monaco, Montenegro, Netherlands, Norway, Poland, Portugal, Romania, San Marino, Serbia, Slovakia, Slovenia, Spain, Switzerland, Sweden, Ukraine and United Kingdom.

7

Directory of Organizations

Afghan Bureau for Reconstruction and Development
Street 3, Part A
Khoshal Maina
Kabul, Afghanistan
Tel: +93 79 934 1118
www.brd.org.af
brd@brd.org.af

The Afghan Bureau for Reconstruction and Development was established in 2002 by Afghans as a non-profit organization for the purpose of assisting and participating in the development and reconstruction of the country. They assist in relief efforts, implement and coordinate development projects, and, through their four key programs—development of a viable civil society, capacity building of the government, capacity building for stable income generation, and human rights—they support the process of developing a strong and pluralistic Afghan society.

Africare Inc.
International Headquarters
440 R Street, N.W.
Washington, DC 20001
Tel: (202) 462-3614
Fax: (202) 387-1034
www.africare.org
info@africare.org
President: Darius Mans

Since its founding in the early 1970s, Africare has been a collaborative effort of Africans and Americans to improve the quality of life in rural Africa. It is now one of the leading NGO's assisting Africa and addresses needs in areas such as health, food security, water resource development, and emergency response, as well as refugee assistance. Africare has worked in 36 African countries and has carried out more than 2,000 assistance projects.

The AMAR International Charitable Foundation
Hope House
45 Great Peter Street
London,
SW1P 3LT
United Kingdom
Tel: +44 (0) 207 799 2217
Fax: +44 (0) 207 222 4665
www.amarfoundation.org
london@amarfoundation.org

Established in London in 1991 to assist Arab refugees, the AMAR International Charitable Foundation now operates in Iran, Iraq, and Lebanon, providing relief as well as professional health and education services to refugee and other communities living in war zones or areas of civil disruption.

American Friends Service Committee
National Headquarters
1501 Cherry Street
Philadelphia, PA 19102
Tel: (215) 241-7000
Fax: (215) 241-7275
www.afsc.org
afscinfo@afsc.org
Presiding clerk: Arlene Kelly

The American Friends Service Committee implements service, development, social justice, and peace programs around the world. They advocate for economic justice, non-heterosexual rights and recognition, refugee and immigrant rights, as well as peaceful and just solutions to conflict situations.

American Jewish Joint Distribution Committee
711 Third Avenue
New York, NY 10036
www.jdc.org
info@jdc.org
Tel: (212) 687-6200
Chief Executive Officer: Steven Schwager

Founded in 1914 to channel financial assistance to starving Jews during World War I, the American Jewish Joint Distribution Committee now provides non-sectarian aid to Jews and non-Jews throughout the world who are the victims of natural and man-made disasters. They also provide long-term development assistance to rural and impoverished communities.

American Red Cross
National Headquarters
2025 E. Street, N.W.
Washington, DC 20006
Tel: (202) 303-5000
www.redcross.org
President: Gail J. McGovern

The American Red Cross is the nation's primary emergency response organization. It also provides international relief and assistance to victims of war and natural disasters. Working in co-operation with the International Federation of Red Cross and Red Crescent Societies it helps refugees find missing family members and assists them to secure basic material needs, as well as supporting worldwide development programs.

American Refugee Committee
World Headquarters
430 Oak Grove Street, Suite 204
Minneapolis, MN 55403
1-800-875-7060
Tel: (612) 872-7060
Fax: (612) 607-6499
www.arcrelief.org
info@archq.org
President: Daniel Wordsworth

The American Refugee Committee is an international non-profit, non-governmental organization that works with refugee communities, providing humanitarian assistance and skills training to refugees and displaced persons in seven countries around the world. They provide shelter, health care, clean water, sanitation, protection, and microcredit education, with the goal of assisting individuals to rebuild their lives after a crisis.

Amnesty International
International Secretariat
1 Easton Street
London WCIX0DW
United Kingdom
Tel: +44 20 741 35500
Fax: +44 20 795 61157
www.amnesty.org
Secretary General: Claudio Cordone

Founded in 1961 as a campaign to stop the abuse of human rights worldwide, Amnesty International now has offices in more than 80 countries. They work to improve internationally recognized human rights through campaigning and international solidarity, advocating for fair trials for political prisoners, the release of prisoners of conscience, and to abolish the use of torture and capital punishment.

American Near East Refugee Aid (ANERA)
1111 14th Street N.W., #400
Washington, DC 20005
Tel: (202) 266-9700
Fax: (202) 266-9701
www.anera.org
anera@anera.org
President: William Corcoran

American Near East Refugee Aid provides assistance to underdeveloped areas throughout the Middle East, especially focusing its services on Palestinian communities. They help local organizations become more effective providers to their communities and also offer development, health, employment, and education programs to communities in need. ANERA is a non-political and non-religious non-profit organization and has been working solely in the Middle East for over 40 years.

Armenian Assembly of America
National Headquarters
1334 G Street, N.W.
Washington, DC 20005
Tel: (202) 393-3434
Fax: (202) 638-4904
www.aaainc.org
info@aaainc.org
Executive Director: Bryan Ardouny

Located in Washington, the Armenian Assembly of America has worked for more than 35 years advocating for a swift and appropriate American and international response to the needs of Armenian refugees, as well as providing humanitarian and development assistance in Armenia and Nagorno Karabakh. They also provide information and resources about Armenian issues.

Boat People S.O.S., Inc.
National Headquarters
6066 Leesburg Pike, Suite 100
Falls Church, VA 22041
Tel: (703) 538-2190
www.bpsos.org
info@bpsos.org
Executive Director: Thang D. Nguyen, Ph.D.

Boat People S.O.S., Inc., works internationally, assisting Vietnamese refugees on the open ocean or in refugee camps, providing them with skill training and support after they relocate.

Bridging Refugee Youth and Children's Services
U.S. Conference of Catholic Bishops
3211 Fourth Street, N.E.
Washington, DC 20017
Tel: 1-888-572-6500
www.brycs.org
info@brycs.org
Senior Program Officer: Lyn Morland, MSW, MA

Bridging Refugee Youth and Children's Services (BRYCS) works to strengthen the capabilities of refugee-serving organizations across the United States. Their mission is to assist these organizations in providing for the successful development of refugee children, youth, and their families. BRYCS provides technical assistance that builds long-term capacity, as well as promoting collaboration between organizations at the local, state, regional, and national levels.

British Refugee Council
Head Office
240-250 Ferndale Road
Brixton
London SW9 8BB
United Kingdom
Tel: 020 7346 6700
Fax: 020 7346 6701
www.refugeecouncil.org.uk
Chair: Douglas Board

The British Refugee Council is a non-profit, non-governmental organization that works to ensure the protection of refugee rights. They provide information resources and direct material support to refugees and asylum seekers.

Canadian Council for Refugees
National Headquarters
6839 Drolet #302
Montreal, Quebec, H25 2T1
Canada
Tel: (514) 277-7223
Fax: (514) 277-1447
www.ccrweb.ca
info@ccrweb.ca
President: Wanda Yamamoto

Founded in 1978, the CCR has been recognized as an important advocate for refugee and immigrant rights in Canada. It is a non-profit organization, committed to the protection and rights of refugees and immigrants in Canada and around the world.

CARE-International
International Secretariat
Chemin de Balexert 7–9
1219 Chatelaine, Geneva
Switzerland
Tel: +41 22 795 10 20

Fax: +41 22 795 10 29
www.care-international.org
Secretary General: Robert Glasser

CARE is an international, non-political humanitarian organization, dedicated to working with individuals and communities in the poorest regions of the world. Often one of the first organizations to provide emergency aid to survivors of wars and natural disasters, CARE remains in the area after the crisis is over to assist people to rebuild their lives. Over 90 percent of their staff are nationals of the countries where their programs are run.

Catholic Relief Services
228 W. Lexington Street
Baltimore, MD 21201-3413
Tel: 1-888-277-7575
www.crs.org
info@crs.org
President: Ken Hackett

Founded in 1943 to assist World War II survivors in Europe, Catholic Relief Services is the official humanitarian arm of the Catholic Church in the United States. Their humanitarian and development programs are aimed at improving the lives of impoverished and disadvantaged individuals and communities around the world. They also develop public policy positions and advocate for them with United States and international governmental officials.

Cefored Institute of Relief and Development
P.O. Box 105020-00100
Nairobi, Kenya
Tel: +254 20 311328
www.cefored.co.ke
info@cefored.co.ke

Cefored Institute of Relief and Development was founded in 1996 and its headquarters is located in Nairobi, Kenya. It provides training to individuals and groups with the goal of establishing a human resource foundation that can respond effectively to emergency and development needs and support human rights worldwide.

Center for Applied Linguistics
4646 40th Street, N.W.
Washington, DC 20016-1859
Tel: (202) 362-0700
Fax: (202) 362-3740
www.cal.org
info@cal.org
President: Donna Christian

The Center for Applied Linguistics is a non-profit organization dedicated to providing research based information and resources related to language and culture. Its Refugee Integration project works with the U.S. government, international organizations, and domestic refugee resettlement agencies to provide them training and assistance with respect to refugee's cultures, languages, and their resettlement needs.

Centers for Disease Control and Prevention
1600 Clifton Road
Atlanta, GA 30333
Tel: 1-800-232-4636
Director: Thomas R. Frieden, M.D., M.P.H.
www.cdc.gov
cdcinfo@cdc.gov

Immigrant, Refugee and Migrant Health
www.cdc.gov/immigrantrefugeehealth/International
    Emergency and Refugee Health Branch
www.cdc.gov/nceh/ierh

The Centers for Disease Control and Prevention is one of the main components of the U.S. Department of Health and Human Services. The branches of the CDC serving immigrants and refugees are the Immigrant, Refugee and Migrant Health, and the International Emergency and Refugee Health Branch. These branches post notices about current health and international issues of concern relating to immigrants and refugees, as well as guidelines regarding refugee health questions.

Center for Migration Studies
27 Carmine Street
New York, NY 10014-4423
Tel: (212) 337-3080

Fax: (212) 255-1771
www.cmsny.org
cms@cmsny.org
Executive Director: Rene Manenti

Founded in 1964 as a non-profit organization dedicated to supporting and undertaking original research, the Center for Migration Studies of New York provides a forum for discussion and debate on international migration. They also publish "International Migration Review," a peer-reviewed scholarly journal about international migration.

Center for Victims of Torture
1875 I Street, N.W., 5th Floor
Washington, DC 20006
1-877-265-8775
Tel: (202) 857-3284
Fax: (202) 429-9574
www.cvt.org
cvt@cvt.org
Executive Director: Douglas A. Johnson, M.P.P.M.

The Center for Victims of Torture has branches in Minneapolis and St. Paul, Sierra Leone, Jordan, and the Democratic Republic of Congo, where they work with victims of torture, providing resources and counseling to aid in the healing process. They also advocate for an end to the use of torture worldwide. Since their founding in 1985, they have assisted over 18,000 torture victims and their families.

Church World Service Immigration and Refugee Program
475 Riverside Drive, Suite 700
New York, NY 10115
Tel: (212) 870-2061
Fax: (212) 870-3523
www.churchworldservice.org/site/PageServer
info@churchworldservice.org
Director: Erol Kekic

The Immigration and Refugee Program of Church World Service is an ecumenical organization that provides resources and information to churches, enabling them to assist refugees and immigrants in the United States and around the world. Through their program, approximately 8,000 refugees are resettled in the United States each year. Their organization provides news and resources advocating for fair and equitable U.S. policies toward refugees and immigrants.

Council for Assisting Refugee Academics
London South Bank University
Technopark
90 London Road SE1 6LN
London
United Kingdom
Tel: +44 (0) 207 021 0880
Fax: +44 (0) 207 021 0881
www.academic-refugees.org
info.cara@lsbu.ac.uk
President: Sir John Ashworth

Council for Assisting Refugee Academics was founded in 1933 in response to news that leading academics in Germany were being removed from their posts, due to their race or their politics, under the Nazi regime. The organization's goal is to assist university teachers and investigators in any country who are unable to work because of their race, religion, or politics. In the past 75 years, the organization has provided assistance to over 9,000 academics and their dependents.

Cultural Survival
215 Prospect Street
Cambridge, MA 02139
www.culturalsurvival.org
Executive Director: Ellen Lutz

For 37 years, Cultural Survival has worked with indigenous peoples in dozens of countries around the world, helping them protect their lands, languages, and cultures. They advocate for indigenous issues and work to end rights abuse.

Danish Refugee Council
Borgergade 10, 3rd Floor
1300 Copenhagen K.

Denmark
Tel: +45 3373 5000
www.drc.dk
id@drc.dk

Founded in 1956, the Danish Refugee Council is a private, non-profit organization, committed to the realization of durable solutions to refugee crises. They are comprised of 30 member organizations working to provide relief and development services, refugee support, and community rehabilitation worldwide.

Direct Aid Iraq
MECCS/Direct Aid Iraq
P.O. Box 382425
Cambridge, MA 02238
Tel: (802) 659-4281
www.directaidiraq.org
info@directaidiraq.org

Direct Aid Iraq is a program of the Middle East Cultural and Charitable Society, and is a non-profit organization that supports peace in Iraq through education, aid provision, and advocacy work.

Direct Relief International
27 S. La Patera Lane
Santa Barbara, CA 93117
Tel: (805) 964-4767
Fax: (805) 681-4838
www.directrelief.org
President: Thomas Tighe

Established in 1948, Direct Relief International provides medical assistance for individuals affected by poverty, war, and disaster both in the United States and abroad. They partner with domestic organizations, providing them with direct material assistance, including medicines, equipment, and other supplies.

Episcopal Migration Ministries
815 Second Avenue
New York, NY 10017
1-800-334-7626
Tel: (212) 716-6000

www.episcopalchurch.org/emm
emm@episcopalchurch.org
Director: Deborah Stein

Episcopal Migration Ministries is one of the humanitarian arms of the Episcopal Church. They work to ensure the basic civil and human rights of immigrants and refugees, and provide assistance with refugee resettlement.

Eritrean Relief Association
Robin House
2A Iverson Road
London NW6 2HE
United Kingdom
Tel: 00 44 20 7328 7888
www.era-uk.org
info@era-uk.org

The Eritrean Relief Association is a United Kingdom based organization dedicated to providing relief and development assistance to individuals and communities within Eritrea, as well as providing resources to Eritreans in the United Kingdom.

Ethiopian Community Development Council
901 South Highland Street
Arlington, VA 22204
Tel: (703) 685-0510
Fax: (703) 685-0529
www.ecdcinternational.org
info@ecdeinternational.org
President: Tseheye Teferra, Ph.D.

The Ethiopian Community Development Council's goal is to facilitate the integration of Ethiopian refugees into the United States. They provide educational and social programs to assist refugees in acculturation, resettlement, and healing from past traumas.

European Council on Refugees and Exiles
ECRE Brussels Office Secretariat
Rue Royale 146
2nd Floor 1000
Brussels, Belgium
Tel: +32 (0) 2 234 3800

Fax: +32 (0) 2 514 5922
www.ecre.org
ecre@ecre.org

The ECRE is a diverse network composed of 69 non-profit, non-governmental organizations dedicated to assisting refugees and advocating for the improvement of European asylum policies.

European Refugee Fund
European Commission
DG Justice, Freedom, and Security
B-1049
Brussels
Belgium
Tel: +32 2.299.96.96
http://ec.europa.eu/justice_home/funding/refugee/funding
_refugee_en.htm

Created in 2000 to help member states of the European Union share the costs of reception and integration of refugees, the European Refugee Fund supports and improves the efforts of European Member States to apply fair and effective asylum procedures and good practices in their reception of refugees.

Exodus World Service
P.O. Box 620
Itasca, IL 60143-0620
Tel: (630) 307-1400
Fax: (630) 307-1430
www.e-w-s.org
Director: Heidi Moll Schoedel

Exodus World Service trains volunteers in the Chicago area, providing them with the necessary information to intervene for and assist newly arrived refugees. They also provide tools and training for local refugee organizations to help with resettlement and other service projects.

Georgetown University Institute for the Study of International Migration
Georgetown University
Harris Building
3300 Whitehaven Street, N.W.

Third Floor
Washington, DC 20007
Tel: (202) 687-2258
Fax: (207) 687-2541
www.isim.georgetown.edu
Executive Director: Susan Martin

The Institute for the Study of International Migration is part of the Edmund A. Walsh School of Foreign Service at Georgetown University. They conduct research and provide analysis on all aspects of international migration, including the causes of and potential responses to migration, immigration and refugee law and policy, comparative migration studies, and the effects of migration on national and international concerns.

Grassroots International
179 Boylston Street, Fourth Floor
Boston, MA 02130
Tel: (617) 524-1400
Fax: (617) 524-5525
www.grassrootsonline.org
info@GrassrootsOnline.org
Director of Global Programs: Maria Aguiar

Grassroots International is a development and human rights organization that builds alliances between social movements and progressive organizations. Their goal is to support a global movement for social justice through advocacy, education, and the support of community led initiatives.

HealthRight International
80 Maiden Lane, Suite 607
New York, NY 10038
Tel: (212) 226-9890
Fax: (212) 226-7026
www.healthright.org
info@healthright.org
Executive Director: Mila Rosenthal, Ph.D.

HealthRight International was founded in 1990 to be a global health and human rights organization, addressing health and social crises, and working to create permanent access to health care for marginalized communities. They take a rights-based approach aimed at improving conditions in impoverished and marginalized areas, aiming to create projects that enable communities to advocate for themselves.

Hebrew Immigrant Aid Society
333 Seventh Avenue, 16th Floor
New York, NY 10001-5019
Tel: (212) 967-4100
www.hias.org
President: Gideon Aronoff

As the international migration agency of the American Jewish community, the Hebrew Immigrant Aid Society provides assistance to refugees and endangered communities worldwide regardless of their ethnic or religious background, and advocates for fair refugee and immigration policies in the United States.

Holt International Children's Services
1195 City View
Eugene, OR 97402
Tel: (541) 687-2202
Fax: (541) 683-6175
www.holtintl.org
info@holtinternational.org
President: Kim Brown

Holt International is an international adoption and child-care agency, focused on protecting the rights of children, as well as both the birth and adoptive parents. They also run facilities and programs overseas to ensure safe and nurturing environments for children at risk.

Human Rights Documentation Exchange
P.O. Box 2327
Austin, TX 78768
Tel: (512) 476-9841
Fax: (512) 476-0130
www.handplant.com/mockups/hrde/default.htm
mail@hrde.org
Executive Director: Rebecca Hall

The Human Rights Documentation Exchange provides information on human rights abuses and country specific conditions to persons applying for asylum and in the United States, assisting them to verify their claim of reasonable fear of persecution in his or her own country.

Human Rights First
333 Seventh Avenue, 13th Floor
New York, NY 10001-5108
Tel: (212) 845-5200
Fax: (212) 845-5299
www.humanrightsfirst.org
feedback@humanrightsfirst.org
President: Elisa Massimino

Human Rights First was founded in 1978 as a non-profit organization dedicated to promoting human rights and respect for the rule of law. They work to ensure the rights and dignity of persons through advocacy, litigation, coalition-building, and research.

Human Rights Internet
1 Nicholas Street, Suite 1105
Ottawa, ON K1N 7B7
Canada
Tel: (613) 789-7407
Fax: (613) 789-7414
www.hri.ca
info@hri.ca
Executive Director: Dr. Corinne Packer

Human Rights Internet is committed to the advancement of social justice and human rights. They work with governmental, international, and non-governmental actors and organizations to support marginalized groups, provide research and information, and to push for policy changes, good governance, and institutional development.

Human Rights Watch
350 Fifth Avenue, 34th Floor
New York, NY 10118-3299
Tel: (212) 290-4700

Fax: (212) 736-1300
www.hrw.org
hrwnyc@hrw.org
Executive Director: Kenneth Roth

Human Rights Watch has been one of the world's principal organizations devoted to protecting and advancing human rights for 30 years. They investigate and expose human rights violations, employing a "naming and shaming" approach, and work to bring perpetrators of violations to justice through the use of international law.

Immigrant and Refugee Community Organization
Central Office
10301 N.E. Glisan Street
Portland, OR 97220
Tel: (503) 234-1541
Fax: (503) 234-1259
www.irco.org
Executive Director: Mr. Sokhom Tauch

The Immigrant and Refugee Community Organization is a Portland, Oregon-based service provider for newly arrived immigrants and refugees. Their goal is to promote the integration of immigrants, refugees, and their adopted community.

Immigrant and Refugee Rights Project
Washington Lawyers' Committee
Attn: Immigrant and Refugee Rights Project
11 Dupont Circle, N.W., Suite 400
Washington, DC 20036
Tel: (202) 319-1000 ext. 120
www.washlaw.org/projects/immigrants_refugees_eng/
    default.htm
immigrant@washlaw.org
Director: Laura E. Varela

The Washington Lawyers' Committee Immigrant and Refugee Rights Project works to protect and support the rights of immigrants and refugees who are discriminated against in violation of state and federal law.

InterAction
1400 16th Street N.W., Suite 210
Washington, DC 20036
Tel: (202)667-8227
www.interaction.org
ia@interaction.org
President: Samuel Worthington

InterAction is a coalition of more than 180 member organizations working to assist the poorest individuals and communities in the world. They promote an agenda, focused on development and humanitarian assistance, to United States and international policy makers, as well as creating a forum for leading NGO's and other leaders in various fields to share expertise and ideas on poverty reduction.

Internal Displacement Monitoring Centre
Chemin de Balexert, 7–9
1219 Chatelaine
Geneva, Switzerland
Tel: +41 (22) 799 07 00
Fax: +41 (22) 799 07 01
www.internal-displacement.org
Head: Kate Halff

The Internal Displacement Monitoring Centre was established by the Norwegian Refugee Council in 1998, and has evolved into the leading international organization monitoring conflict-induced internal displacement around the world. They run an online database at the request of the United Nations that provides information and analysis on internal displacement and use the data they gather to effectively advocate on an international level for lasting solutions to the needs of internally displaced persons in accordance with international law.

International Alert
346 Clapham Road
London SW9 9AP
United Kingdom
Tel: 44 (0) 20 7627 6800
Fax: 44 (0) 20 7627 6900
www.international-alert.org
Secretary General: Dan Smith, OBE

International Alert is a non-profit organization committed to the prevention and end of violent conflict worldwide. Based in London, International Alert works in over 20 countries. They combine local work with persons directly affected by violence with advocacy at governmental and international levels to support the creation of sustainable peace.

International Catholic Migration Commission
1, Rue de Varembe
P.O. Box 96
CH 1211 Geneva 20
Switzerland
Tel: 41 (0) 22 919 10 20
Fax: 41 (0) 22 919 10 48
www.icmc.net
info@icmc.net
President: John Klink

The International Catholic Migration Commission was established in 1951 to serve the needs and protect the rights of refugees, internally displaced persons, and migrants worldwide. They have 172 member organizations in 30 countries around the world, with expertise in refugee resettlement, local integration, emergency response, and advocacy.

International Center for Migration and Health
11, Route du Nant d'Avril
CH-1214 Geneva
Switzerland
Tel: 41 (22) 783 10 80
Fax: 41 (22) 783 10 87
www.icmh.ch
admin@icmh.ch
President: Dr. Eamon Kelly

Established in 1995, the International Center for Migration and Health's mission is to work for the protection of health and welfare of refugees, internally displaced persons, and migrants. They collaborate with the World Health Organization by generating research and advocating for international public policy in all areas related to migration and health.

International Committee of the Red Cross
19 avenue de la Paix
CH 1202 Geneva
Switzerland
Tel: 41 (22) 733 20 57
Fax: 41 (22) 734 60 01
www.icrc.org
President: Jakob Kellenberger, Ph.D.

Established in 1863, the International Committee of the Red Cross (ICRC) is a non-political organization working to ensure humanitarian protection and assistance for victims of conflict. The ICRC has a legal mandate from the international community, sourced from both the Geneva Convention and the Statutes of the International Red Cross and Red Crescent Movement. This mandate tasks the ICRC with working impartially for prisoners, wounded, and civilians affected by both armed conflicts and situations of internal violence.

International Council of Voluntary Agencies
26-28 avenue Giuseppe Motta 1202
Geneva
Switzerland
Tel: 41 (0) 22 956 9600
Fax: 41 (0)22 950 9609
www.icva.ch
secretariat@icva.ch
Coordinator: Ed Schenkenberg van Mierop

The International Council of Voluntary Agencies (ICVA) is a network of organizations focused on humanitarian, human rights, and refugee policy issues. As an advocacy alliance, the ICVA provides a means for both extensive collaboration between NGOs and for the improvement of individual organizations.

International Federation of Red Cross and Red Crescent Societies
P.O. Box 372
CH-1211 Geneva 19
Switzerland
Tel: 41 22 730 42 22

Fax: 41 22 733 03 95
www.ifrc.org
Secretary General: Bekele Geleta

With 186 member societies, the International Federation of Red
Cross and Red Crescent Societies is the largest humanitarian
organization in the world, carrying out relief operations to assist
victims of conflict and natural disaster, and providing development assistance to strengthen the abilities of its national societies.

International Organization for Migration
17 Route des Morillons
Ch-1211 Geneva 19
Switzerland
Tel: 41 22 717 9111
Fax: 41 22 798 6150
www.iom.int
info@iom.int
Director General: William Lacy Swing

Established in 1951 as the Intergovernmental Committee for
European Migration, the International Organization for Migration is the leading organization specializing in migration issues.
By collaborating with the international community to advance
understanding of migration issues, they assist in meeting the
challenges posed by migration in the 21st century, and work for
the protection of the rights and well-being of migrants.

International Refugee Rights Initiative
866 United Nations Plaza, Suite 4018
New York, NY 10017
Tel: (212) 453 5853
Fax: (212) 310 0100
www.refugee-rights.org
info@refugee-rights.org
Co-Directors: Déirdre Clancy and Dismas Nkunda

The International Refugee Rights Initiative is a non-profit, non-
governmental organization that is committed to the protection of
human rights in conflict situations and of the rights of displaced
individuals. They are an advocacy organization, focused on
Africa, which conducts research on the effects of national and

international policy on affected groups and brings their findings to policy makers with the aim of improving and creating laws and policies that best guarantee human rights.

International Rescue Committee
122 East 42nd Street
New York, NY 10168-1289
Tel: (212) 551-3000
Fax: (212) 551-3179
www.theirc.org
President: George Rupp

The International Rescue Committee is a global network of individuals and organizations working in 42 countries to provide emergency relief, refugee relocation and resettlement, and post-conflict development. They assist individuals uprooted by violence and conflict, as well as those fleeing racial, ethnic, or religious persecution.

International Social Service—United States of America Branch, Inc.
200 E. Lexington Street, Suite 1700
Baltimore, MD 21202
Tel: (443) 451-1200
Fax: (443) 451-1220
www.iss-usa.org
iss-usa@iss-usa.org
Executive Director: Julie Gilbert Rosicky

An international network composed of 150 national branches, the International Social Service provides assistance to individuals who encounter socio-legal problems worldwide. They are a non-profit, non-religious organization, with each national branch operating autonomously.

Iraqi Refugee Assistance Project
www.iraqirefugee.us
iraqi.refugee.assistance@gmail.com

Founded by students in 2008, the Iraqi Refugee Assistance Project is student-run organization working to facilitate the resettlement of refugees and advocating for improved U.S. refugee policies.

Jesuit Refugee Service
National Headquarters
1016 16th Street, N.W., Suite 500
Washington, DC 20036
Tel: (202) 462-0400
Fax: (202) 328-9212
www.jrs.net

The Jesuit Relief Service is an international Catholic organization with programs in over 50 countries. Their mandate is to provide assistance to, and defend the rights of, refugees and internally displaced persons (IDP). They also contribute to research on refugee issues at Oxford University and advocate internationally for greater international protection for refugees and IDPs.

Lutheran Immigration and Refugee Service
Headquarters
700 Light Street
Baltimore, MD 21230
Tel: (410) 230-2700
Fax: (410) 230-2890
www.lirs.org
lirs@lirs.org
President: Linda Hartke

Advocacy
122 C Street, N.W., Suite 125
Washington, DC 20001
Tel: (202) 783-7509
Fax: (202) 783-7502
dc@lirs.org

Lutheran Immigration and Refugee Service works with churches across the United States to assist in refugee resettlement. They work within the community receiving the refugees to create a welcoming and compassionate environment. The organization also advocates for improved U.S. policies concerning immigration and refugees.

Lutheran World Relief
700 Light Street
Baltimore, MD 21230
Tel: (410) 230-2800

Fax: (410) 230-2882
www.lwr.org
President: John Arthur Nunes

Lutheran World Relief works with churches in the United States and partners around the world to facilitate international relief and development programs.

Mapendo International Inc
689 Massachusetts Avenue, Second Floor
Cambridge, MA 02139
Tel: (617) 864-7800
Fax: (617) 864-7802
www.mapendo.org
info@mapendo.org
Executive Director: Sasha Chanoff

Mapendo International works to provide assistance to the refugees that the UNHCR is unable to help, those that live in urban areas, often illegally, rather than in refugee camps. They are an independently funded organization that targets those individuals that have been largely unnoticed by the international community.

Mennonite Central Committee
21 S. 12th Street
P.O. Box 500
Akron, PA 17501-0500
1-888-563-4676
Tel: (717) 859-1151
www.mcc.org
mailbox@mcc.org
Executive Director: Arli Klassen

Mennonite Central Committee is a worldwide ministry of Anabaptist churches, dedicated to addressing basic human needs such as food, water, and shelter. They work with local churches internationally to build peace and provide disaster relief and sustainable community development.

Minnesota Advocates for Human Rights
650 3rd Avenue South, Suite 1240
Minneapolis, MN 55402-1940

Tel: (612) 341-3302
Fax: (612) 341-2971
www.mnadvocates.org
hrights@advrights.org
Executive Director: Robin Phillips

The Minnesota Advocates for Human Rights works to promote and support a movement to protect human rights, nationally and internationally. Their work with refugees and immigrants is based in advocacy and research, as well as the provision of free legal assistance to refugees and immigrants in need.

Minority Rights Group International
54 Commercial Street
London E1 6LT
United Kingdom
Tel: 44 (0) 20 7422 4200
Fax: 44 (0) 20 7422 4201
www.minorityrights.org
minority.rights@mrgmail.org
Executive Director: Mark Lattimer

The Minority Rights Group International mounts campaigns that target governments and communities in which discriminatory attitudes against disadvantaged minorities. The group seeks to eradicate such attitudes, and works with around 130 partner organizations in over 60 countries, utilizing education, legal cases, publications, and the media to secure equal opportunities and rights to minorities.

Muslim Aid
PO Box 3
London E1 1WP
United Kingdom
Tel: +44 (0)20 7377 4200
Fax: +44 (0)20 7377 4201
www.muslimaid.org
CEO: Syed Sharfuddin

Committed to poverty eradication and community empowerment, Muslim Aid works with its partners in over 70 countries around the world. They provide assistance to individuals and communities after natural disasters and conflict situations, and implement development programs focused on education, sanitation, health care, and skill development.

National Immigration Forum
50 F Street, N.W., Suite 300
Washington, DC 20001
Tel: (202) 347-0040
Fax: (202) 347-0058
www.immigrationforum.org
Executive Director: Ali Noorani

The National Immigration Forum is the leading immigrant advocacy organization in the United States. Established over 25 years ago, the Forum emphasizes the value of immigrants and immigration to American society, and advocates for immigration policies that protect the rights and dignity of immigrants and refugees, while at the same time upholding American ideals.

Nationalities Service Center
1216 Arch Street
Fourth Floor
Philadelphia, PA 19107
Tel: (215) 893-8400
Fax: (215) 735-9718
www.nationalitiesservice.org
Executive Director: Dennis Mulligan

The Nationalities Service Center (NSC), located in Philadelphia, is a non-profit organization that assists approximately 4,000 area refugees and immigrants per year. The NSC focuses on the provision of services such as legal assistance, translation and interpretation, and educational assistance.

Norwegian Refugee Council
P.O. Box 6758
St Olavs plass
0130 Oslo
Norway
Tel: (47) 23 10 98 00

Fax: (47) 23 10 98 01
www.nrc.no
nrc@nrc.no
Secretary General: Elisabeth Rasmusson

The NRC is an independent, non-profit organization focused on the international promotion and protection of the rights of refugees and internally displaced persons and returning refugees. They are the only organization of this kind in Norway, and they operate with about 2,600 staff members in over 20 countries. They provide humanitarian assistance in the form of education, distribution of food, water, and other necessities, building homes and schools, and refugee camp management. The NRC also engages in advocacy on these issues, both in Norway and internationally.

Office of Refugee Resettlement
Administration for Children and Families
Office of Refugee Resettlement
U.S. Department of Health and Human Services
Aerospace Building
901 D Street, S.W.
Washington, DC 20447
Tel: (202) 401-9246
Fax: (202) 401-5487
www.acf.hhs.gov/programs/orr
Director: Eskinder Negash

Part of the U.S. Department of Health and Human Services, the Office of Refugee Resettlement provides assistance and resources to refugees, with their aim being the successful integration of these refugees into American society.

Office of United Nations High Commissioner for Refugees
Case Postale 2500
CH-1211
Geneva 2 Depot
Switzerland
Tel: 41 22 739 8111
www.unhcr.org
High Commissioner: António Guterres

Established by the UN General Assembly in 1950, the Office of the UN High Commissioner for Refugees (UNHCR) is tasked with the coordination of international action to protect refugees. Its mission is to ensure the rights and well-being of refugees, including the right to seek asylum. It has a staff of over 6,600 individuals in more than 110 countries. The Office of the United Nations High Commissioner has been awarded the Nobel Peace Prize twice, in 1954 and 1981.

Operation USA
3617 Hayden Avenue, Suite A
Culver City, CA 90232
1-800-678-7255
Tel: (310) 838-3455
Fax: (310) 838-3477
www.opusa.org
info@opusa.org
President: Richard Walden

Operation USA is an international humanitarian agency that works with local organizations to provide relief, reconstruction, and development operations. They promote long-term programs such as education, health services, and leadership development, as well as support the building of grassroots advocacy movements.

Oxfam America
226 Causeway Street
Fifth Floor
Boston, MA 02114-2206
(617) 728-2594
Tel: 1-800-776-9326
www.oxfamamerica.org
info@oxfamamerica.org
President: Raymond C. Offenheiser

Oxfam America is one of 13 worldwide affiliates of Oxfam International, a relief and development organization that has for 20 years set the standard for the delivery of clean water and sanitation supplies in emergency situations. Oxfam responds to every major refugee crisis, anywhere in the world, and their affiliates come together to provide the most efficient response. Oxfam International also works for change in international laws and policies that allow poverty to remain endemic to certain regions of the world.

Project ROSE
SEARAC-Head Office
1628 16th Street, N.W., Third Floor
Washington, DC 20009-3099
Tel: (202) 667-4690
Fax: (202) 667-6449
www.searac.org/rose.html
searac@searac.org
Contact: Bach Pham

A collaboration between Mosaica: The Center for Nonprofit Development and Pluralism, and the South East Asia Resource Action Center (SEARAC), Project Refugee Organization and Service Enhancement (ROSE) works to build the capacity of refugee service agencies and organizations. Project ROSE provides technical assistance and information resources to international refugee organizations, as well as conducting regional trainings, to help new or struggling refugee organizations provide the most effective and efficient services.

Rav Tov International Jewish Rescue Operation
500 Bedford Avenue
Brooklyn, NY 11211
Tel: (718) 963-1991
www.allbusiness.com/4035145-1.html
Contact: Divid Niederman

Rav Tov is an international network that provides immigration and resettlement assistance to refugees immigrating to Western countries. They have financial assistance available to bridge the gap before an immigrant is able to be self-sufficient, and connects immigrants to educational and employment services.

Refugee Action
The Old Fire Station
150 Waterloo Road
London SE1 8SB
UK
Tel: +44 (0)20 7654 7700
Fax: +44 (0)20 7654 0696
www.refugee-action.org.uk
info@refugee-action.org.uk
Chief Executive: Jill Roberts

Founded over 25 years ago in the United Kingdom, Refugee Action works to create a society where refugees are welcome and safe in their adopted communities. They seek to empower refugees through their resettlement and integration services, independent advice, and advocacy.

Refugee and Migrant Justice
Nelson House
153-157 Commercial Road
London E1 2DA
Tel: 020 7780 3200
Fax: 020 7780 3201
www.refugee-migrant-justice.org.uk
rlc@rmj.org.uk
Chief Executive: Caroline Slocock

Established in 1992 as the Refugee Legal Centre, Refugee and Migrant Justice is a non-profit UK-based legal organization that works to procure legal justice for refugees, asylum seekers, and other migrants in the United Kingdom. They are the largest provider of advice and representation to these groups in the United Kingdom, and have built a solid reputation as effective legal advocates in their area. In 2005, Refugee and Migrant Justice won the Liberty/Justice Human Rights Award for their work.

Refugee Assistance Project
City Bar Justice Center
42 West 44th Street
New York, NY 10036
Tel: (212) 382-6600
www.nycbar.org/citybarjusticecenter/projects/immigrant-justice/
    refugee-assistance-projectinfo@nycbar.org

The Refugee Assistance Project is part of the City Bar Justice Center in New York City. They recruit and train volunteer attorneys to assist refugees seeking political asylum in the United States.

Refugee Council of Australia
Head Office
410 Elizabeth Street, Suite 4 A6
Sury Hills NSW 2010

Australia
Tel: 02 9211 9333
Fax: 02 9211 9288
www.refugeecouncil.org.au
info@refugeecouncil.org.au
CEO: Paul Power

The Refugee Council of Australia is a network of 130 Australian organizations assisting refugees and asylum seekers. As the umbrella organization, the council conducts research, provides information, and advocates for the development of improved refugee and immigration policies.

Refugee Health—Office of Global Health Affairs
U.S. Department of Health and Human Services
Room 639H
200 Independence Avenue, S.W.
Washington, DC 20201
Tel: (202) 690-6174
Fax: (202) 690-7127
www.globalhealth.gov
Director: Dr. Nils Daulaire

Part of the U.S. Department of Health and Human Services, the Office of Global Health Affairs assists in the coordination of refugee health policies nationally and internationally. Among their collaborative initiatives is the Refugee Health Promotion and Disease Prevention Initiative, a project coordinated between several offices of Health and Human Services that is intended to increase refugee health awareness.

Refugee Relief International
2995 Woodside Road # 400–244
Woodside, CA 94062
www.refugeerelief.org
info@refugeerelief.org

Refugee Relief International is an independent humanitarian relief organization that conducts missions to provide medical and relief assistance in crisis situations. They are staffed by volunteer doctors, nurses, and medics who have experience working in war zones and emergency environments.

Refugee Studies Centre
Oxford Department of International Development
University of Oxford
3 Mansfield Road
Oxford OX1 3TB
United Kingdom
Tel: +44 (1865) 281720
Fax: +44 (1865) 281730
www.rsc.ox.ac.uk
rsc@gch.ox.ac.uk

Established in 1982, the Refugee Studies Centre has earned an international reputation as the premier center for research on the causes and consequences of forced migration. The center provides degrees and individual courses to individuals wishing to gain a greater understanding of refugee issues.

Refugee Women's Alliance
4008 Martin Luther King, Jr. Way South
Seattle, WA 98108
Tel: (206) 721-0243
Fax: (206) 721-0282
www.rewa.org
Executive Director: Someireh Amirfaiz

The Refugee Women's Alliance is an independent, non-profit organization in the Seattle that provides support services to refugee and immigrant women, including education and vocational training, family and parenting support classes and counseling, and domestic violence awareness programs.

Refugee Women's Network
4151 Memorial Drive
Suite 103F
Decatur, GA 30032
Tel: (404) 299-0180
Fax: (404) 296-9118
www.riwn.org
info@riwn.org
Executive Director: Dr. BryAnn Chen

Founded in 1995 by women who immigrated to the United States as refugees, the Refugee Women's Network provides services to support and empower refugee and immigrant women in the Atlanta area. They provide leadership training, educational assistance, and advocacy to promote independence and self-sufficiency.

Refugees International
2001 S Street, N.W., Suite 700
Washington, DC 20009
Tel: (202) 828-0110
Fax: (202) 828-0819
www.refugeesinternational.org
ri@refintl.org
President: Dan Glickman

Refugees International is a leading independent advocacy organization that makes recommendations to governments, international organizations such as the United Nations, and aid organizations to improve the quality of life for refugees and internally displaced persons. They conduct field missions each year in critical areas of the world to identify the needs of individuals in crisis situations.

Salvation Army World Service Office
P.O. Box 1428
615 Slaters Lane
Alexandria, VA 22313
Tel: (703) 684-5528
Fax: (703) 684-5536
www.SAWSO.org
sawso@usn.salvationarmy.org
Executive Director: Lt. Colonel Daniel Starrett

The Salvation Army World Service Office was established in 1977 to develop permanent solutions to poverty in third world countries. They work to increase community preparedness for emergency situations, institute development programs, and provide relief services after a disaster.

SAMHSA–Refugee Mental Health Program
Substance Abuse and Mental Health Services Administration
Center for Mental Health Services
Refugee Mental Health Program
1 Choke Cherry Road

Room 6-1099
Rockville, MD 20857
Tel: (240) 276-1845
Fax: (240) 276-1890
www.refugeewellbeing.samhsa.gov
Director: Captain John J. Tuskan, Jr., USPHS

The Refugee Mental Health Program, part of the National Center
for Mental Health Services, works in cooperation with the Office
of Refugee Resettlement to assess the needs of refugees and
migrants in the United States. They provide mental health information and technical assistance to federal, state, and other agencies
with programs directed at improving the quality of care and access
to mental health services.

Save the Children Federation
54 Wilton Road
Westport, CT 06880
1-800-728-3843
Tel: (203) 221-4030
www.savethechildren.org
CEO: Jasmine Whitbread

Save the Children Federation is the largest independent organization in the world working for children's rights. It is comprised of
29 national organizations and provides assistance to other organizations working to support children's health and educational
needs. Save the Children delivers emergency relief after disasters
and implements development programs targeted toward children's
needs.

Southeast Asia Resource Action Center
1628 16th Street, N.W., 3rd Floor
Washington, DC 20009-3099
Tel: (202) 667-4690
Fax: (202) 667-6449
www.searac.org
searac@searac.org
Executive Director: Doua Thor

Founded in 1979 as an independent organization facilitating the successful relocation of Southeast Asian immigrants to the United
States, the Southeast Asia Resource Action Center now serves as an

advocate for Southeast Asian Americans at the national level. They also work to build coalitions of community-based organizations supporting the needs of Southeast Asian immigrants and refugees.

Tolstoy Foundation
P.O. Box 578
104 Lake Road
Valley Cottage, NY 10989
Tel: (845) 268-6722
Fax: (845) 268-6937
www.tolstoyfoundation.org
info@tolstoyfoundation.org
Executive Director: Victoria Wohlsen

Founded in 1939 to assist individuals fleeing war and political persecution, the Tolstoy Foundation today provides relief assistance internationally with emphasis on building the capacity of individuals and communities to be self-reliant.

UN Office for Coordination of Humanitarian Affairs
United Nations Secretariat
New York, NY 10017
Tel: (212) 963-1234
Fax: (212) 963-1013
ochaonline.un.org
ochany@un.org
Under Secretary General: John Holmes

The UN Office for the Coordination of Humanitarian Affairs is responsible for the mobilization and coordination of national and international organizations and other actors to facilitate relief and development activities internationally.

UNICEF
New York Headquarters
UNICEF House
3 United Nations Plaza
New York, NY 10017
Tel: (212) 326-7000
Fax: (212) 887-7465
www.unicef.org
Executive Director: Anthony Lake

UNICEF has a mandate from the United Nations General Assembly to work for the protection of children's rights and to assist in the provision of basic needs such as health care and education for children internationally. They have the ability to mobilize both governmental and non-governmental actors to protect children in underdeveloped areas and in crises.

UNRWA
Gaza Headquarters
P.O. Box 61
Gaza City
Tel: 972 8 288 7333
Fax: 972 8 288 7555
www.unrwa.org
Commissioner General: Filippo Grandi

New York Office
One United Nations Plaza
Room DC1-1265
New York, NY 10017
Tel: (212) 963-2255
Fax: (212) 935-7899
Director: Andrew Whitley

The UN Relief and Works Agency for Palestinian Refugees in the Near East was established in 1949 to carry out relief programs for new Palestinian refugees in the aftermath of the 1948 Israeli-Arab conflict. Now, the organization is the primary provider of services such as education, health care, social services, and relief to 4.6 million Palestinian refugees in the Middle East.

United States Catholic Conference, Migration and Refugee Services (USCCB)
3211 Fourth Street, N.E.
Washington, DC 20017
Tel: (202) 541-3352
Fax: (202) 722-8755
www.usccb.org/mrs/
mrs@usccb.org
Executive Director: Johnny Young

The United States Catholic Conference Migration and Refugee Services works with and for the rights of refugees, immigrants, and displaced persons nationally and internationally. They advocate at the national level for improved immigration and refugee policies, and work to provide information to individuals and organizations about immigrant and refugee rights.

United States Citizenship and Immigration Services (USCIS)
20 Massachusetts Avenue, N.W.
Washington, DC 20529
Tel: 1-800-375-5283
www.uscis.gov
Director: Alejandro Mayorkas

With 250 offices worldwide, the U.S. Citizenship and Immigration Services is the government agency that oversees immigration to the United States. They provide information about immigration, promote an understanding of citizenship in the United States, and grant citizenship and immigration benefits.

U.S. Committee for Refugees and Immigrants
2231 Crystal Drive, Suite 350
Arlington, VA 22202-3711
Tel: (703) 310-1130
Fax: (703) 769-4241
www.refugees.org
uscri@uscridc.org
President: Lavinia Limón

The U.S. Committee for Refugees and Immigrants provides direct assistance to refugees fleeing their country as well as supporting them during relocation and resettlement in a new homeland. They also advocate for refugee rights and improved immigration and refugee policies nationally, and work for refugees' successful integration into their new communities.

U.S. Department of State—Bureau of Population, Refugees, and Migration
2201 C Street, N.W.
Washington, DC 20520
Tel: (202) 647-4000
www.state.gov/g/prm
Assistant Secretary: Eric P. Schwartz

The U.S. State Department's Bureau of Population, Refugees, and Migration provides assistance internationally through a multilateral system of organizations including the UNHCR and the International Committee of the Red Cross. They also provide solutions for refugees through assistance with repatriation or resettlement in the United States.

U.S. Fund for UNICEF
125 Maiden Lane
New York, NY 10038
Tel: 1-800-486-4233
www.unicefusa.org
President: Caryl M. Stern

Utilizing advocacy, fundraising, and education in the United States, the U.S. Fund for UNICEF supports UNICEF's mission to provide for and protect children worldwide.

U.S. House Judiciary Committee
Subcommittee on Immigration, Citizenship, Refugees, Border Security, and International Law Membership
2138 Rayburn House Office Building
Washington, DC 20515
Tel: (202) 225-3951
www.judiciary.house.gov/about/subimmigration.html
Chairman: Zoe Lofgren

The U.S. House Judiciary Committee Subcommittee studies and makes recommendations on immigration, citizenship, refugees, border security, treaties, conventions and international agreements, and other relevant matters.

U.S. Senate Judiciary Committee
Subcommittee on Immigration, Refugees, and Border Security
224 Dirksen Senate Office Building
Washington, DC 20510
Tel: (202) 224-8352
Fax: (202) 228-2260
www.judiciary.senate.gov/about/subcommittees/
    immigration.cfm
Chairman: Chuck Schumer

The U.S. Senate Subcommittee on Immigration, Refugees, and Border Security has jurisdiction over immigration, citizenship, and refugee laws nationally, as well as over international laws and policy concerning international migration, internally displaced persons, and refugees.

Women's Refugee Commission
122 East 42nd Street
New York, NY 10168
Tel: (212) 551-3115
www.womensrefugeecommission.org
info@wrcommission.org
Executive Director: Carolyn Makinson

The Women's Refugee Commission is an independent advocacy organization, working nationally and internationally for improved laws and policies for refugees and internally displaced persons. They conduct research and fact-finding missions to identify both the critical problems facing refugee women and children as well as successful policies and practices.

World Concern International
International Headquarters
19303 Freemont Avenue North
Seattle, WA 98133
Tel: 1-800-755-5022
Fax: (206) 546-7269
www.worldconcern.org
info@worldconcern.org
President: David Eller

World Concern is an international non-profit organization working to relieve poverty through development programs and to assist in the provision of health care and social services through better community organization and preparation.

World Food Programme
Via CG Viola 68
Parco dei Midici
00148 Rome
Italy

Tel: +39 06 65131
Fax: +39 06 6590632
Executive Director: Josette Sheeran

As the world's largest humanitarian organization fighting hunger, the World Food Programme provides food and services during and after emergencies to ensure that every individual has access to food. They also work to prevent hunger in the future by implementing programs the help communities become more food secure. The World Food Programme is part of the United Nations system.

World Learning
P.O. Box 676
1 Kipling Road
Brattleboro, VT 05302-0676
1-800-257-7751
Tel: (802) 257-7751
Fax: (802) 258-3248
www.worldlearning.org
info@worldlearning.org
President: Adam Weinberg

World Learning is a non-profit organization that works in 75 countries creating international education programs to strengthen cross-cultural understanding, collaboration, and global citizenship. They both teach and implement community-driven international development and exchange projects.

World Relief
7 East Baltimore Street
Baltimore, MD 21202
Tel: 1-800-535-5433
www.worldrelief.org
worldrelief@wr.org
President: Sammy Mah

World Relief is an international faith-based organization that provides training, education, and resources to local churches in impoverished and volatile areas. They create grassroots development and relief programs that are community centered and directed.

World Vision
P.O. Box 9716, Dept W
Federal Way, WA 98063-9716
Tel: 1-888-511-6548
www.worldvision.org
info@worldvision.org
President: Richard Stearns

Founded in 1950 to help children orphaned in the Korean War, World Vision is a Christian international aid organization that now primarily works to protect children in any region of the world where their health and safety are jeopardized. They also equip teams to provide disaster and emergency relief in crisis situations.

Young Professionals in Foreign Policy—Refugee Assistance Program
1800 K Street, N.W., Suite 400
Washington, DC 20006
www.ypfp.org/rap
info@ypfp.org
President: Joshua Marcuse

The Young Professionals in Foreign Policy Refugee Assistance Program recruits and trains volunteers to work with resettled refugee families for six months to assist them in integrating into American society. They partner with the International Rescue Committee, The List Project, and Lutheran Social Services. Since 2007, the Refugee Assistance Program has assisted over 250 individuals in the greater Washington, DC, area.

8

Resources

Print Resources

There are thousands of publications on refugees, and the number is rapidly expanding. In this chapter we offer a brief annotated bibliography of the leading journals, major references, books, and reports in the field and non-print sources so that readers can quickly identify the sources most important and useful to them.

Journals

There are many periodicals that carry material related to refugees, a highly interdisciplinary topic. Below, we provide information on those that are either specifically dedicated to those purposes or those that quite often carry stories on the topic.

AWR Bulletin
Association for the Study of the World Refugee Problem
Wilhelm Braumüller
Universitäts-Verlagsbuchandlung
A-1092 Vienna
Servite-casse 5
Austria
www.awr-int.de

This quarterly publication is devoted to the study of refugee problems. It includes articles, speeches, book reviews, legislative materials, and other writings of concern to refugees.

Human Rights Quarterly
The Johns Hopkins University Press
2715 North Charles Street
Baltimore, MD 21218-4363
(410) 516-6900
Fax: (410) 516-6968
http://www.press.jhu.edu/journals/human_rights_quarterly/

This quarterly journal specializes in human rights, including refugee issues.

Immigrants and Minorities
Taylor & Francis Group
Mortimer House
37–41 Mortimer Street
London W1T 3JH
United Kingdom
http://www.tandf.co.uk/journals/fimm

Immigrants and Minorities is a British quarterly that focuses on immigrant minorities in Western societies.

International Journal of Refugee Law
Human Rights Centre
University of Essex
Wivenhoe Park
Colchester
Essex CO4 3SQ
United Kingdom
http://ijrl.oxfordjournals.org

This quarterly journal publishes articles about refugee law and policy. It also includes legislation, documentation, and abstracts of recent publications in the field.

International Migration
International Organization for Migration
17, Route des Morillons
CH-1211 Geneva 19
Switzerland
http://www.iom.int/jahia/jsp/index.jsp

This intergovernmental quarterly includes documents, conference reports, and articles.

International Migration Review
Center for Migration Studies
27 Carmine Street
New York, NY 10014-4423
http://www.wiley.com/bw/journal.asp?ref=0197-9183

The leading quarterly journal in the field of migration, *International Migration Review* contains current research articles, book reviews, documents, and bibliographies.

International Review of the Red Cross
International Committee of the Red Cross
19 Avenue de la Paix
CH-1201 Geneva
Switzerland
http://www.icrc.org/Web/eng/siteeng0.nsf/htmlall/review?OpenDocument

This journal, published six times a year, contains articles on international humanitarian law.

Journal of Refugee Studies
Refugee Studies Programme
Oxford University Press
Walton Street
Oxford OX2 6DP
England
http://jrs.oxfordjournals.org

The quarterly *Journal of Refugee Studies* covers all aspects of refugee issues from a multidisciplinary perspective.

Netherlands Quarterly of Human Rights
Netherlands Institute of Human Rights
Drift 15
3512 BR Utrecht
The Netherlands
http://www.nqhr.net

This quarterly journal covers refugees and other human rights issues and problems.

Refuge
Room 845, Centre for Refugee Studies
York Research Tower

4700 Keele Street
Toronto, ON M3J 1P3
Canada
http://pi.library.yorku.ca/ojs/index.php/refuge/index

This publication discusses Canadian refugee policy and reviews recent developments in refugee problems around the world.

Refugee Reports
U.S. Committee for Refugees
2231 Crystal Drive, Suite 350
Arlington, VA 22202-3711
http://www.refugees.org/article.aspx?id=1175&rid=1178

Refugee Reports is an essential monthly source of information and documentation about refugees and legislation and programs affecting them. A special year-end statistical issue is published every December.

Revue Européenne des Migrations Internationales
MSH
Bâtiment A5–5, rue Théodore Lefebvre
86000 Poitiers
France
http://remi.revues.org/

Issues of this biannual publication, published by the university's geography department, focus on subjects such as Antilleans in Europe and immigration in the Americas.

World Disasters Report
International Federation of Red Cross and Red Crescent Societies
P.O. Box 372
CH-1211 Geneva 19
Switzerland
http://www.ifrc.org/publicat/wdr2009/index.asp

This report is the only annual report focusing on disasters—from earthquakes to epidemics and conflict to economic crises—and on the millions of people affected by them.

World Refugee Survey
U.S. Committee for Refugees
2231 Crystal Drive, Suite 350

Arlington, VA 22202-3711
http://www.wiley.com/bw/journal.asp?ref=0197-9183

World Refugee Survey is an indispensable annual survey that identifies and reviews refugee problems in the world and provides authoritative statistics.

Important Document Sources

International Migration Outlook
Organization for Economic Cooperation and Development
2 rue André-Pascal, 75116
Paris
France
http://www.oecd.org/dataoecd/30/13/41275373.pdf

This annual publication has articles and important statistical information on migration flows into the industrialized states of the world.

Refugee Report
Bureau for Refugee Resettlement
Administration for Children and Families
U.S. Department of Health and Human Services
Aerospace Building
901 D Street, S.W.
Washington, DC 20447
http://www.acf.hhs.gov/programs/orr/data/arc.htm

This is the official annual report to Congress concerning the world refugee situation.

Refugee Survey Quarterly
Center for Documentation on Refugees
United Nations High Commissioner for Refugees (UNHCR)
Case Postale 2500
1211-Geneva 2 Dépôt
Switzerland
http://rsq.oxfordjournals.org

This quarterly lists the abstracts of many of the publications about refugees. In addition, it contains a selection of country reports and a section on refugee- or human rights-related legal documentation.

Sri Lanka Monitor
The Refugee Council
3 Bondway
London SW8 1SJ
England
http://brcslproject.gn.apc.org

Sri Lanka Monitor contains information about Tamil refugees and developments in Sri Lanka affecting refugee flows.

The State of World Population
UN Population Fund
220 East 42nd Street
New York, NY 10017
http://www.unfpa.org/swp

This annual publication discusses world population growth and related problems, and it contains useful statistics. UN Population Fund also publishes: *World Population Trends, Reports, World Foreign-Born Populations*, and *World Migration Studies*.

Reference Works

This section provides a select listing of key reference resources that are useful in the study of refugees. Although some of the titles may not deal specifically with refugees, they are included here because they have sections on refugees or are valuable introductions to refugee-related issues.

Aitchison, Jean. *International Thesaurus of Refugee Terminology.* **Dordrecht, Netherlands: Martinus Nijhoff, 1989. 476 p. ISBN 0-7923-0504-3.**

This thesaurus covers a wide range of subjects central to or impinging on the field of refugees. It is intended for use by organizations that are active in documentation work concerning refugees.

American Immigrant Lawyers Association. *The Law of Asylum: A Manual for Practitioners and Adjudicators.* **Washington, DC: American Immigrant Lawyers Association, 1989. 81 p.**

An indispensable resource for lawyers involved in asylum work, this resource analyzes and explains the legal basis for asylum, the withholding of deportation and application processes, cessation of asylum status, the rights of applicants, and the handling of persecution claims.

Refugees in Africa. Berlin: Edition Parabolis, 1993. 140 p.

This bibliography includes the major works on refugee movements in Africa.

Refugees in Asia and Australia/Oceania. Berlin: Edition Parabolis, 1992. 144 p.

This is a listing of 1,283 titles covering refugee movements in Asia and Australasia since the end of World War II.

Refugees in Latin America and the Caribbean. Berlin: Edition Parabolis, 1993. 140 p.

This is a bibliography of the research on refugees in Latin America and the Caribbean.

Refugees in Northern America. Berlin: Edition Parabolis, 1993. 300 p.

This listing of books, articles, research reports, dissertations, and reports of aid agencies on refugee issues covers all of North America.

Refugees in Western Europe. Berlin: Edition Parabolis, 1992. 176 p.

Refugees in Western Europe lists the literature on the refugee and asylum issue in Western Europe, excluding Germany. It includes studies on refugee movements, immigration and asylum policy, the social situation of refugees, and their integration and legal status.

Boyer, Laura M. *The Older Generation of Southeast Asian Refugees, An Annotated Bibliography.* Minneapolis, MN: Southeast Asian Refugee Studies Project, Center for Urban and Regional Affairs, University of Minnesota, 1991. 61 p.

This is an annotated listing of sources on older Southeast Asian refugees.

Center for Human Rights, United Nations. *Human Rights Bibliography: United Nations Documents and Publications, 1980–1990.* New York: United Nations, 1993. 5 volumes. ISBN 92-1-100377-6.

This bibliography presents all UN instruments, documents, and publications on human rights.

Center for the Study of Human Rights, Columbia University, New York. *Human Rights: A Topical Bibliography.* Boulder, CO: Westview Press, 1983. 297 p. ISBN 0-86531-571-X.

A bibliography consisting of scholarly books and articles on human rights, *Human Rights* draws primarily from the disciplines of law, the social sciences, and philosophy. It includes a list of the agencies that provide documentary resource materials on a continuing basis.

Central America Refugee Policy Research Project. *Sourcebook on Central American Refugee Policy: A Bibliography.* Austin, TX: Lyndon B. Johnson School of Public Affairs, University of Texas, 1985. 68 p.

This bibliography contains almost 800 items, including books, articles, newsletters, and other reports and resources on Central American refugees.

Davies, Julian, and Refugee Studies Programme, University of Oxford. *Displaced Peoples and Refugee Studies, A Resource Guide.* London: Hans Zell Publishers, 1990. 219 p. ISBN 0-905450-76-0.

This resource guide includes a comprehensive and well-annotated list of manuals, reference works, periodicals, dissertations, and books. There are also useful directories of libraries, documentation centers, research and teaching centers, and organizations concerned with all aspects of the refugee issue, arranged alphabetically by country of location.

Enrostat. *Asylum Seekers and Refugees: A Statistical Report.* Luxembourg: Office for Official Publications of the European Communities, 1994. 157 p. ISBN 92-826-7623-4.

This publication is an important resource of statistics providing up-to-date figures on asylum-seekers and refugees for the European Union and European Free Trade Association countries.

Fenton, Thomas, and Mary Heffron, eds. *Third World Resource Directory.* Maryknoll, NY: Orbis Books, 1984. 283 p. ISBN 0-88344-509-3.

This comprehensive resource guide is divided into geographical areas and themes. It covers resources, organizations, and printed and audiovisual materials.

Hammond, Ruth E., and Glenn L. Hendricks, eds. *Southeast Asian Refugee Youth: An Annotated Bibliography.* Minneapolis, MN: Southeast Asian Refugee Studies Project, Center for Urban and Regional Affairs, University of Minnesota, 1988. 143 p. Publication No. CURA 88-2.

This annotated bibliography lists 372 works about Southeast Asian young people who are refugees in the United States.

Human Rights Internet. *Africa: Human Rights Directory and Bibliography.* Ottawa: Human Rights Internet, University of Ottawa, 1989. 304 p. ISBN 0-939338-04-1.

This directory of human rights organizations in Africa is concerned with human rights and social justice.

Human Rights Directory: Eastern Europe. Ottawa: Human Rights Internet, University of Ottawa, 1987. 210 p. ISBN 0-939338-03-3.

This resource lists organizations in Eastern Europe that are working on human rights and social justice.

Human Rights Directory: Latin America and the Caribbean. Ottawa: Human Rights Internet, University of Ottawa, 1990. 526 p. ISBN 0-939338-05-X.

This directory describes nearly 800 organizations concerned with human rights and humanitarian issues in Latin America and the Caribbean. Available in English and Spanish, it is an excellent source for networking, research, and policymaking.

Human Rights Directory: North America. Ottawa: Human Rights Internet, University of Ottawa, 1984. 300 p. ISBN 0-939338-02-5.

This directory lists organizations in North America concerned with human rights and social justice.

Human Rights Directory: Western Europe. Ottawa: Human Rights Internet, University of Ottawa, 1982. 335 p. ISBN 0-939338-01-7.

This directory focuses on organizations in Western Europe that deal with human rights and social justice issues.

International Committee of the Red Cross (ICRC). *Bibliography of International Humanitarian Law Applicable in Armed Conflicts.* Geneva: ICRC and Henry Dunant Institute, 1987. 605 p. ISBN 2-88044-017-3.

An indispensable bibliography, this book covers international humanitarian law, international armed conflicts, non-international armed conflicts, and protection of noncombatants in warfare.

International Refugee Integration Resource Centre. *International Bibliography of Refugee Literature.* Geneva: IRIRC, 1985. 152 p.

This bibliography includes 850 titles covering refugee situations according to the following categories: international organizations, exodus, asylum, resettlement, and integration.

Newman, Frank, and David Weissbrodt, eds. *Selected International Human Rights Instruments.* Cincinnati: Anderson Publishing Co., 1990. 812 p. ISBN 0-87084-368-0.

This handbook lists and describes the principal international human rights instruments.

Refugee Studies Programme, University of Oxford. *The Directory of Research on Refugees and Other Forced Migrants.* 3d ed. Oxford, UK: Refugee Studies Programme, 1993. 184 p. ISBN 0-9512260-0-2.

This directory contains information on the research and publications of about 400 scholars working in the refugee field. It gives the cultural origin, discipline, and research topic for each entry and provides telephone and fax numbers where applicable. Cross-referencing is facilitated by lists based on geographical area and discipline of each person listed.

Segal, Aaron. *An Atlas of International Migration.* London: Hans Zell, 1993. 233 p. ISBN 1-873836-30-9.

This atlas details various kinds of migration patterns and their effects on sending and receiving countries. It contains much useful documentation.

Schorr, Alan. *Refugee and Immigrant Resource Directory, 1990–1991.* Juneau, AK: Denali Press, 1990. 349 p. ISBN 0-938737-19-8.

This invaluable resource includes information on 958 local, regional, and national organizations, research centers, academic programs, foundations, museums, government agencies, and other groups in the United States that offer services or provide information about refugees and immigrants.

United Nations High Commissioner for Refugees (UNHCR). *Collection of International Instruments concerning Refugees.* Geneva: UNHCR, 1979. 335 p.

This is a collection of the international legal instruments (concerning refugees, stateless persons, and human rights), regional legal instruments (for Africa, Europe, and the Americas), and other instruments.

UNHCR. *Conclusions on the International Protection of Refugees Adopted by the Executive Committee on International Protection of Refugees of the UNHCR Program.* Geneva: UNHCR, 1980. 91 p.

This compendium comprises the conclusions on the international protection of refugees as adopted by UNHCR's Executive Committee up to 1980.

UNHCR Centre for Documentation on Refugees and Refugee Policy Group. *Bibliography on Refugee Children.* Geneva: UNHCR, 1987. 138 p.

This is an annotated bibliography on refugee children categorized under protection and assistance; national policies; refugee camps; placement and fostering; integration; education; health; and psychological problems.

UNHCR. *Bibliography on Refugee Women.* Geneva: UNHCR, 1989. 122 p.

This annotated bibliography focuses on current research on refugee women and is arranged geographically.

UNHCR. *Bibliography Prepared for the Excom Working Group on Solutions and Protection.* Geneva: UNHCR, 1990. 85 p.

This is an annotated bibliography of literature on refugees divided into four sections: (1) refugee and related migratory movements; (2) solutions; (3) early warning and prevention; and (4) refugee law and policies.

UNHCR Liaison Section with Non-Governmental Organizations. *Directory of Non-Governmental Organizations.* Geneva: UNHCR, 1992. 240 p.

This directory contains the names and addresses of over 500 institutions working with refugees and asylum-seekers.

Williams, Carolyn. *An Annotated Bibliography on Refugee Mental Health.* Washington, DC: Department of Health and Human Services, 1987. 335 p. DHHS Publication No. (ADM) 87-1517.

This bibliography of 666 items is organized under four main headings: (1) understanding refugees in context; (2) specific mental health issues and refugees; (3) concerns of selected subgroups of refugees; and (4) other bibliographies on refugees or related topics.

Books

Adelman, Howard, ed. 1991. *Refugee Policy: Canada and the United States.* Toronto: York Lanes Press.

This book, a collection of papers presented at a conference at York University in 1990, compares the refugee policies of Canada and the United States. It includes contributions by many of the leading North American researchers in refugee studies and has chapters on the normative and political aspects of refugee policy, root causes, refugee relief and development assistance, refugee law and practice, and resettlement policies.

Agier, Michel. 2008. *On the Margins of the World: The Refugee Experience Today.* Cambridge, UK: Polity Press.

This provides a look at the refugee phenomenon from the vantage point of an anthropologist who has long studied exiled peoples.

Alborzi, M. R. 2006. *Evaluating the Effectiveness of International Refuge Law: The Protection of Iraqi Refugees.* **Leiden, Netherlands: Martinus Nijhoff Publishers.**

This book uses the current refugee crisis in Iraq to analyze the effectiveness (or ineffectiveness) of the 1951 Refugee Convention.

Baines, Erin K. 2004. *Vulnerable Bodies: Gender, the UN, and the Global Refugee Crisis.* **Burlington, VT: Ashgate Publishing Company.**

Employing a comparative analysis of Bosnia, Rwanda, and Guatemala, Baines explores the ravages of the refugee experience from an international, national, and local level.

Baker, Ron, ed. 1983. *The Psychological Problems of Refugees.* **London: The British Refugee Council.**

As the title indicates, this book provides important data and analysis on the myriad of mental health problems experienced by almost every single refugee.

Bariagaber, Assefaw. 2006. *Conflict and the Refugee Experience: Flight, Exile, and Repatriation in the Horn of Africa.* **Burlington, VT: Ashgate Publishing Company.**

This book uses the conflicts in the Horn of Africa to provide an important analysis of the seemingly never-ending mass migrations in this part of the world.

Basoglu, Metin. 1992. *Torture and Its Consequences.* **Cambridge: Cambridge University Press.**

Basoglu gives an account of victims of torture, many of whom are refugees, and the challenges of providing treatment for these individuals.

Beatrice, Marie, and Umutesi Madison. 2000. *Surviving the Slaughter: the Ordeal of a Rwandan Refugee in Zaire.* **Madison: University of Wisconsin Press.**

Surviving the Slaughter: The Ordeal of a Rwandan Refugee in Zaire provide an important micro-level analysis of the horrific experience of Marie Béatrice Umutesi, a Hutu woman from Rwanda who had fled to a refugee camp in Zaire.

Bixler, Mark. 2005. *The Lost Boys of Sudan: an American Story of the Refugee Experience*. Athens, GA: University of Georgia Press.

The author provides a first hand account of a group of the "Lost Boys" who land in Atlanta, as they attempt to make a new life for themselves in their new homeland.

Black, Richard, and Khalid Koser, eds. 1999. *The End of the Refugee Cycle?: Refugee Repatriation and Reconstruction*. New York: Berghahn Books.

With the fall of communism in Eastern Europe in the late 1980s and early 1990s, there was renewed enthusiasm for a "new world order" that would translate into greatly reduced refugee flows. The reality, however, has been something altogether different and this volume explains how and why this is.

Bookman, Milica Zarkovic. 2002. *After Involuntary Migration: The Political Economy of Refugee Encampments*. Lanham, MD: Lexington Books.

As increasing numbers of refugees are being "warehoused," scholars such as Bookman are beginning to study the inner workings of these new refugee communities.

Bramwell, Anna, ed. 1987. *Refugees in the Age of Total War: Twentieth Century Case-Studies of Refugees in Europe and the Middle East*. London: Unwin Hyman.

These 20 chapters analyze refugee movements in Europe and the Middle East generated by the two world wars and their aftermaths. They also examine the responses of international organizations and governments to the movements.

Bread for the World Institute on Hunger and Development. 1992. *Hunger 1993: Uprooted People*. Washington, DC: Bread for the World Institute on Hunger and Development.

This book focuses on the special circumstances of refugees and displaced people and the problems of hunger and malnutrition.

It is a useful overview of the issues and contains many helpful tables and graphs, as well as a bibliography.

Byrne, Rosemary, Gregor Noll, and Jens Vedsted-Hansen, eds. *New Asylum Countries?: Migration Control and Refugee Protection in an Enlarged European Union.*

The book focuses on the rapid expansion of the European Union and analyzes how this might transform the nature of refugee protection throughout Europe.

Cahill, Kevin, ed. 1993. *A Framework for Survival: Health, Human Rights, and Humanitarian Assistance in Conflicts and Disasters.* **New York: Basic Books and the Council on Foreign Relations.**

This book, with 20 chapters by practitioners, focuses on legal and economic issues, health issues, and the responses of private voluntary agencies and the United Nations to humanitarian crises. It illustrates the interdependence of conflict, famine, health care, and refugee crises and underscores the importance of a comprehensive approach to these problems.

Cohen, Roberta and Frances Deng. 1998. *Masses in Flight: The Global Crisis of Internal Displacement.* **Washington DC: Brookings Institute.**

Masses in Flight was one of the earliest treatments of the IDP phenomenon and it remains a seminal text on the subject.

Collinson, Sarah. 1993. *Beyond Borders: West European Migration Policy towards the 21st Century.* **London: Royal Institute of International Affairs and Wyndham Place Trust.**

This book focuses on some of the major policy challenges confronting European governments: immigrant integration, immigration controls, proposals to alleviate the root causes of migration, and refugee and asylum policies.

Collinson, Sarah. 1993. *Europe and International Migration.* **London: Pinter Publishers.**

This book highlights elements of continuity and change in European states' involvement in migration policies. It places the problem of migration within an international, historical process and focuses on the integration of immigrant and ethnic minorities. Finally, it discusses Europe's efforts to harmonize their asylum and migration policies.

Crew, Linda. 1991. *Children of the River.* **New York: Dell Publishing.**

Children of the River is a novel for young adults about Sundra, a teenage Cambodian refugee, who is torn between her loyalty to her family and cultural traditions and her love for an American boy.

Damrosch, Lori. 1993. *Enforcing Restraint: Collective Intervention in Internal Conflicts.* **New York: Council on Foreign Relations Press.**

This is a collection of case studies—from the former Yugoslavia, Somalia, Haiti, Liberia, and Cambodia—that examines the efforts by the international community to intervene to end political conflict and provide humanitarian relief in the post-Cold War era.

Deng, Francis. 1993. *Protecting the Dispossessed: A Challenge for the International Community.* **Washington, DC: The Brookings Institution.**

This book details the difficulties the international community confronts trying to protect the approximately 25 million internally displaced people in the world today. It includes case studies from the former Yugoslavia, Russia, Somalia, Sudan, El Salvador, and Cambodia.

Dowty, Alan. 1987. *Closed Borders: The Contemporary Assault on Freedom of Movement.* **New Haven, CT: Yale University Press.**

Dowty traces how different governments throughout history have dealt with populations both entering and exiting their countries and explores the reasons for past and present government policies designed to restrict entry. He also analyzes the political and economic consequences of such policies and argues for a policy of open borders that would allow individuals to emigrate or immigrate at will.

Druke, Louise. 1990. *Preventive Action for Refugee-Producing Situations.* **Frankfurt: Peter Lang.**

Preventive Action for Refugee-Producing Situations examines situations where refugees are exploited as a weapon for political purposes and suggests ways to prevent situations that lead to refugee flows.

Ebadi, Shirin. 2008. *Refugee Rights in Iran*. Berkeley: University of California Press.

Ebadi is the winner of the 2003 Nobel Peace Prize and her book chronicles the lack of refugee protection for Afghan refugees in Iran.

Feller, Erika, Volker Turk, and Frances Nicholson, eds. 2003. *Refugee Protection in International Law: UNHCR's Global Consultations on International Protection*. Cambridge: Cambridge University Press.

The book provides some of the expert opinions that are part of the UNHCR's Global Consultations on International Protection.

Ferris, Elizabeth. 1993. *Beyond Borders: Refugees, Migrants and Human Rights in the Post–Cold War Era*. Geneva: World Council of Churches Publications.

This book examines the international context within which forced migration occurs and discusses the role of international organizations, governments, and nongovernmental organizations in assisting and protecting refugees.

Forbes Martin, Susan. 2004. *Refugee Women*. 2nd edition. Lanham, MD: Lexington Books.

This book focuses on the particular circumstances of refugee women and shows how they have to cope with additional traumas, such as rape.

Foster, Michelle. 2007. *International Refugee Law and Socioeconomic Rights: Refuge from Deprivation*. Cambridge: Cambridge University Press.

This book questions the theoretical justifications for making such a sharp distinction between civil and political rights and economic, social and cultural rights and questions the manner in which the Refugee Convention applies to the former but not the latter.

Frank, Anne. 1990. *The Diary of a Young Girl*. New York: Random House.

This is the remarkable story of a young Jewish girl and two families who hid from the Nazis in a house in Amsterdam from 1942 to 1944. It is a poignant account of the thoughts and expressions of a young teenager living under extraordinarily difficult conditions.

Gallagher, Dennis, ed. 1986. *Refugees: Issues and Directions. International Migration Review*. Volume 20. New York: Center for Migration Studies.

This is a special edition of the *International Migration Review* dealing with refugees. Eighteen essays by refugee specialists analyze the causes and characteristics of refugee movements worldwide, asylum and protection issues, refugee issues in developing countries, and adjustment and resettlement matters.

Gammeltoft-Hansen, Thomas. 2009. *Access to Asylum: International Refugee Law and the Offshoring and Outsourcing of Migration Control*. Ph.D. thesis, Aarhus University.

The author examines the manner in which Western states have continued to move the asylum experience further and further from their own national borders and it analyzes the legal implications of this.

Gibney, Mark. *Strangers or Friends: Principles for a New Alien Admission Policy*. Westport, CT: Greenwood Press.

This book provides an analysis of the normative basis for a country's alien admission policy—both immigration and refugee—and argues that refugee admissions should be promoted over other national ends such as family reunification and employment-related migration.

Gibney, Mark, ed. 1988. *Open Borders? Closed Societies? The Ethical and Political Questions*. Westport, CT: Greenwood Press.

This collection of essays addresses many of the legal and ethical questions regarding policy on immigration and refugee admissions. Although these issues are of concern to most states, the focus of the authors in this volume is U.S. policy.

Gibney, Mark, and Sigrun Skogly, eds. 2010. *Universal Human Rights and Extraterritorial Obligations*. Philadelphia: University of Pennsylvania Press.

This edited volume examines the extraterritorial application of several areas of human rights including refugee protection.

Gibney, Matthew. 2004. *The Politics and Ethics of Asylum: Liberal Democracy and the Response to Refugees*. Cambridge: Cambridge University Press.

Matthew Gibney provides the most thorough theoretical examination of the moral basis for refugee protection and this is greatly informed by his case studies of state practice in Germany, the United Kingdom, the United States, and Australia.

Gondek, Michal. 2009. *The Reach of Human Rights in a Globalising World: Extraterritorial Application of Human Rights Treaties*. Antwerp: Intersentia.

Gondek provides a detailed and intelligent examination of the geographic scope of the leading international human rights treaties.

Goodwin-Gill, Guy. 1996. *The Refugee in International Law*. 2nd Edition. Oxford, UK: Clarendon Press.

This is a classic sourcebook for international refugee law. It describes the framework of refugee law and covers the definitions of terms such as refugee, refoulement, refugee asylum, and refugee protection. The author examines the evolution and effectiveness of treaties and organizations, state policies, and responsibilities, and he includes an appendix of key texts.

Gordenker, Leon. 1987. *Refugees in International Politics*. New York: Columbia University Press.

This study explores the nature of forced migration and sets forth a framework that examines the causes of refugee movements. The author also covers the responses of states and international organizations to refugee flows and examines the traditional solutions—repatriation, local resettlement, and third-country resettlement—to refugee incidents. The study concludes with recommendations regarding early warning and a preventive framework for dealing with future refugee flows.

Gorman, R. F. 1987. *Coping with Africa's Refugee Burden: A Time for Solutions*. Dordrecht, Netherlands: Martinus Nijhoff.

This book focuses on the recommendations of the Second International Conference on Assistance to Refugees in Africa (ICARA II). The author analyzes the policies, organizational constraints, and roles of international agencies, governments, and nongovernmental organizations in responding to the refugee crisis, as well as the related development needs of host countries.

Grahl-Madsen, Atle. 1966. *The Status of Refugees in International Law*. Leyden, Netherlands: A. W. Sijthoff.

This two-volume work investigates the international framework of refugee law. It examines refugee status determination, refugee definitions, refugee rights and obligations, and international and national law.

Haddad, Emma. 2008. *The Refugee in International Society: Between Sovereigns*. Cambridge: Cambridge University Press.

Emma Haddam employs an historical analysis to analyze the depiction of the "refugee" and to explore the whole notion of the "refugee problem."

Hakovirta, H. 1986. *Third World Conflicts and Refugeeism: Dimensions, Dynamics and Trends of the World Refugee Problem*. Helsinki: Finnish Society of Science and Letters.

This study attempts to develop a social science model for analyzing the causes, dimensions, trends, and consequences of contemporary refugee movements.

Hannum, H. 1987. *The Right To Leave and Return in International Law and Practice*. Leyden, Netherlands: Martinus Nijhoff.

This study examines the international formulation, historical evolution, and jurisprudence of the right to leave and return. The author also analyzes state practice toward the right to movement in various countries throughout the world.

Hansen, Art, and A. Oliver-Smith, eds. 1982. *Involuntary Migration and Resettlement: The Problems and Responses of Dislocated People*. Boulder, CO: Westview Press.

This volume examines a number of migration and resettlement schemes. The authors look at individual, group, and state reactions to the stresses of involuntary dislocation and resettlement and compare these to the stresses of voluntary migration.

Harrell-Bond, Barbara. 1986. *Imposing Aid: Emergency Assistance to Refugees.* **Oxford, UK: Oxford University Press.**

This study appraises the assistance program mounted by international agencies in response to an emergency influx of Ugandan refugees into Sudan starting in early 1982. Using the findings of this case study, the author questions the effectiveness of current refugee assistance strategies. In particular, the book argues that relief workers easily become part of the problem they set out to solve and finds that in the search for solutions, the needs and skills of refugees are often overlooked.

Hathaway, James. 1991. *The Law of Refugee Status.* **Toronto: Butterworths.**

This book explains the scope of the definition of the term refugee as embodied in the United Nations Convention Relating to the Status of Refugees (1951) and as it has evolved in practice. This is an excellent resource for international refugee law and is particularly useful to those concerned about the legal determination of refugee status.

Hathaway, James. 2005. *The Rights of Refugees Under International Law.* **Cambridge: Cambridge University Press.**

This work immediately gained its status as one of the leading treaties on international refugee law.

Hitchcox, Linda. 1990. *Refugees.* **New York: Franklin Watts.**

One of the "Issues" series on current problems, this work is aimed at primary school children. It uses text, maps, and photographs to present the subject and includes a section on refugee children, a page of useful facts and statistics, and an index.

Holborn, Louise W. 1956. *The International Refugee Organization: A Specialized Agency of the United Nations, Its History and Work, 1946–1952.* **Oxford, UK: Oxford University Press.**

This book details the history and activities of the United Nations' first refugee organization, the International Refugee Organization, between 1946 and 1952.

Holborn, Louise. 1975. *Refugees: A Problem of Our Time: The Work of the United Nations High Commissioner for Refugees.* **Metuchen, NJ: Scarecrow Press.**

These two volumes detail the history of the first 20 years of the Office of the United Nations High Commissioner for Refugees (UNHCR). Considered to be the official history of the early development of UNHCR, it contains extensive country-by-country case studies and provides useful historical documentation.

Holm, Anne. 1965. *North to Freedom.* **San Diego, CA: Harcourt Brace Jovanovich.**

This novel for young adults recounts the story of David, a 12-year-old boy, who escapes from a prison camp in Eastern Europe during the Cold War and makes his way on foot across Europe until he finds freedom.

Independent Commission on International Humanitarian Issues. 1986. *Refugees: Dynamics of Displacement.* **London: Zed Books.**

This is the official report on refugees from the Independent Commission on International Humanitarian Issues. The report focuses on mass expulsion, forcible relocation programs, and internally displaced people. It also highlights the increasingly restrictive policies of Western governments toward asylum-seekers, the responsibilities of governments worldwide in causing involuntary migration, and the inadequacy of international law in the prevention and resolution of problems of involuntary migration.

Joly, Daniele, Clive Nettleton, and H. Poulton. 1992. *Refugees: Asylum in Europe?* **London: Minority Rights Publications.**

This book examines the causes of refugee flight in both Western and Eastern Europe, the acceptance and settlement of refugees, international conventions and state legislation, and the racist backlash against refugees. It suggests how individuals, organizations, and governments can protect and assist refugees.

Kent, Randolph. 1987. *The Anatomy of Disaster Relief: The International Network in Action.* **London: Pinter Publishers.**

This study analyzes the causes and consequences of disasters, including man-made ones, and investigates the structure of the international disaster relief process. The author discusses specifically the role of international organizations and governments. He argues that some disaster relief aid is ineffective because many aid workers have skills unsuited to the disaster environment, pay little attention to the culture and traditions of aid recipients, and fail to learn from earlier mistakes.

Kibreab, Gaim. 1985. *African Refugees: Reflections on the African Refugee Problem.* **Trenton, NJ: Red Sea Press.**

This work critically examines assumptions about refugee rehabilitation in African host countries and suggests the adoption of measures to make refugees active and useful participants in the development process.

Kidd, Diana. 1989. *Onion Tears.* **New York: Orchard Books.**

This novel for young readers tells the story of Nam-Houng, a Vietnamese refugee, and the difficult adjustments she has to make integrating into her new homeland in the United States.

Koehn, Peter. 1991. *Refugees from Revolution: U.S. Policy and Third World Migration.* **Boulder, CO: Westview Press.**

This study examines the causes of recent refugee migrations to the United States and the underlying connections between U.S. foreign and domestic policies regarding immigration, refugee resettlement, and human rights. The author focuses on Cuban, Indochinese, Ethiopian, Eritrean, and Iranian exile communities in the United States and examines their treatment under U.S. policy, their social and economic adaptation, and the factors that influence their decisions to return home.

Kourula, Pirkko. 1997. *Broadening the Edges: Refugee Definition and International Protection Revisited.* **The Hague: Martinus Nijhoff Publishers.**

Broadening the Edge attempts to place international refugee law and protection within the broader realm of international law and international relations.

Kritz, Mary, ed. 1983. *U.S. Immigration and Refugee Policy: Global and Domestic Issues*. Lexington, MA: D. C. Heath.

This book is an anthology of many theoretical and policy issues that confront scholars concerned with international migration. The editor stresses the importance of identifying the causes of population flows.

Kunz, Egon F. 1988. *Displaced Persons: Calwell's New Australians*. Sydney: Australian National University Press.

This history details Australia's immigration policy during and after World War II, when displaced Estonians, Latvians, Lithuanians, Poles, Ukranians, Russians, Czechs, Slovaks, Hungarians, Croats, Serbs, and Bulgarians were transported to Australia to increase its population and work force.

Lake, Anthony, et al., eds. 1991. *After the Wars: Reconstruction in Afghanistan, Indochina, Central America, Southern Africa and the Horn of Africa*. New Brunswick, NJ: Transaction Publishers.

Five policy analysts examine the political and economic costs of rebuilding the regions that experienced geopolitical rivalries and long-standing and destructive wars during the 1980s. Policy suggestions include creating an international fund to finance the reconstruction of war-torn areas of the Third World.

Larkin, Mary Ann, Frederick Cuny, and Barry Stein. 1991. *Repatriation under Conflict in Central America*. Washington, DC, and Dallas: Georgetown University and Intertecht.

This multi-authored volume examines the issue of repatriation in Central America. Experts examine the motivations of Salvadoran, Guatemalan, and Nicaraguan refugees from their initial flight through repatriation. Conditions in exile and at home, as well as assistance policies, are analyzed in light of their influence on the repatriation decision.

Lawless, Richard, and Laila Monahan, eds. 1987. *War and Refugees: The Western Sahara Conflict*. London: Pinter Publishers.

This is a study of the Western Sahara conflict and the long-standing refugee problem it created. The book analyzes the economic and political interests behind the war and the legal basis for occupation by Morocco, and it describes the life of a largely forgotten group of refugees.

Lischer, Sarah Kenyon. 2005. *Dangerous Sanctuaries: Refugee Camps, Civil War, and the Dilemmas of Humanitarian Aid.* Ithaca, NY: Cornell University Press.

One of the things that hinders refugee protection is the concern that aid and assistance is being provided to so-called "refugee warriors." Sarah Kenyon Lischer's book is an attempt to systematically study this phenomenon.

Loescher, Gil. 1993. *Beyond Charity: International Cooperation and the Global Refugee Crisis.* New York: Oxford University Press.

This book is an extensive overview of the global refugee situation in the post-Cold War era. The author presents the contemporary crisis in a historical framework, examining both the rise of refugee problems in the last 70 years and the roles of international agencies, particularly the UNHCR, in responding to those problems. The book concludes with short- and long-term measures that might help address various aspects of the refugee problem.

Loescher, Gil. 1992. *Refugee Movements and International Security.* Adelphi Paper 268. London: Brassey's for International Institute for Strategic Studies.

This study examines the relationship between refugee movements and national and international security in the post-Cold War period. The author offers an overview of the contemporary refugee situation, outlines the political and strategic causes and consequences of refugee flows, and suggests a policy framework for dealing with the global refugee problem.

Loescher, Gil, ed. 1992. *Refugees and the Asylum Dilemma in the West.* University Park, PA: Pennsylvania State University Press.

This book examines the historical background and contemporary significance of the asylum and refugee issue confronting Western governments and draws lessons for future policymaking. Seven experts look at asylum policy in the United States, Canada, and Western Europe and the development of an international response to the global refugee problem.

Loescher, Gil, Alexander Betts, and James Milner. 2008. *The United Nations High Commissioner for Refugees (UNHCR): The Politics and Practice of Refugee Protection into the Twenty-First Century.* **New York: Routledge**.

Written by a group of refugee experts, this book examines the relationship between states, international relations, and the United Nations, especially the Office of the High Commissioner for Refugees.

Loescher, Gil, and Ann Loescher. 1982. *The World's Refugees, A Test of Humanity.* **San Diego, CA: Harcourt Brace Jovanovich**.

Written for high school students and the uninitiated, this book provides an insightful introduction to the world refugee problem. It looks at what life is like for refugees in different regions of the world and at the international response to the problem. It also includes useful appendixes.

Loescher, Gil, and James H. S. Milner. 2005. *Protracted Refugee Situations: Domestic and International Security Implications.* **New York: Routledge**.

This book is one of the first systematic studies of "warehousing" of refugees and all the social, political, and security dislocations that this has brought about.

Loescher, Gil, and Laila Monahan, eds. 1989. *Refugees and International Relations.* **Oxford, UK: Oxford University Press**.

This study contains 17 essays by experts in the field of refugee protection and assistance. It examines the international context and the political, legal, and economic dimensions of the global refugee problem, as well as the search for appropriate policy responses to this growing problem. Among the specific subjects addressed are military attacks on refugee camps, voluntary repatriation, restrictionism in Europe, women refugees, the role of the churches, the future of third-country settlement, and the problems of development and repatriation.

Loescher, Gil, and John Scanlan. 1986. *Calculated Kindness: Refugee and America's Half-Open Door 1945–Present.* **New York: Free Press**.

This study documents the political history of American refugee policy from 1945 until 1986. The authors focus on the factors that have influenced the refugee admissions policy of the United States: Cold War foreign policy that views refugees as symbols and instruments of anti-communism, restrictionist forces that contend that refugees are difficult to assimilate and that they take jobs away from Americans, religious and ethnic groups that lobby for displaced persons and co-ethnics abroad, and humanitarian interests that advocate admission for persecuted groups and individuals abroad.

Loescher, Gil, and John Scanlan, eds. 1983. *The Global Refugee Problem: U.S. and World Response.* **Special Issue of the Annals of American Academy of Political and Social Science 467. Beverly Hills, CA: Sage Publications**.

This collection of 13 essays by leading experts in the field addresses the causes and consequences of refugee movements in the United States and the world as they appeared in the early 1980s. Chapters focus on the scope of the problem, the international framework, the politics of refugee flows, and legal and resettlement issues.

Macalister-Smith, Peter. 1985. *International Humanitarian Assistance: Disaster Relief Action in International Law and Organisation.* **Dordrecht, Netherlands: Martinus Nijhoff**.

This book details the legal principles and instruments applied in historical and contemporary relief operations, with particular reference to the operations of the International Committee of the Red Cross, the Federation of Red Cross and Red Crescent Societies, and various agencies of the United Nations, including the UNHCR. It also offers suggestions about how to improve the implementation of international humanitarian norms.

Marrus, Michael R. 1985. *The Unwanted: European Refugees in the Twentieth Century.* **Oxford, UK: Oxford University Press**.

This book tells the story of the refugee problem throughout the twentieth century, particularly during the Nazi era. It examines the impact of refugee movements on the conduct of international relations and diplomacy, outlines the growth of international agencies designed to help refugees, and assesses the work of those agencies.

Martin, David A., ed. 1989. *The New Asylum-Seekers: Refugee Law in the 1980s.* **Dordrecht, Netherlands: Martinus Nijhoff.**

This book addresses the legal and political issues raised by growing numbers of asylum-seekers and the increasingly restrictive measures introduced by Western governments during the 1980s.

Martin, Susan F., Patricia Weiss Fagen, Kari Jorgensen, Lydia Mann-Bondat, and Andrew Schoenholtz. 2005. *The Uprooted: Improving Humanitarian Responses to Forced Migration.* **Lanham, MD: Lexington Books.**

The Uprooted seeks to provide a broader conception of the forces of forced migration to go beyond the narrow political confines of the international refugee law and it does so through the use of five case studies: Burundi, Colombia, East Timor, Georgia, and Sri Lanka.

Mason, Linda, and Roger Brown. 1983. *Rice, Rivalry and Politics.* **South Bend, IN: University of Notre Dame Press.**

The Khmer Rouge reign of terror and the subsequent invasion of Cambodia by Vietnam generated hundreds of thousands of refugees. This book tells the story of the international relief effort for these people, focusing in particular on the Thai-Cambodian border.

McAdam, Jane. 2007. *Complementary Protection in International Refugee Law.* **Oxford, UK: Oxford University Press.**

This book represents one of the first attempts to systematically study "other" firms of protection short of being granted refugee status under the 1951 Convention.

Mertus, Julie, Jasmina Tesanovic, Habiba Metikos, and Rada Boric, eds. 1997. *The Suitcase: Refugee Voices from Bosnia and Croatia.* **Berkeley: University of California Press.**

This book gives voice to voiceless refugees by simply asking them about themselves, their lives, their suffering—and their aspirations.

Minear, Larry. 1993. *Humanitarian Action in Times of War.* **Boulder, CO: Lynne Rienner.**

This is a handbook for practitioners providing humanitarian relief in armed conflict situations around the world.

Morgan, Scott, and Elizabeth Colson, eds. 1987. *People in Upheaval.* **Staten Island, NY: Center for Migration Studies.**

This collection of 11 essays addresses the issue of displaced people. Key topics include the ambiguity between involuntary and voluntary migration, the interaction of refugees and host communities, the growth of national and international agencies, the support of kin and community, and the effects of resettlement.

Morris, Benny. 1987. *The Birth of the Palestinian Refugee Problem, 1947–1949.* **Cambridge: Cambridge University Press.**

Palestinian refugees constitute one of the oldest continuous refugee problems in the world. This book examines the roots of the Palestinian refugee problem by examining the exodus of 1947 to 1949 in the context of the first Arab-Israeli War. The author analyzes the reasons behind the Palestinian flight and uncovers some new views about it.

Morsink, Johannes. 1999. *The Universal Declaration of Human Rights: Origins, Drafting, and Intent.* **Philadelphia: University of Pennsylvania Press.**

Johannes Morsink's book provides the definitive study of the drafting of the UDHR, which was the genesis of the present-day human rights revolution.

Muntarbhorn, Vitit. 1992. *The Status of Refugees in Asia.* **Oxford, UK: Oxford University Press.**

This work is an analysis of the national laws and regulations concerning the admission and treatment of refugees and aliens in Asia. It provides useful documentation.

Musalo, Karen, Jennifer Moore, and Richard A. Boswell. 2007. *Refugee Law and Policy: A Comparative and International Approach.* **3rd Edition. Durham, NC: Carolina Academic Press.**

This is one of the law school texts commonly used in the United States (and elsewhere) on immigration law.

Naidoo, Beverley, and Kate Holt, eds. 2004. *Making It Home: A Childs Eye of Life As a Refugee*. London: Puffin Books.

These stories are written by refugee children, providing some insight into what the refugee experience is like for the young and the seemingly powerless. What emerges from these stories of both lives of ordinariness but also courage and conviction.

Nichols, Bruce. 1988. *The Uneasy Alliance: Religion, Refugee Work and U.S. Foreign Policy*. New York: Oxford University Press.

U.S. refugee policy has always relied on the successful co-operation of government and voluntary agencies, especially religious groups. This study traces the history of cooperation and conflict between government policy and religious agencies regarding refugee work.

Nichols, Bruce, and Gil Loescher, eds. 1989. *The Moral Nation: Humanitarianism and U.S. Foreign Policy Today*. South Bend, IN: University of Notre Dame Press.

This book critically examines the roles of U.S. government and private agencies in providing relief to human rights victims, refugees, and famine victims. Contributors examine the moral and political philosophy of humanitarianism and its relationship to the conduct of U.S. foreign policy, the political and legal factors involved in the formulation of humanitarian policy, and case studies involving asylum, sanctuary, and famine relief in Central America and the Horn of Africa.

Nicholson, Frances, and Patrick M. Twomey, eds. 1999. *Refugee Rights and Realities: Evolving International Concepts and Regimes*. Cambridge: Cambridge University Press.

This edited collection brings together a number of academics, representatives of NGOs, and policymakers as they systematically analyze the gap between the promise of the 1951 Refugee Convention and the reality of state practice.

Ogata, Sadako N. 2005. *The Turbulent Decade: Confronting the Refugee Crises of the 1990s*. New York: W. W. Norton and Company.

Ogata is the former High Commissioner for Refugees and her book seeks to provide insight into the refugee crises that she faced under her tenure and the rationales for responding as the UNHCR did.

Plender, Richard, ed. 1988. *Basic Documents on International Migration Law.* **Dordrecht, Netherlands: Martinus Nijhoff.**

This book lists the principal international conventions, declarations, and instruments governing the laws of international migration. It includes extracts from some of the instruments governing human rights and full texts of the principal treatises and declarations governing nationality, the protection of refugees, and migrant labor. There are also texts of the principal items of legislation of the European Communities and the instruments adopted by the Council of Europe, the Benelux Community, and the economic communities of West and Central Africa and the Caribbean.

Plender, Richard. 1988. *International Migration Law.* **Dordrecht, Netherlands: Martinus Nijhoff.**

This is a comprehensive review of the rights of aliens under international law. It not only includes chapters on the rights of aliens but also on the powers of states to restrict aliens. The book also includes a table of cases, statutes, and other internal instruments regarding migration.

Ressler, Everett, Neil Boothby, and David Steinbeck. 1987. *Unaccompanied Children: Care and Placement in Wars, Natural Disasters and Refugee Movements.* **Oxford, UK: Oxford University Press.**

This book provides a history of unaccompanied children and the assistance given them in the past. Based upon research conducted on the Thai-Cambodian border, the authors explain child development both within the family and community and outside these frameworks; the major legal issues involved concerning this group; and the roles of international and voluntary organizations.

Rogers, Rosemarie, and Emily Copeland. 1993. *Forced Migration: Policy Issues in the Post–Cold War World.* **Medford, MA: The Fletcher School of Law and Diplomacy, Tufts University.**

This book is a good introduction to many of the policy issues involved in forced migration. It discusses the international political context of population movements and the limitations of traditional responses to refugee problems. It also proposes a more comprehensive approach to refugees for the future. The book has useful tables and references.

Rutter, Jill. 1991. *We Left Because We Had To: An Educational Book for 14–18 Year Olds.* **London: Refugee Council.**

This is an excellent educational resource for teachers offering lessons or courses on refugees. It discusses who refugees are, the causes of refugee movements, and the difficulties most refugees encounter as they resettle into new homelands.

Rutter, Jill. 2003. *Supporting Refugee Children in 21st Century Britain: A Compendium of Essential Information.* **Staffordshire, UK: Trentham Books Limited.**

Using the United Kingdom as the basis of her study, Jill Rutter provides an insightful overview of what refugee children experience.

Schuster, Lisa. 2003. *The Use and Abuse of Political Asylum in Britain and Germany.* **London: Frank Cass Publishers.**

Lisa Schuster provides a provocative account of the manner in which asylum policies have been used as a political tool of Western states who, she argues, were only interested in upholding the principle of asylum when and if it meant that few people could actually file for refugee status in those countries.

Shawcross, William. 1984. *The Quality of Mercy: Cambodia, Holocaust and Modern Conscience.* **New York: Simon & Schuster.**

Written by a British journalist, this book examines the political disputes surrounding the worldwide relief effort aimed at Cambodia from the late 1970s to 1983. William Shawcross tells the story of the workings of major relief agencies such as UNHCR and UNICEF and the political pressures exerted on them by the Thai, Vietnamese, and Western governments, as well as by the coalition government promoted by the various resistance groups within Cambodia.

Simpson, John Hope. 1939. *The Refugee Problem.* **London: Oxford University Press**.

This book is an account written in 1939 of the refugee problems in Europe during the preceding 20 years and of the international community's response to these problems.

Skogly, Sigrun. 2006. *Beyond National Borders: States' Human Rights Obligations in International Cooperation.* **Antwerp: Intersentia**.

Sigrun Skogly's work remains the seminal text on the extraterritorial effect of international human rights law.

Skran, Claudena. 1994. *Refugees in Inter-War Europe.* **Oxford, UK: Clarendon Press**.

An analysis of the refugee problem in Europe from 1921 to 1939, this volume gives a particularly useful account of the growth and evolution of the international community's response to refugees during the interwar period.

Spijkerboer, Thomas. 2000. *Gender and Refugee Status.* **Burlington, VT: Ashgate Publishing Company**.

Focusing on law and practice, this represents the first comprehensive socio-legal study of the interrelation between gender and the law of refugee status.

Steiner, Niklaus. 2000. *Arguing about Asylum: The Complexity of Refugee Debates in Europe.* **New York: St. Martins Press**.

Niklaus Steiner offers an insightful comparative analysis of the legislative debates concerning asylum issues in Switzerland, Germany, and the United Kingdom.

Steiner, Niklaus. 2009. *International Migration and Citizenship Today.* **New York: Routledge**.

The book offers a very readable and succinct analysis of the world's migration issues by focusing on immigrants, refugees, and citizenship and the rise of nationalism.

Steiner, Niklaus, Mark Gibney, and Gil Loescher (ed.). 2003. *Problems of Protection: The UNHCR, Refugees, and Human Rights.* **New York: Routledge.**

Although the volume touches upon a number of different refugee issues, many of the contributions focus on the UNHCR itself and the roles it plays and the obligations it is bound by.

Stoessinger, John. 1956. *The Refugee in the World Community.* **Minneapolis, MN: University of Minnesota Press.**

This book is a history of the International Refugee Organization, which resettled over one million displaced persons between 1947 and 1951, and the motivations of states in accepting large numbers of refugees as immigrants.

Strom, Margot Stern, and William Parsons. 1982. *Facing History and Ourselves: Holocaust and Human Behavior.* **Watertown, MA: Intentional Educations, Inc.**

This educational book, aimed at high school and older students, considers the holocaust of Armenians at the hands of the Ottoman Empire and of Jews at the hands of the Third Reich. An important feature of this book is the material on the social and political attitudes that lead to persecution of minorities and to political tyranny.

Sutter, Valerie. 1990. *The Indochinese Refugee Dilemma.* **Baton Rouge: Louisiana State University Press.**

Between 1975 and 1990, well over 1.5 million refugees poured out of Indochina. This book offers a concise history of the complex national issues surrounding the Indochina refugee problem. It examines the domestic and foreign policy interests of the Indochinese states, Thailand and other Southeast Asian states, China, the United States, and the Soviet Union

Ung, Loung. 2000. *First They Killed My Father: A Daughter of Cambodia Remembers.* **New York: HarperCollins Publishers.**

The author, a survivor of the Cambodia genocide, reflects on the horrors of her country and her life.

Van Arsdale, Peter, W. 2006. *Forced to Flee: Human Rights and Human Wrongs in Refugee Homelands*. Lanham, MD: Lexington Books.

Peter Van Arsdale puts his longstanding first-hand knowledge of forced migration to good use in this volume that combines field work with a significant policy analysis of the world's refugee situation.

Van Selm, Joanne, et al., eds. 2003. *The Refugee Convention at Fifty: A View from Forced Migration Studies*. Lanham, MD: Lexington Books.

The book uses the 50th anniversary of the Refugee Convention to explore what the treaty has achieved, but also where it has not fulfilled its mandate. The book offers a nice blend of work by academics, NGO workers, and international organization professionals.

Vernant, Jacques. 1953. *The Refugee in the Post-War World*. New Haven, CT: Yale University Press.

This is an account of the growth of refugee problems in the early post–World War II period, when large numbers of refugees fled communist regimes in Europe and the Soviet Union.

Walzer, Michael. 1983. *Spheres of Justice: A Defense of Pluralism and Equality*. Oxford, UK: Martin Robertson.

Michael Walzer provides the touchstone for normative analysis of asylum and immigration policy as he sets forth the moral reasoning that should guide the policies of nation-states.

Watters, Charles. 2008. *Refugee Children: Towards the Next Horizon*. New York: Routledge.

Nearly half the refugee and IDPs in the world are children and this book is devoted to providing an in-depth analysis of children who are caught up in this hell.

Weiner, Myron, ed. 1993. *International Migration and Security*. Boulder, CO: Westview Press.

This collection of essays analyzes the security consequences of international population movements. There are individual chapters on Europe, the former Soviet Union, Asia, Africa, and Central America.

White, James D., and Anthony J. Marsella, eds. 2007. *Fear of Persecution: Global Human Rights, International Law, and Human Well-Being*. **Lanham, MD: Lexington Books**.

As the title would suggest, this edited collection places refugee protection within a broader human rights context. Another added feature to this volume is the manner in which it takes up both macro-level and micro-level phenomena.

Williams, Carolyn, and Joseph Westermayer, eds. 1986. *Refugee Mental Health in Resettlement Countries*. **Washington, DC: Hemisphere Publishing Corporation**.

Refugees often suffer trauma and severe psychological problems as a result of being uprooted and displaced. This work summarizes research literature dealing with refugee health problems and explains the acculturation process, highlighting the behavioral and mental health problems of refugees. Case studies include Cambodians, the Falasha of Israel, Laotians, and Cubans. The book also offers suggestions for treatment and assessment.

Woodbridge, George. 1950. *The History of UNRRA*. **New York: Columbia University Press**.

This is a history of the United Nations Relief and Rehabilitation Administration, which provided relief assistance to war victims and displaced people in Europe from 1943 to 1947. The book also recounts the repatriation of East Europeans and Russians after the end of World War II.

Wyman, David. 1985. *The Abandonment of the Jews: America and the Holocaust, 1941–1945*. **New York: Pantheon**.

This is a critical analysis of the failure of the United States to rescue more Jews from certain death in the Holocaust from 1941 to 1945.

Wyman, David. 1968. *Paper Walls: America and the Refugee Crisis 1938–1945*. **Amherst, MA: University of Massachusetts Press**.

This is a moving and critical account of the ineffective and harsh U.S. policy toward Jews in Germany and the rest of Europe during the early years of World War II.

Zolberg, Aristide, Astri Suhrke, and Sergio Aguayo. 1989. *Escape From Violence: Conflict and the Refugee Crisis in the Developing World.* **New York: Oxford University Press.**

This book is one of the most systematic analyses of refugee movements in the Third World up to the late 1980s. The authors attempt a comprehensive, theoretically grounded, structural explanation for refugee movements and highlight the relationship between social conflict and refugee flows. All major regions of the world are covered, except the Middle East, Eastern Europe, and the former Soviet Union.

Zucker, Norman, and Naomi Zucker. 1987. *The Guarded Gate: The Reality of American Refugee Policy.* **San Diego, CA: Harcourt Brace Jovanovich.**

This book tells the story of U.S. refugee and asylum policy up to the mid-1980s. The authors trace the origins of U.S. refugee policy to immigration restrictionism in American history and offer constructive suggestions for reform in refugee and asylum policy.

Zucker, Norman, and Naomi Zucker. 1996. *Desperate Crossings: Seeking Refuge in America.* **Armonk, NY: M. E. Sharpe.**

The Zukers provide a rich and in-depth analysis of American immigration/refugee policy from the beginnings of the Republic.

Selected Articles and Essays

Aleinikoff, T. Alexander. 1991. The Meaning of "Persecution" in United States Asylum Law. *International Journal of Refugee Law* **3: 5–29.**

Anker, Deborah E. 2002. Refugee Law, Gender, and the Human Rights Paradigm. *Harvard Human Rights Journal.*

Barnes, R. 2008. Refugee Law at Sea. *International Journal of Refugee Law.*

Barnett, L. 2002. Global Governance and the Evolution of the International Refugee Regime. *International Journal of Refugee Law.*

Carens, Joseph. 1987. The Case for Open Borders. *The Review of Politics* 49: 251–73.

Chimni, B. S. 1998. The Geopolitics of Refugee Studies: A View from the South. *Journal of Refugee Studies* 4: 350–374.

Gibney, Mark, Vanessa Dalton, and Marc Vockell. 1992. USA Refugee Policy: A Human Rights Analysis Update. *Journal of Refugee Studies* 5: 33–46.

Hailbronner, Kay. 1990. The Right to Asylum and the Future of Asylum. *International Journal of Refugee Law* 3: 341–60.

Helton, Arthur. 1984. Political Asylum under the 1980 Refugee Act: An Unfulfilled Promise. *University of Michigan Journal of Law Reform* 17: 243–264.

Krenz, F. E. 2008. The Refugee as a Subject of International Law. *International and Comparative Law Quarterly*.

Malkki, Lisa H. 1995. Refugees and Exile: From "Refugee Studies" to the National Order of Things. *Annual Review of Anthropology* 24: 495–523.

Martin, David. 1990. Reforming Asylum Adjudication: On Navigating the Coast of Bohemia. *University of Pennsylvania Law Review* 138: 1247–1381.

Montes, Segundo. 1988. Migration to the United States as an Index of the Intensifying Social and Political Crises in El Salvador. *Journal of Refugee Studies* 1: 107–126.

Musalo, Karen. 2007. Protecting Victims of Gendered Persecution: Fear of Floodgates or Call to (Principled) Action? *Virginia Journal of Social Policy* 14: 119.

Ramji-Nogales, Jaya, Andrew Schoenholtz, and Philip G. Schrag. Refugee Roulette: Disparities in Asylum Adjudication. Stanford Law Review, Vol. 60, 2008.

Shacknove, Andrew. 1985. Who is a Refugee? *Ethics* 95:274–284.

Stanley, William. 1987. Economic Migrants or Refugees from Violence? A Time Series Analysis of Salvadoran Migration to the U.S. *The Latin American Research Review* 22: 132–154.

Reports

Amnesty International. *Amnesty International Report*. London: Amnesty International.

This annual report of worldwide human rights violations is produced by a prominent human rights monitoring organization.

Amnesty International. 2007. *Migration Related Detention*.

Burr, Millard. *1993. Sudan 1990–1992: Food Aid, Famine and Failure*. Washington, DC: U.S. Committee for Refugees.

About five million Sudanese have been internally displaced and more than half a million are refugees. This report provides a detailed historical review of Western food relief efforts and diplomatic maneuvering toward Sudan and looks at the Sudanese government policies that have persistently undermined relief efforts.

Canada Immigration and Refugee Board. 1999. *Weighing Evidence*.

Chesnais, Jean-Claude. 1990. *Migration from Eastern to Western Europe, Past (1946–1989) and Future (1990–2000)*. Strasbourg: Council of Europe.

This is an analysis of past and future trends of East-West flows. The main objective of this work is to reduce some of the uncertainty about the potential size of such movements in the future. It includes tables and documentation.

Childers, Erskine, and Brian Urquhart. 1991. *Strengthening International Response to Humanitarian Emergencies*. New York: Ford Foundation.

Two experienced former UN officials propose a comprehensive set of policy recommendations to expedite and make more effective the response of international organizations to humanitarian crises in the post–Cold War era.

Clark, Jeffrey. 1992. *Famine in Somalia and the International Response: Collective Failure*. Washington, DC: U.S. Committee for Refugees.

This paper reviews the history of missed opportunities and strategic and operational blunders in Somalia during 1990–1992.

Cohen, Roberta. 1991. *Human Rights Protection for Internally Displaced Persons.* **Washington, DC: Refugee Policy Group.**

This report analyzes the dimensions of the human rights problems confronting people displaced within their own countries and the lack of national and international protection for these people. It proposes a number of institutional and legal changes that would improve the protection of the internally displaced.

Cohen, Roberta. 1992. *United Nations Human Rights Bodies: An Agenda for Humanitarian Action.* **Washington, DC: Refugee Policy Group.**

This is an analysis of the ways in which United Nations human rights bodies can more effectively respond to the humanitarian problems of the post–Cold War period.

Forbes Martin, Susan. 1989. *Emigration, Immigration and Changing East-West Relations.* **Washington, DC: Refugee Policy Group.**

This report examines the massive flow of refugees from Eastern Europe toward the West in 1989, the policy responses to this situation by Western countries, the movement of refugees within Eastern Europe, and the institutional and policy structures available for dealing with refugee matters.

Frelick, Bill. 1992. *Croatia's Crucible: Providing Asylum for Refugees from Bosnia and Herzegovina.* **Washington, DC: U.S. Committee for Refugees.**

This report discusses the failures of the United Nations, the European Community, and the United States to respond to the humanitarian challenges in the former Yugoslavia.

Georgetown University Law Center, Human Rights Institute Fact Finding Group. 2006. *Unintended Consequences: Refugee Victims of the War on Terror.*

Human Rights Watch. *Human Rights Watch Report.* **New York: Human Rights Watch.**

This annual report by a prominent human rights organization documents human rights violations worldwide.

Human Rights Watch. 2009. *Jailing Refugees.*

Human Rights Watch. 2010. *Genocide, War Crimes, and Crimes Against Humanity.*

INS. 1982. *Asylum Adjudications: An Evolving Concept for the Immigration and Naturalization Service.*

International Crisis Group. 2008. *Failed Responsibility: Iraqi Refugees in Syria, Jordan, and Lebanon.*

International Development Research Centre. 2001. *The Responsibility to Protect: Report of the International Commission on Intervention and State Sovereignty.*

International Displacement Monitoring Center. 2006. *Displaced by the Wall: Forced Displacement as a Result of the West Bank Wall and its Associated Regime.*

International Displacement Monitoring Center. 2009. *Monitoring Disaster Displacement in the Context of Climate Change.*

International Rescue Committee. 2010 *A Tough Road Home: Uprooted Iraqis in Jordan, Syria, and Iraq.*

Jacobson, Jodi. 1988. *Environmental Refugees: A Yardstick of Habitability.* **Washington, DC: World Watch Institute.**

Throughout the world, vast areas are becoming unfit for human habitation. This report argues that the growing number of people fleeing from environmental degradation adds a new dimension to the global refugee problem.

Joly, Daniele, and Clive Nettleton. 1990. *Refugees in Europe.* **London: Minority Rights Group.**

This report offers a useful outline of some of the issues surrounding the current situation faced by refugees in Europe.

Keely, Charles. 1981. *Global Refugee Policy: The Case for a Development Oriented Strategy.* **New York: Population Council.**

This report was one of the first accounts that drew attention to the need to provide refugees with long-term development assistance rather than short-term relief assistance.

Kirk, Robin. 1991. *The Decade of Chaqwa: Peru's Internal Refugees.* **Washington, DC: U.S. Committee for Refugees.**

This report describes the causes of internal displacement in Peru and the plight of indigenous populations at the center of the fighting between the government and guerrillas.

Kirk, Robin. 1993. *Feeding the Tiger: Colombia's Internally Displaced People.* **Washington, DC: U.S. Committee for Refugees.**

Robin Kirk discusses the plight of internally displaced people in Colombia, the causes of their flight, and the inadequacies of the responses by Colombia and the international community.

Lawyers' Committee for International Human Rights. 1990. *The Implementation of the Refugee Act of 1980: A Decade of Experience.* **New York: Lawyers' Committee for International Human Rights.**

This is a critical review of the first 10 years of U.S. asylum policy after the passage of the Refugee Act of 1980.

Lawyers' Committee for International Human Rights. 1990. *Refugee Refoulement: The Forced Return of Haitians under the U.S. Haitian Interdiction Agreement.* **New York: Lawyers' Committee for International Human Rights.**

This report discusses the U.S. policy of interdicting Haitian boat people and returning them to Port-au-Prince.

Lawyers' Committee for International Human Rights. 1991. *Uncertain Haven.* **New York: Lawyers' Committee for International Human Rights.**

A critical assessment of asylum and refugee policy in the 1980s in Asia, Africa, Latin America, Western Europe, and North America, this report also discusses the difficulties confronting the United Nations High Commissioner for Refugees (UNHCR) in providing protection.

Lawyers' Committee for International Human Rights. 1991. *The UNHCR at 40: Refugee Protection at the Crossroads.* **New York: Lawyers' Committee for International Human Rights.**

This report examines the work of the Office of the United Nations High Commissioner for Refugees (UNHCR) at the time of its 40th anniversary. It focuses on the 1980s and discusses the institutional organization of the UNHCR, recent arrangements regarding its funding and oversight by governments, and efforts to work with nongovernmental organizations.

Loescher, Gil. 1993. *Forced Migration within and from the Former USSR: The Policy Challenges Ahead.* **Santa Monica, CA: The Rand Corporation.**

This report examines displacement within the former Soviet Union and the policy challenges it poses to the West. It sets out the range of policy responses that the international community should consider in the future.

Refugees International. 2009. *Nationality Rights for All: A Progress Report and Global Survey on Statelessness.*

Ruiz, Hiram. 1992. *Left Out in the Cold: The Perilous Homecoming of Afghan Refugees.* **Washington, DC: U.S. Committee for Refugees.**

This report analyzes the plight of Afghan refugees who have returned home following the withdrawal of Soviet forces from their country. It also documents the donor countries' poor financial support, which has left returnees, displaced people, and other war victims at risk in Afghanistan.

Ruiz, Hiram. 1993. *Repatriation: Tackling Protection and Assistance Concerns.* **Washington, DC: U.S. Committee for Refugees.**

This report discusses many of the issues surrounding the return home of refugees, in particular the problems of assisting and protecting them.

Ruiz, Hiram. 1993. *El Retorno: Guatemalans' Risky Repatriation Begins.* **Washington, DC: U.S. Committee for Refugees.**

This documents the problems and risks associated with the repatriation of Guatemalan refugees during a time of continued conflict and political uncertainty in Guatemala.

Ruiz, Hiram. 1992. *Uprooted Liberians: Casualties of a Brutal War.* **Washington, DC: U.S. Committee for Refugees.**

This report reviews and analyzes the situation of Liberian refugees both inside their home country and in neighboring Sierra Leone, Guinea, and the Ivory Coast.

Select Commission on Immigration and Refugee Policy. 1981. *U.S. Immigration Policy and the National Interest.*

Tamari, Salim. 1996. Institute for Palestinian Studies. *Palestinian Refugee Negotiations: From Madrid to Oslo II.*

UNHCR. 1993. *Note on International Protection.*

UNHCR. 1998. *Note on Burden and Standard of Proof in Refugee Claims.*

UNHCR. Annual. *The State of the World's Refugees.*

UNHCR. 2006. *Note on HIV and AIDS and the Protection of Refugees, IDPs, and Other Persons of Concern.*

UNHCR. 2007. *The Protection of Internally Displaced Persons and the Role of UNHCR.*

Wasem, Rush Ellen and Karma Ester. Congressional Research Service. 2008. *Temporary Protected Status: Current Immigration Policy and Issues.*

Women's Commission for Refugee Women and Children. 1992. *Balkan Trail of Tears Revisited: Living with the Nightmare.* New York: International Rescue Committee.

This report on former Yugoslavia focuses on the use of rape as a weapon of war and on the current needs of refugee and internally displaced women and children.

Women's Commission for Refugee Women and Children. 1992. *Going Home: the Prospect of Repatriation for Refugee Women and Children.* New York: International Rescue Committee.

This report contains the proceedings of a conference held to investigate the problems that refugee women and children face when returning home after years, or sometimes decades, of war.

Cases and Administrative Decisions

Bankovic et al. v. Belgium et al., App. No. 52207/99 Eur. Ct. H.R. (2001) (Dec. on admissibility).

Chahal v. United Kingdom, 108 ILR 385 (2007).

General Accounting Office, "Asylum: Approval Rates for Selected Applicants," (Washington DC: GAO 1987).

Human Rights Committee, *Concluding observations of the Human Rights Committee: Canada.* (2006) CCPR/C/CAN/CO/5 20 April 2006.

INS v. Cardoza-Fonseca, 480 U.S. 421 (1987).

INS v. Cardoza-Fonseca, 480 U.S. 421 (1987).

INS v. Elias-Zacarias, 502 U.S. 478 (1992).

Issa v. Turkey, App. No. 31821/96 Eur. Ct. H.R. (2000) (Dec. on admissibility).

Matter of Pula, 19 I. & N. Dec. 467 (BIA 1987).

Ocalan v. Turkey, App. No. 46221/99 Eur. Ct. H.R. (2000) (Dec. on admissibility).

Soering v. United Kingdom, App. No. 4038/88 [1989] ECHR 14 (July 7, 1989).

Suresh v. Canada (Minister of Citizenship and Immigration) [2002] 1 S.C.R. 3, 2002 SCC 1.

Selected Non-Print Resources

Online Resources

European Council on Refugees and Exiles
http://www.ecre.org/

The Political Terror Scale 1976–2008
www.politicalterrorscale.org

United Nations High Commissioner for Refugees
The UN Refugee Agency
www.unhcr.org

The U.S. Committee for Refugees and Immigrants
http://www.refugees.org/

U.S. Department of State
Bureau of Population, Refugees, and Migration
http://www.state.gov/g/prm/

U.S. Department of Health and Human Services
Office of Refugee Resettlement
http://www.acf.hhs.gov/programs/orr/

DVD Resources

El Norte (Gregory Nava 1983). This film from the 1980s is not a "refugee" film as such—but it should be. At the outset, the movie depicts a small community in Guatemala where a small group of Mayan peasants are attempting to organize themselves. The government responds by carrying out a massacre in the village and two teenagers, a brother and a sister, are among the only survivors. Their hope for survival hinges on being able to travel to the United States: El Norte. The two are able to overcome a host of obstacles, but their short-lived happiness comes to a tragic end.

14 Kilometers (Gerardo Olivares 2007). What is the meaning of the title? At its shortest point, the distance between North Africa and the southern part of Spain—between the Third World and the First World—is only 14 kilometers. Following a group of teenagers hoping to make the journey, what the film effectively shows is how close these two worlds are, but also how far away they remain.

In this World (Michael Winterbottom 2002). This documentary-style film follows the journey of two young Afghan boys who abandon their refugee camp in Pakistan and attempt to make their way to another world: the United Kingdom. What follows is a harrowing flight that gives a strong sense of the enormous dangers facing those who make such a flight, but also the reasons propelling otherwise hopeless people to do so.

Mrs. Goundo's Daughter (Barbara Attie and Janet Goldwater 2009). Mrs. Goundo is from Mali and she and her daughter face the specter of being sent back to Mali. Her fear is not war but the very real likelihood that her daughter will be subjected to female genital mutilation (FGM). In this documentary the viewer is not only given privy to Mrs. Goundo attempt to gain refugee status in the United States, but it also depicts the FGM ceremony itself and those who perform it.

Sierra Leone Refugee All-Stars (Zach Niles and Banker White 2007). This documentary follows a group of musicians from Sierra Leone who have been living in various refugee camps in the Republic of Guinea, and what helps them cope with their lives is their music. What the viewer gets is a sense of the horrors these individuals have lived through, but also the enormous will to move forward. The music alone is reason to see this documentary.

Well-Founded Fear (Michael Camerini and Shari Robertson 2000). The refugee standard is that the applicant must prove a "well-founded fear" of persecution and this absorbing documentary gives an in-depth and emotional portrayal of the obstacles and difficulties that asylum seekers must overcome. What is so effective about this documentary is that the human-side of the asylum process comes fully to life, and the individuals who the viewer meets will remain with them for a long period of time. One of the subjects is an elegant Chinese poet who is forced to recount the horrible torture that he was repeatedly subjected to. Another is an East European engineer who when he first arrived in the United States was relegated to folding newspapers—but now that he has advanced himself and achieved the American Dream, he is on the verge of being sent back home. Another story involves a pregnant young woman from Algeria who has led a life of hell in her home country, but because of translation difficulties very little of this is conveyed to the hearing examiner. Without question, this is the single best portrayal of what the asylum process looks like. But perhaps the most startling, but also most satisfying, moment in the entire film occurs as the credits are rolling at the end.

Glossary

1951 Refugee Convention   As of September 1, 2007, there were 144 state parties to this treaty, which governs international treaty law. The Refugee Convention is the key document setting forth the rights of refugees and asylum seekers as well as obligations for member states. The Convention is reproduced in Chapter 6.

1965 Immigration Act (U.S.)   Established for the first time under U.S. law a permanent category for refugee admissions. However, the act restricted admission to refugees fleeing from communist or Middle Eastern states.

1967 Protocol Relating to the Status of Refugees   This treaty eliminated the geographic (Europe) and temporal (before 1951) elements in 1951 Refugee Convention. The Protocol is reproduced in Chapter 6.

1980 Refugee Act (U.S.)   The Act reformed U.S. law and made it consonant with international law. Most notably, it removed ideological and geographic restrictions in the previous law.

Alien   A term commonly used for foreign nationals.

Asylum   The protection given by one country to refugees from another. First-country asylum refers to a country granting a refugee first or temporary asylum. Third-country asylum refers to a country granting permanent asylum to a refugee transferring or resettling from a first country of asylum.

Asylum-seeker   Someone who has fled from his or her home country and is seeking refugee status in another country.

B-status   Used in Scandinavian and some other European countries to grant a form of temporary asylum. *See also*, Complementary protection.

Boat people   Haitians, Vietnamese, Somalis, Albanians, Afghanis, and so on, who have attempted to rely on ocean voyages in small boats to emigrate. Frequently such people are denied asylum.

Border camp   A refugee camp or settlement situated along the borders between a host country and country of origin.

Brain drain Emigration of highly qualified persons, also known as reverse transfer of technology and transfer of talent.

Burden-sharing Sharing of responsibilities by states in funding refugee programs or admitting refugees for resettlement.

Carrier sanctions Fines or other sanctions inflicted on airlines or other transport firms for knowingly carrying international passengers lacking visas or other documentation.

Cartegena Declaration The refugee convention for Latin America that extends the meaning of "refugee" to include broader societal violence. The Declaration is reproduced in Chapter 6.

Cessation clauses Under the Refugee Convention, an individual ceases to be a "refugee" if he or she has availed himself or herself of protection in some other state (including the former state of nationality), or because of improved conditions in the country of former habitual residence.

Citizenship Legal granted status as a member of a particular nationality, obtained through birth and registration or through a procedure of nationalization prescribed by national authorities.

Complementary protection A form of protection for those who are determined not to meet the "refugee" standard under the 1951 Convention. *See also* B-status.

Convention on the Rights of the Child The most widely adopted international human rights treaty, it serves to protect all children—including refugee children.

Credibility determination Such a determination is often used to test whether an asylum seeker can prove the subjective component of having a "well-founded fear."

Credible fear Under U.S. law, those who arrive at the country's borders either with no documents or forged documents must first go through a "credible fear" hearing before being allowed proceed with asylum claim.

Deportation Act of sending people back home or to another country against their will.

Detention Increasingly, states are resorting to detaining asylum seekers during refugee proceedings, often as a way of trying to prevent further flows.

Durable solution Permanent settlement of refugees, whether through repatriation to their homeland, resettlement in a third country, or settlement in the first country of asylum.

Early warning Attempts and methods to detect a possible refugee exodus and to take appropriate measures to avoid or minimize it.

Economic migrant Someone who has left his or her home to look for better work and a higher standard of living in another place.

Emigration   Act of leaving one country or region to settle in another.

Environmental refugee   Person displaced by natural disaster, such as drought, deforestation, or other environmental degradation.

Ethnic cleansing   Forcible expulsion of one ethnic group from an area and their replacement by another ethnic group.

Ethnic minority   A group of people who share a distinctive culture, usually different from the culture of the majority of people in a region.

Exilic bias   Term used to describe efforts by Western states to encourage refugee flows, especially from communist countries, in 1970s and 1980.

Expatriate   Person who leaves his or her homeland and establishes temporary residence in another country.

Expedited removal   U.S. law allows for an expedited removal of those who fail to convince administrative officials of having a "credible fear" of persecution.

Expulsion   Forced removal of legal and undocumented foreigners.

Extraterritorial obligations   The human rights obligations that states have outside their own territorial borders.

Family reunification   Highest preference in many countries for legal immigration of divided spouses, siblings, or other family members.

Forced migration   Compelling refugees or other persons to migrate by massive coercion. May also refer to internally displaced persons moving as a result of political violence or natural disasters. Also referred to as involuntary migration.

Genocide   The deliberate and systematic murder of one ethnic or religious group.

Humanitarian concern   Under U.S. law, preference in terms of refugee admissions given to those who meet this standard.

Illegal immigrant   A person who has entered a country without the proper legal documentation or permission.

Immigration   The act of entering a country with the intention of settling there.

Immigration preferences   Criteria used to select immigrants by host countries, eg, family reunification, skills.

Integration policy   Policy to provide immigrants with equal status as citizens without their having to relinquish previous ethnic or other identities.

Interdiction   The act of intercepting boatloads of refugees and returning them to their homeland. One example is the U.S. Coast Guard program against Haitian boat people in the 1990s.

Intergovernmental organization An international organization containing representatives of national governments.

Internal conflict A war or dispute that takes place within the borders of a country.

Internally displaced person Someone who is forcibly displaced from his or her place of residence but remains within the country.

International Flight Alternative (IFA) Refugee status might be denied if it can be proven that there were other locales in this person's country of nationality where safety could have been sought.

International conflict A war that takes place between two or more countries.

International humanitarian law The laws and conventions that regulate the conduct of parties at war, including the treatment of prisoners of war and noncombatants or civilians. Also known as the Geneva Conventions, international humanitarian law is implemented by the International Committee of the Red Cross.

International migration The movement of people across national borders, usually for economic reasons.

International refugee law The laws and conventions that regulate the treatment and protection of refugees. They are implemented by the office of the United Nations High Commissioner for Refugees.

Irregular migration A population movement, not regulated by agreements between governments, that occurs outside of the normal state-to-state migration.

Local settlement The integration of refugees in the societies and economies of host countries.

Manifestly unfounded asylum application An application for political asylum in which there is no credible evidence of persecution against the applicant.

Man-made disaster A disaster that occurs as a result of the actions of man, such as war, persecution, human rights abuses, and sometimes famines.

Mass expulsion The sudden forced displacement of large numbers of people across borders, usually as a result of war or persecution.

Migrant worker A person, sometimes recruited, who is seeking employment for temporary periods in another country. Known also as guest workers, contract workers, temporary workers, and *braceros* (the Spanish term for unskilled workers).

Migration The permanent movement of people from one place to another.

Natural disaster A disaster that occurs as a result of natural causes, such as hurricanes, earthquakes, floods, and typhoons.

Naturalization   Procedure whereby the foreign-born can acquire the nationality and citizenship of another country.

Nexus requirement   Under the 1951 Refugee Convention, in order to qualify as a refugee, there must be a nexus between the feared persecution and one of five listed factors.

Nongovernmental organization (NGO)   A private rather than governmental organization. A number of NGOs, such as the International Committee of the Red Cross and Oxfam, work with refugees.

Nonrefoulement   From the French word *refouler*, this is a policy of the 1951 UN Convention Relating to the Status of Refugees that commits contracting states to not expel or return a refugee whose life or freedom would be threatened due to race, religion, membership of a social group, or political opinion.

Organization of African Unity (OAU)   Like the Cartagena Declaration, the OAU Convention governing the specific aspects of refugee problems in Africa extends the meaning of "refugee" under the 1951 Refugee Convention to include those fleeing from wars and generalized political violence. The OAU Convention is reproduced in Chapter 6.

Overseas Refugee Program   Under this program, the United States admits tens of thousands of refugees each year, some from refugee camps while others come directly from their country of nationality.

Parole authority   This administrative procedure was frequently used by the Attorney General in the United States to admit hundreds of thousands of refugees, primarily from Cuba and Vietnam.

Persecution   Unjust harassment, including threats of death or imprisonment, usually used for political, religious, or racial reasons.

Preference system   Under U.S. law, preference for refugee admissions is given to certain refugees, particularly those with some pre-existing connection to American citizens or U.S. business interests.

Pull factors   Forces in a country of destination, such as a higher standard of living, jobs, or freer communities, that attract people to the country. Pull factors are sometimes regarded as the variables that explain international voluntary migration.

Push factors   Negative forces, such as conflict, political instability, social inequalities, or poor economic opportunities, which compel people to leave their countries.

Quota   Number of immigrants, refugees, or asylum-seekers allowed in by a receiving state under their immigration policies.

Receiving country   A country that receives incoming refugees.

Reception policy   State policy regarding the admission and integration of incoming refugees.

Refugee Person who has left his or her country of origin and has a well-founded fear of persecution if they return (according to the 1951 UN Convention Relating to the Status of Refugees and the 1967 Protocol Relating to the Status of Refugees).

Refugee camp A temporary settlement established to receive and house refugees, frequently along the borders of the state from which they have fled.

Refugee in transit Refugee who is still in the process of flight from a home country to a country of asylum.

Refugee-warrior Armed guerrilla who lives in or close to a refugee camp, eg, Afghans in Pakistan or Cambodians in Thailand.

Refugees in orbit Term used to describe asylum seekers who are sent from one country to the next on the grounds that they should have applied for refugee status in the first safe country that they passed through.

Repatriation Returning a person to his or her home country. People can be forced to go against their will (forcible repatriation) or they can go voluntarily.

Resettlement The transfer of refugees from a first country of asylum to a third country of permanent resettlement, eg, Laotians from Thailand to the United States.

Return migration The voluntary return of immigrants, migrant workers, or other persons to their country of origin.

Root causes The underlying causes of refugee flight, such as political persecution or conflict.

Safe areas Policy adopted by the UNHCR as an alternative to offering refugee protection, this consists of creating "safe areas" in a country experiencing gross and systematic human rights violations.

Safe country of origin A number of Western states have compiled lists of countries considered "safe," from which asylum seekers will either be denied the ability to file a refugee claim altogether or will be subject to expedited proceedings.

Safe haven Temporary asylum subject to restrictions, e.g., Temporary Protected Status in the United States. Safe haven asylum may or may not allow persons to seek employment, housing, and welfare benefits.

Safe third country A number of Western states will either deny the ability of asylum seekers to file a claim or subject an asylum seeker to expedited procedures if they had first passed through a country considered "safe."

Self-determination The act of a national group deciding its own political future.

Stateless persons   Individuals who have been denied national identity documents or have had them removed. After World War I, the League of Nations created special passports, called Nansen passports, for such persons.

Third World   The developing countries of Africa, Asia, and Latin America.

Torture Convention   An international treaty that proscribes torture and other cruel, inhuman or degrading treatment and punishment. Like the Refugee Convention, the Torture Convention also has a nonrefoulement provision.

Travel documents   Passports and visas.

Undocumented alien   Person whose status does not meet a host country's legal conditions for immigration. Undocumented aliens are also known as illegal aliens, illegals, and irregular migrants.

UNHCR Handbook   This document provides an in-depth analysis of the 1951 Refugee Convention and it has had an enormous influence in terms of how states have interpreted their obligations under the treaty.

United National High Commissioner for Refugees (UNHCR)   This is the principal officer in the United Nations dealing with international refugee issues.

Visa   A stamp on a passport that allows a person to enter a particular country.

Well-founded fear   The standard by which refugee determinations are made. There remains debate whether both a subjective and objective element are needed.

Withholding of deportation   Under U.S. law, a person who can prove that his or her life or freedom would be threatened in another state will not be sent there. This is considered mandatory while those who only meet the lower "refugee" standard might be returned.

Index

Page numbers followed by t indicate table

About the Author

Mark Gibney is the Belk Distinguished Professor at the University of North Carolina-Asheville. His most recent book publications include the edited volume (Gibney & Skogly) *Universal Human Rights and Extraterritorial Obligations* (University of Pennsylvania Press) and *International Human Rights Law: Returning to Universal Principles* (Rowman & Littlefield, 2008). He also has a forthcoming book (with Sabine Carey and Steve Poe) entitled *The Politics of Human Rights: The Quest for Dignity* (Cambridge University Press). Since 1984, Gibney has directed the Political Terror Scale (PTS), one of the world's most widely used human rights datasets (www.politicalterrorscale.org).